The Freudian Mystique

The Freudian Mystique

Freud, Women, and Feminism

Samuel Slipp, M.D.

New York University Press
NEW YORK AND LONDON

NEW YORK UNIVERSITY PRESS
New York and London

Library of Congress Cataloging- in-Publication Data
Slipp, Samuel.
The Freudian mystique : Freud, women, and feminism / Samuel Slipp.
  p. cm.
Includes bibliographical references and index
ISBN 0–8147–7968–9 (hard) ISBN 0–8147–8014–8 pbk.
1. Femininity (Psychology)—History. 2. Freud, Sigmund,
1856–1939—Contributions in psychology of femininity. 3. Freud,
Sigmund, 1856–1939—Relations with women. 4. Psychoanalysis and
feminism. 5. Women—Psychology—History. 6. Psychoanalysis—
History. I. Tittle.
BF175.5.F48S55 1993
150.19′52′082—dc20   92–35872 CIP

New York University Press books are printed on acid-free paper,
and their binding materials are chosen for strength and durability.

Manufactured in the United States of America

10 9 8 7 6 5 4 3 2

To my wife, Sandra,
and my daughter, Elena

Contents

PART THREE   *Current Issues*

Acknowledgments

My initial interest in the history of psychiatry was stimulated by Sheldon T. Selesnick, and my attention to feminine psychology was fostered by Esther Greenbaum, Malvina W. Kremer, and Ann R. Turkel. I also wish to acknowledge the help of Marianne Horney Eckardt and Richard C. Friedman, who read the early manuscript and made valuable suggestions. The initial editorial review of the book by Joan Langs served to help organize the manuscript. Most of all I wish to thank Jason Renker, my editor at New York University Press, who worked patiently and carefully with me to strengthen the book. I would also like to mention Jules Bemporad, Harry Hardin, William Niederland, Donald Rinsley, and Paul Roazen who offered information, advice, and sent me material for the book. I especially want to express my deep appreciation to my wife, Sandra, for her help as the book was being written in connecting the dots of knowledge together to infer meaning about Freud and feminine psychology and for her critique of the manuscript. Finally, I wish to thank her and my daughter, Elena, for the loyal support and loving encouragement that made this book possible.

The Freudian Mystique

Introduction

How could Freud, one of the great geniuses of our modern age, be so wrong about women? This is particularly puzzling because out of his sensitive introspection into his own and others' emotional difficulties, he was able to create a universal understanding of personality functioning, psychopathology, and treatment.

Many writers have contended that Freud's views on feminine psychology were erroneous because they basically reflected and perpetuated the Victorian bias against women. This is in all likelihood true, but the picture is more interesting than this simple explanation alone. To understand how Freud developed his views on female development, it is important to explore not only the patriarchal and phallocentric Victorian society of Vienna but Freud's own personal conflicts as well.

These influences on Freud cannot be reduced to the narrow confines of even several parallel explanations, since personal and familial dynamics as well as cultural and social forces are closely intertwined and influence one another. In this book I will attempt to show how the effects of all these factors played roles in shaping Freud's personality and his theory about women. These factors include losses of important early childhood attachment figures; unconscious conflicts with his mother, who appeared to be seductive, aggressive, intrusive, and exploitative; his mother's own frustrations as a person and her constricted social role; and anti-Semitism, which contributed to his father's economic failure and Freud's own professional difficulties.

Unfortunately, some writers, in rejecting Freud's theories about women, have rejected all of psychoanalysis, as if no new developments had occurred in psychoanalysis since the turn of the century. In fact, there have been profound and sweeping changes. Like its cultural context, psychoanalysis had been patriarchal and phallocentric, but it is now mother-centered.

Freud's views on feminine psychology provoked controversy within the psychoanalytic establishment itself around 1922, and became increasingly widespread in the wake of the feminist movement of the 1960s. Thus Freud's early works regarding women must be delineated from the markedly different psychoanalytic thinking on feminine psychology today.

How were Freud's views on feminine psychology influenced by the Victorian attitudes toward women in Europe? How did the Victorian cultural bias against women evolve in Western civilization? Although this book is not an in-depth historical study, it will contain a broad overview from ancient times to the turn of the century and will trace why women and their sexuality were feared and needed to be demeaned and controlled. In addition, the existing economic and political forces around the turn of the century in Vienna, Austria, and Europe in general will be reviewed, as will the impact they had on the lives of Freud and his parents. All these factors affected Freud's psychological development, and appear to have had a profound influence on the formulation of his theories about women.

To support the hypotheses that are developed in the book, I have used a wide variety of evidence from a number of fields. This interdisciplinary perspective will include anthropology, biology, economics, history, individual and group psychology, mythology, religion, philosophy, politics, psychoanalysis, and sociology. Each discipline is seen not in isolation from the other, but as woven into an interactive and interdependent fabric or system.

I will also develop the thesis that the emotional traumas Freud suffered with his mother and mother-surrogate when he was a very small child shaped his personality and influenced his subsequent relations with all women. In addition, I will show that the specific form of family constellation that Freud experienced throughout the rest of his childhood and into adulthood perpetuated his unconscious ambivalent relationship to his mother and to women in general.

In Freud's theoretical work he ignored the early preoedipal period—from birth to three years of age—as well as the later postoedipal phase from six years to adulthood; he focused primarily on the time between them, the oedipal period. Why was this the case? Freud's own analysis focused primarily on his relationship to his father during the oedipal period, while his early and later relationship to his mother remained unanalyzed. During the oedipal period, Freud depicted the mother as primarily an object of incestuous desire for whom the father was a rival.

Why did Freud even name the Oedipus complex after the old Greek tragedy of Oedipus Rex? Why did he show such interest in ancient cultures in his writings and in his art collection? And why did he give rings with engraved Roman stones to members of his secret circle? His classical education undoubtedly stimulated his interest in Egyptian, Greek, and Roman societies. He was also fascinated with pictures of ancient Egyptians in the Philippson Bible he read as a child with his father, and this interest was furthered by the important archeological discoveries being made at the time. Freud compared psychoanalysis to archeology: buried remnants of the past are unearthed, examined, and new knowledge is obtained from them. Thus he made the analogy between an individual's early childhood and the ancient past. I will show that Freud's strong interest in ancient cultures was probably more related to his attempt to master his own deeply repressed early-childhood conflicts with his mother.

In this book we will investigate Freud's preoedipal and postoedipal experiences with his mother and how they influenced his work in feminine psychology. The book reflects an object-relations perspective in modern psychoanalytic theory, not only with individuals but also with families.

The book is divided into three parts: Part One presents Freud's ideas about feminine psychology and traces the controversy about them that grew within the psychoanalytic movement. It then explores the historical-cultural antecedents of Victorian society and their profound influence on ideas about women. The fear and need to control women and their sexuality are shown as having no rational basis but stem from the magical way of adapting to nature in ancient and primitive societies. Women and their sexuality were associated with the great mother goddess (Mother Nature) who was believed to control fertility, life, death, and rebirth. Women and their mysterious sexuality were feared and had to be controlled. This magical form of adaptation to helplessness in life and death was a major factor in the evolution of a *patriarchal* social structure.

In their historical evolution, cultures have employed ways of adaptation similar to those found in each human individual's development. Individual child development is used as a template for cultural evolution. Adaptation in periods of history are traced and compared to stages of individual child development. However, even though cultural adaptation may use magical thinking and defense mechanisms similar to those individuals use in coping with their helplessness in early childhood, the culture becomes a force in itself and in turn influences the individual.

The evolution of a *phallocentric* society is traced to men's attempt to gain further mastery over nature by replacing the female goddess with male gods. The magical power of the phallus was substituted for the womb as responsible for fertility and life. Women's sexuality was now less feared and demeaned. Even though women apparently have always been controlled in Western society, the power derived from their role in pagan religion was now diminished as well.[1]

The continuation of pre-Christian fertility worship persisted in the form of witchcraft during the Middle Ages. All women were considered as potential witches, and women's sexuality was considered evil and related to the devil. During the Inquisition in the fifteenth century, many Jews, who were also nonbelievers in Christianity, and women, who were convicted as witches, were blamed for magically causing natural calamities and diseases and persecuted and killed. Part One traces how aspects of the human condition, such as emotionality, dependency, and sexuality, associated with the flesh, human frailty, and mortality, were denied by men and through the defense mechanism of projective identification placed into women and Jews. The result was pervasive misogyny and anti-Semitism that extended through the Enlightenment into the Victorian European culture. These biases stemmed from magical forms of thinking and primitive defense mechanisms used during early childhood and formed the basis for the patriarchal and phallocentric society in which Freud lived and worked.

Part Two follows the significant psychological events in Freud's early childhood that served to shape his psychological theories about women. It examines the preoedipal and postoedipal family dynamics of Freud in relation to his mother and its effect on feminine theory, his relationships with women, and his collection of antiquities.

Freud's personal life remained obscure until his definitive three-volume biography was written by Ernest Jones (1953, 1955, 1957). This biography was written despite Freud's strong objections, claiming that only his ideas and not his personal life were significant. But Freud did reveal a good deal of his personal life in his professional work and letters. This

---

1. It is noteworthy that a revival of interest in ancient myths and rituals associated with the great mother goddess has recently surfaced among some feminists. Their search is for a form of spirituality that empowers women through the worship of this powerful female deity.

self-revelation further served to stimulate interest and to create an air of mystery about him as a person.

The greatest mystery is Freud's relationship to his mother, which has remained vague in Freud's own writings as well as in those of his biographers. Peter Gay (1988), in his biography of Freud, comments on Freud's persistent evasion of his feelings about his mother, and on the fact that there is no evidence for any systematic self-analysis of his relationship to her. Freud's ambivalent feelings toward his mother were defended against and remained repressed in what he called the "deeper layers" of his unconscious. His understanding of women remained shrouded in obscurity, like a "dark continent."

In this book we will explore the major traumatic events and losses that Freud suffered during his preoedipal period. These include his feeling of being emotionally abandoned by his mother, the seductive-aggressive experience he had with her, and her later intrusiveness and exploitation of his success. Consciously, Freud idealized his mother, but his split-off and repressed aggression toward her was unconsciously expressed through behavior. I will present evidence that he emotionally distanced himself from his mother and may have unconsciously punished her through behavior. He did not attend her funeral, and did not mourn her death. Probably because of his repression of the trauma with his preoedipal mother, Freud omitted the role of the mother in his theory of early child development. In addition, this early childhood trauma is one of several explanations I will explore about Freud's rejection of his early seduction theory of neurosis.

Freud's idea that bisexuality was the foundation for female development will be rejected here. Freud did not differentiate sexual orientation from gender identity in his work. Sexual orientation is now generally considered to be genetic, with homosexuality being a normal inborn variant. Studies do show, however, that core gender identity is a psychological phenomenon that is learned around two years of age. This is based on the cultural ideas that define masculinity and femininity. Recent research notes that gender instability may develop in boys who experience a traumatic loss of their mothers around two years of age. To deal with their annihilation anxiety, these boys do not individuate from the mother; their orientation is bisexual and later as adults becomes mostly homosexual. However, these gender-identity disordered boys represent *only a small subgroup* of all homosexual men.

Freud was also two years old when he suffered emotional abandonment by his mother and physical abandonment by his nanny, which would account for his own bisexual conflicts. Freud stated that he analyzed and resolved his latent homosexual feelings in his self-analysis, in which his friend Wilhelm Fliess served as analyst, though he still suffered from latent homosexual conflicts in his relationship with Jung. Perhaps using himself as a model, he considered bisexuality to be universal, and the libido for both sexes to be masculine. Cultural stereotypes, that define gender identity, were also used in his theory. He felt that women needed to overcome their active masculine strivings (clitoral masturbation) to become passive and feminine. Freud also equated latent male homosexuality with passivity, which he considered feminine.

Freud's early oedipal experience with a dominant mother and a passive father probably led him to the conclusion that male homosexuality was due to lack of resolution of the Oedipus complex and failure to identify with the father. His ambivalent relationship with his mother was not limited to early childhood, but continued into the postoedipal period and adulthood. This situation may have been due to his family's dynamics, which were of the kind that often leads to depression. In patriarchal Victorian society, women were deprived of an individual identity and needed to achieve a sense of self by identifying with the social and economic successes of their husbands. Because Freud's father was considered a failure, his mother appears to have established a close-binding, intrusive, and exploitative relationship with Sigmund, her eldest son. With Freud serving as the family savior, his mother could sustain her self-esteem and identity by living vicariously through the achievements of her son instead of her husband. This responsibility for preserving his mother's ego, as well as his earlier preoedipal annihilation anxiety, probably prevented Freud from dealing with his unconscious ambivalence toward her. He resented the fact that he could not experience love that "cost him nothing."

Freud's unconscious conflicts with his mother will be shown to have affected his adult relationships with women. He experienced a diminished interest in his wife after she became a mother, and this conflict may have contributed to the fact that his daughter Anna never became a mother. Although Freud's theoretical position was biased against women, in psychoanalysis he encouraged them to develop professionally. This paradox was probably possible because these women were interested mainly in their careers, not in motherhood.

In 1920 Freud published his essay, *Beyond the Pleasure Principle,* which dealt with the repetition compulsion and a child's efforts to master separation from the mother. We will provide evidence that Freud's analysis of his daughter Anna during this time was an unconscious repetition of a seductive and aggressive experience he had had with his mother around four years of age. It was during the time he analyzed his daughter that Freud wrote his essay "A Child Is Being Beaten." Just as Freud had been overwhelmed by his "awesome" seductive experience with his mother, his daughter had difficulty with her own sexuality, which apparently remained sublimated for the rest of her life.

Part Three elaborates on revisions and changes in psychoanalytic theory and technique. Some women have recently turned to Jungian analytic psychology, since it emphasizes that masculine and feminine elements exist in each gender and retains a strong interest in religion and spirituality. Ironically, Freud welcomed Carl Jung, who was Christian, into the psychoanalytic movement, so that it would not be dismissed as a Jewish-feminine-sexual science. However, Jung rejected sexuality in personality development, and he considered the "collective unconscious" of Aryans to be superior to those of Jews. He compared Jews to women, since he felt they both manipulate and control men. Jung identified strongly with the attitudes of misogyny and anti-Semitism that were so prevalent in Victorian society.

In chapter 16, on modern changes in psychoanalysis, I will elaborate on the influence of women patients on Freud. Later in life Freud changed his psychoanalytic theory and technique from a mechanistic (male) id psychology to a more relationship-oriented (female) ego psychology. We will review object-relations psychoanalytic theory, which emphasizes the dyadic relationship between mother and child. We will review the contributions of a number of women psychoanalysts, especially those concerning relationship issues between patient and analyst.

The final chapter concludes with an attempt to develop a new scientific feminine psychology that encompasses inborn biological factors and how they are shaped by the environment. These include human and animal research into the mother-child relationship, gender differences, female personality development, and the question of whether men are innately more aggressive than women. The chapter ends with some new evidence that as society and gender development change, both sexes should be able to become more complete as individuals. Each gender will be able to achieve, as well as to relate more intimately with others.

In the epilogue I will give a brief history of modern feminism and summarize some current feminist thought, followed by a discussion of the two leading approaches that combine feminist theory with psychoanalysis. One is based on object-relations theory, which emphasizes the mother-child attachment, separation, and individuation. The other is reflected in the writings of female proponents of Lacanian theory, which rejects biology and uses linguistics and logic to understand female development. Both emphasize the preoedipal period of development, although from markedly different perspectives. Some female Lacanians advocate the form of thinking found in the preoedipal stage to subvert patriarchy, since it is not based on the dualistic division of subject and object. However, as discussed in Part One, this preoedipal thinking, with its use of magic and primitive defenses, is itself historically responsible for the suppression of women and the institution of patriarchy and phallocentrism. The usefulness of the object-relations family typology presented in this book is suggested as a means of integrating individual, interpersonal, family, and social perspectives.

My hope is that this book will bring a greater understanding of why Freud developed his theories on feminine psychology. He has been sharply criticized by feminists because of his views on women, yet he himself acknowledged that his writings on women were the weakest part of his work. His great genius had a flaw—his misunderstanding of women. Despite this imperfection, we cannot discount the inestimable value of his other contributions—the understanding of the development and workings of the human mind as well as the healing of its afflictions. We now need to proceed to develop new understandings of feminine psychology based on our current knowledge.

PART ONE

Historical-Cultural Background

1. Psychoanalysis and Feminine Psychology

Freud and Feminine Psychology

In this chapter we will look at some of Freud's key views on feminine psychology, as well as the major criticisms of his theories. Certain questions still remain unanswered about his theoretical understanding of feminine psychology, for example:

Why did Freud ignore the role of the mother in early child development?

Why did Freud consider the libido to be a masculine force in both sexes?

Why were only the male genitals and castration anxiety a model for both sexes, and the female genitals ignored?

Why did Freud think that women felt castrated already, did not suffer castration anxiety, and thus did not resolve the Oedipus complex as readily as men?

Why did Freud think that the superego developed only *after* the resolution of the Oedipus complex, and was a result of internalization of the father and not the mother?

Why did Freud consider the superego development in the personality of women to be less complete than in men?

Why did Freud write that women suffered penis envy and never overcame their sense of inferiority because of it?

Why did Freud think it was penis envy that led women to turn to their fathers, become feminine, and to desire a baby?

Why were men and women considered to be bisexual by Freud?

Why did Freud say that women need to give up active clitoral stimulation, which he considered masculine, and replace it with passive vaginal orgasm to be feminine?

Why were passivity, narcissism, and masochism primarily associated with femininity, and activity with masculinity?

Freud's final statement about feminine psychology appeared in his *New Introductory Lectures on Psychoanalysis* (1933), where he wrote:

Girls remain in it [the Oedipus complex] ... they demolish it late and, even so, incompletely. In these circumstances the formation of the super-ego must suffer ... and feminists are not pleased when we point out to them the effects of this factor upon the average feminine character. (129)

The fact that women must be regarded as having little sense of justice is no doubt related to the predominance of envy in their mental life. ... We also regard women as weaker in their social interests and as having less capacity for sublimating their instincts than men. ... A woman of the same age (as a man of 30) ... frightens us by her psychical rigidity and unchangeability. ... There are no paths open to further development ... the difficult development to femininity had exhausted the possibilities of the person concerned. (135)

Why did Freud make such grossly biased and incorrect statements about women, when in other areas he was such a perceptive and accurate observer? This is a mystery that cried for explanation. Unfortunately, it was precisely because of Freud's genius and his monumental discoveries in other areas of mental functioning that credibility was lent to his psychoanalytic theory of women. This book will provide evidence on how the prevailing Victorian cultural world in which Freud lived, as well as Freud's conflictual relationship with his mother, strongly influenced his thinking about women.

This book is a psychohistory, in which we will analyze Freud's inner life as well as the cultural context of the Victorian society that influenced him. Indeed, Freud was the father of psychohistory, having written about Leonardo da Vinci, Paul Schreber, Moses, and Woodrow Wilson. Psychohistory not only offers a historical chronicle of events but also tries to provide an in-depth analytic understanding of them. Freud did not interview any of the men in these studies, but he used the insights of psychoanalysis to gain an understanding of each man from his actions, creative works, and written documents. Psychohistory uses such sources, yet the resulting psychological understanding is still speculative.

In this book I also have not used direct psychoanalysis or interviews with people. The autobiographical materials were derived from Freud's letters, dreams, and other writings, and I use biographical materials as well. In addition, I make an attempt to link Freud's actual behavior toward women and his choice of art collection to the hypotheses developed in this book. Despite my efforts to make the most accurate analytic constructions, the analyses developed rest on speculations and cannot be presented with certainty. However, the insights that are developed should bring together events in a creative way to provide fresh perspectives and new meanings.

One subject we will deal with is the paradox between what Freud wrote about women and his relationships with his female colleagues. Though he considered the personality of woman to be inferior to that of man in theory, Freud actually opened up psychoanalysis to women, respected their contributions, nurtured their careers, and developed strong personal friendships with many of them. Despite his shortcomings on feminine theory, Freud was a genius who had a profound influence on modern society. Not only did he provide us with a method to analyze the human mind and a way to heal emotional suffering, but he advanced an understanding of child development that fosters healthier child rearing. Freud sensitized society to a greater acceptance of human sexuality and aggression, as well as an acknowledgment of the influence of unconscious determinants on personality formation and relationships. Literature and art, as well as the behavioral and social sciences, have been profoundly enriched by the contributions of psychoanalysis.

Feminism and Psychoanalysis

The renaissance of the feminist movement in the 1960s ignited a controversy about Freud's theory and treatment of women. Feminists such as Simone de Beauvoir (1961) and Betty Friedan (1963) believed that Freud's feminine psychology did not promote gender equality but perpetuated the age-old suppression of women. Most of the early feminist writers rejected classical psychoanalytic theory, since they felt it represented a direct reflection of the Victorian bias against women. Instead, feminists turned to anthropology, history, philosophy, politics, and sociology for explanations about feminine psychology and gender relations. However,

Betty Friedan, in *The Feminine Mystique* (1963), acknowledged the debt the feminist movement owed to other aspects of Freud's work. Psychoanalysis contributed significantly toward emancipating women from existing repressive Victorian sexual morality. However, Friedan posited that Freud's psychology of women created "a new tyranny of the shoulds, which chains women to an old image, prohibits choice and growth, and denies them individual identity." Thinly disguised cultural prejudices that consider "women are animals, less than human, unable to think like men, born merely to breed and serve men" were simply reinforced.

One of the early feminist defenders of Freud's psychoanalytic feminine psychology was Juliet Mitchell (1974), who noted its usefulness as a method of understanding gender development. Mitchell rejected the notion that classical psychoanalytic theory was subjective and influenced by Victorian culture. She viewed psychoanalysis as a value-free science, immune from the investigator's personal influence. However, as Remmling (1967) and Spence (1987) have noted, no science is value-free. This is particularly the case for the softer behavioral sciences, such as psychoanalysis. All scientific theory is influenced by the personal issues of the theorist, as well as the social and cultural forces of a particular time and place. In addition, the linguistic philosopher Ludwig Wittgenstein even questioned the objectivity of all scientific theory, despite following the rigorous requirement of the logical positivists that theory be based solely on empirical observation (Janik and Toulmin 1973). Wittgenstein noted that language is not a clear window through which to view the world. Because language is another variable that shapes perception, scientific theory can provide only a symbolic description of the world that is pragmatically useful.

Within psychoanalysis, similar disagreements about Freud's feminine psychology had been strongly voiced much earlier, especially by female analysts such as Karen Horney (1922), Melanie Klein (1928), and Clara Thompson (1950). Beginning in the 1930s in England, Melanie Klein departed from Freud's ideas about the entire early period of child development for both sexes. Freud had not acknowledged the role of the mother and emphasized the relationship to the father in the child's personality development. Klein, on the other hand, found that the child's relationship to the mother during the first three years of life was the most significant factor in personality development. This was the preoedipal period. Problems in this phase resulted in more psychopathology than during the oedipal period.

The cornerstone of Freud's theory of neurosis rested on the lack of resolution of the relationship to the father during the *oedipal* period. The oedipal period, from three to six years of age, resulted from biologically inborn sexual instincts and occurred universally in every child's development. During this period the child became sexually attracted to the parent of the opposite sex and wished to eliminate the parent of the same sex. Klein's reformulation, which stressed the earlier *preoedipal* period of child development and the role of the mother rather than the father, was a radical departure. Klein also felt that the child's fantasy was more significant than biological instincts in personality development. She further diminished the importance of instincts by relegating them to another form of fantasy experienced in the child-mother relationship.

Klein then went on to construct her own timetable for child development, quite different from that of Freud. Hers was less biological and more relational. It included a two-person psychology: an interpersonal relationship between mother and child, and a one-person psychology that was intrapsychic. She observed that oedipal fantasies and even superego development became manifest as early as the first three years of life for both sexes. In Freud's formulation, the development of a conscience, the superego, rested on the resolution of the Oedipus complex, which did not occur until five or six years of age. According to Freud, it was only then that the first person was internalized by the child to form the superego. This person was the father and not the mother. Klein disagreed with this formulation and suggested that the infant was relating to and internalizing the mother from birth onward.

The most significant departure by Klein was her belief that the *relationship of the infant's bonding to the mother and later separating* from her is the central issue in infant development. For Klein, the child's *attachment* was paramount, and not the gratifying instincts as Freud believed. Despite Klein's differing position, the psychoanalytic movement in Britain did not break into two groups, as it had in the United States, because of the support of its leader, Ernest Jones. Jones had originally invited Klein to come to London from Berlin in 1926. She treated his children, and he agreed with many of her formulations. After heated conflict and negotiations, the British psychoanalytic movement managed to remain whole, yet it divided into classical, Kleinian, and middle groups in 1946.

Deriving many of their concepts from Melanie Klein, British object-relations analysts from the middle group further elaborated on the effects of the real relationship between the mother and infant on personality formation. While Klein had focused mostly on the child's internal fantasies of greed, envy, destruction, and reparation, the object-relations analysts

nsidered the actual impact of the mother on the child. They em-
d that the mother must be responsive to the developmental needs
of the child. The object-relations group of analysts included Michael Balint,
Ronald Fairbairn, Harry Guntrip, and Donald Winnicott.

In the United States, neo-Freudians such as Karen Horney and Clara
Thompson had objected to Freud's patriarchal and phallocentric orientation in feminine psychology and emphasized *postoedipal* family and cultural factors. Freud held the view that considered penis envy as biological
and universal in all women. Horney and Thompson saw it only as a
symbolic manifestation of a male-oriented Victorian culture. Even before
Karen Horney emigrated from Europe to the United States in 1932, she
had courageously stood up at the International Congress of Psychoanalysis
in Berlin in 1922. With Freud presiding, she strongly objected to the
presentation by Karl Abraham (her former analyst), which elaborated on
Freud's emphasis on penis envy in female psychology (Gay 1988).

Freud had postulated that young girls considered their vagina a wound,
resulting from castration of their penis. The girl then blamed the mother
and turned to her father, hoping to receive a gift of a penis, which later
changed into a gift of a child. The paper Horney presented at the Congress,
"On the Genesis of the Castration Complex in Women" (1922), acknowledged the significance of penis envy and the castration complex in the
oedipal developmental period of women. However, she denied that they
created femininity or that they led women to reject their womanhood:
"But, the deduction that therefore repudiation of their womanhood is
based on that envy by no means precludes a deep and wholly womanly
love attachment to the father, and that it is only when this relation comes
to grief over the Oedipus complex that the envy leads to a revulsion from
the subject's own sexual role." Horney further speculated that it was masculine bias that was responsible for formulating such a theory that considered women, half the world's population, as dissatisfied with the sex
into which they were born.

After Freud published his paper "Some Psychical Consequences of the
Anatomical Distinction between the Sexes" (1925), Horney noted that
psychoanalysis was created by a male genius, and that it was mostly men
who elaborated on Freud's ideas. She felt it was easier for these men to
evolve a masculine than a feminine psychology. She disagreed with Freud's
idea that just because women felt castrated they turned to their fathers
and *then* became feminine. Horney considered femininity as a basic biological given into which women were born, and not an end product
developing out of self-disappointment and envy of men.

In her paper "The Flight from Womanhood" (1926), Horney quoted the eminent German sociologist Georg Simmel to the effect that modern society was essentially masculine and had forced women into an inferior role; this lack of social equality was the cause of women's envy of men. Horney stated male and female biology were equal but different. She boldly suggested that the deprecation of women might be related to men's envy of women's reproductive capacity, or *womb envy*.

In her paper "The Dread of Women" (1932), Horney explored the pervasive fear of women across many cultures. She linked it with the small boy's dread, during the oedipal period, that his penis was too small for his mother's engulfing vagina. The boy anticipated that he would be rejected and humiliated by his mother, and therefore feared and needed to demean women. In her subsequent writings, Horney considered cultural inequality important but not the only cause for emotional difficulties in both men and women, and she searched for more general universals.

Marie Bonaparte, the French analyst who was a descendant of Napoleon and later helped rescue Freud and his family from the Nazis, also felt that Freud's understanding of feminine psychology was deficient (Bertin 1982). Although she remained conflicted about Freud's theory of feminine psychology, she questioned that it was universal and inborn. Instead, Bonaparte looked to transcultural studies to delineate biological factors from the role played by culture in female psychology. Like Horney, Marie Bonaparte also recognized that "man is afraid of woman."

Freud's famous biographer, Ernest Jones, strongly disagreed with Freud's views on feminine psychology, which resulted in the famous Freud-Jones debates in the 1920s and 1930s. Jones defended Karen Horney's position at the 1935 meeting of the Vienna Psychoanalytic Society (Gay 1988). He agreed with Horney that girls envied the penis because it symbolized power and instant sexual gratification. However, Jones believed that the boy envied the girl's sexual organs, which are capable of reproducing life and symbolize instant creativity. Jones insisted that women's femininity was developed out of their genetic constitution: women are born and not made. Femininity was innate and biological, even though it was influenced and shaped by psychological issues.

Clara Thompson (1950) noted that women's subservience to men socially and sexually was simply taken for granted in the patriarchal Victorian culture. As a result, women's envy of men was wholly realistic, in view of men's greater power and freedom in society. The penis, so important in Freud's developmental psychology, was significant only as a symbol of the male's superior condition socially. Thompson stressed that the social devaluation of women and the denial of their sexuality had a more profound effect on personality formation than simply penis envy. Not only was woman placed into an inferior position socially, but the undervaluation of her genitals and the denial of her sexuality made it difficult for her to gain self-acceptance, self-respect, and self-esteem.

Thompson's understanding about women fits in with the general sociological finding of Kurt Lewin (1935). Any group that is devalued by society tends to internalize this assault on its self-esteem and to develop a sense of inferiority. The minority group that suffers prejudice, whether on the basis of ethnicity, race, religion, or sex, tends to identify with the devaluation of it by the larger society. The negative self-image that develops becomes part of one's identity, resulting in self-hatred.

In those early days of psychoanalysis, not only women analysts challenged Freud's patriarchal and phallocentric view of feminine psychology. In 1908 Fritz Wittels delivered a paper before the Vienna Psychoanalytic Society about the role of culture in shaping women's personality (Gay 1988). He maintained that society constricted women and fostered their obsession with personal beauty. It was the culture and not women themselves that contributed to women's dissatisfaction with not having been born men. Wittels acknowledged that social injustice was responsible for the creation of the women's movement as a way to gain social equality.

Also in 1908, Sandor Ferenczi, Freud's closest male colleague, wrote a paper published in Hungarian entitled "The Effect on Women of Premature Ejaculation in Men" (Vida 1989). It stated that not only was women's position in society suppressed by the culture, but their sexuality was as well. Since sexual enjoyment was seen as morally indecent or sinful in society, women felt forced to choose between sexual satisfaction and self-respect. To sustain their self-esteem in this conflict, "good" women could not be active sexually. Instead, they had to assume a passive and masochistic position in sex, and thereby to deny themselves sexual orgasm. Since men also assumed that proper women did not enjoy sex, they made little or no effort to arouse women in sexual foreplay. The result was that most marital sex consisted of premature ejaculation for the male and little or no satisfaction for the female. Ferenczi concluded that the cultural values prohibiting enjoyment of sexuality resulted in incomplete or absent sexual satisfaction for women. He stated that this frustrated sexual satisfaction accounted for so many women suffering anxiety and hysterical neuroses in Europe around the turn of the century. Ferenczi thus implicated the European culture as largely responsible for these neuroses in women.

In 1935 Karen Horney rejected the libido theory, and her specific interest in feminine psychology expanded into a more general inclusion of social and cultural forces in the development of normal personality and psychopathology. She joined forces with Harry Stack Sullivan, Clara Thompson, William Silverberg, and Erich Fromm, all of whom concurred that it was important for psychoanalysis to interact with other scientific disciplines (Eckardt 1978). Horney's two books, *The Neurotic Personality of Our Time* (1937) and *New Ways in Psychoanalysis* (1939), emphasized the cultural issues in psychoanalysis.

On April 29, 1941, at a business meeting of the New York Psychoanalytic Society, Karen Horney was disqualified from being an instructor and training analyst because she was allegedly disturbing students with her cultural ideas. She walked out, accompanied by Clara Thompson, Sarah Kelman, Saul Ephron, and Bernard Robbins, all of whom resigned from the Society.

In 1955 Clara Thompson organized a meeting of eminent psychoanalysts, which included Sandor Rado, Jules Masserman, Franz Alexander, Abram Kardiner, and others, to organize a psychoanalytic organization where a free exchange of ideas coming from many scientific disciplines could occur. On April 29, 1956, the American Academy of Psychoanalysis was created, with Janet Rioch as its first president. The Academy's goal was to take into account not only biological factors and intrapsychic dynamics but also interpersonal, social, and cultural relationships that affected personality development. Although it has markedly changed since then, in the mid–1950s classical psychoanalysis still limited itself to a one-person psychology, focusing on the sexual-libido theory and the internal dynamics of the individual. Since then, object relations and self psychology, which are two-person psychologies, have assumed a prominent position in classical psychoanalysis.

More recently, a growing number of publications have combined feminism and newer aspects of psychoanalytic theory (Miller 1976). This is particularly true for object-relations theory (Chodorow 1989; Dinnerstein 1976) and feminist writers using Lacanian theory (Cixous 1986; Irigaray 1985a and 1985b; Kristeva 1977), which see the preoedipal mother-child relationship as paramount in feminine personality and gender development. These theories will be covered in the Epilogue.

In understanding feminine psychology, a multicausal orientation is essential that includes not only the oedipal but also the preoedipal and postoedipal periods. In this way, the dynamic relationships between the biological, intrapsychic, interpersonal, social, and cultural forces can more readily be taken into account.

2. Magic, the Fear of Women, and Patriarchy

The Origin and Use of Magic

In this chapter we will explore how social attitudes toward women evolved out of an effort to gain magical control over nature and to master existence. Historically, women have been closely associated with nature, since, like nature, their bodies created new life and provided sustenance. This connection to nature was furthered by women's menstrual cycles, which were seen as similar to the cycles of the moon and the seasons. Women were also mysteriously tied to another cycle—life, death, and rebirth. Because of these fantasized ties to nature, women and their sexuality were feared and had to be controlled.

We will review how various ancient civilizations adapted to nature, and how this led to the evolution of the patriarchal society in Freud's fin-de-siècle Vienna. Although Victorian society is usually blamed by feminists to explain Freud's attitude toward women, it is important to view this time and place from a broader historical and cultural perspective. We need to understand why these primitive attitudes toward women continued through the Middle Ages, the Enlightenment, and into Victorian society. These views of women, based on irrational, magical forms of adaptation to nature, persisted even when rationality became supreme. Vienna, like other nineteenth-century European societies, remained patriarchal and phallocentric and felt the need to control women and their sexuality.

Freud himself tried to understand the ancient origins of patriarchal society in his book *Civilization and Its Discontents* (1930). However, he justified the existence of patriarchy as essential in sustaining civilization. The father's law in society restricted sexuality and aggression in exchange for security. Freud considered that men were better able to renounce and sublimate their instincts to support civilization's "higher psychical activities, scientific, artistic, or ideological." On the other hand, he perpetuated the association of women with nature and instinctual life. When men withdrew from sexual life to be with other men, Freud stated, "the woman finds herself forced into the background by the claims of civilization, and she adopts a hostile attitude toward it."

Freud also recognized that religion was an adaptive mechanism to deal with human helplessness against nature. Here again Freud minimized the role of women, and he saw religion as a longing for a protective father to shield against Mother Nature. Freud also condemned religious feelings as a mass delusion based on the oceanic feeling experienced by the infant at the mother's breast. He considered religion as infantilizing and an escape from painful reality. Freud's views of civilization are based on his instinct theory, with emphasis on the Oedipus complex and the father. This same issue of human adaptation can be viewed from the perspective of object relations, taking into account the mother, and the magical form of cognition found in preoedipal development.

Women and Primitive Religions

To cope with its helplessness in facing the forces of nature, each society develops its own myths and rituals. These inventions enable individuals to survive emotionally, not to feel totally helpless and hopeless, and to deal with the many vicissitudes of life and the reality of death. Although we are consciously aware of our mortality, we also have the ability to use magical thinking, to fantasize and create myths and rituals to deal with anticipated trauma and loss. In primitive societies these myths were institutionalized and expressed in communal rituals, which strengthened the protection of each individual against nature. In addition, by people sharing the myths and rituals, the fabric of society was cemented into a cohesive whole and provided a continuity with the past.

What has been the historical development of magical thinking and the effect on women of primitive religions? Homer Smith (1952) noted that during the prehistoric era of civilization, people tried to control their destiny by anthropomorphizing the forces of nature. They fantasized that their physical surroundings were inhabited by sacred powers, which could be either protective or destructive. The ultimate symbol for these powers in their religion was the great mother goddess, despite the fact that these societies were *patriarchal* in their power structure.

During the Stone Age, idols of the great mother goddess had been worshiped, and sacrifices were made to her to insure fertility, life, and rebirth. Excavations of Mesopotamian settlements along the Tigris and Euphrates rivers, which date back to 5000 B.C., such as at Kish, Ur, Susa, and Tell al-Ubaid, as well as others along the Nile valley in Egypt, provide us with information about the great mother goddess. These excavated figures depict her body as a pregnant woman with large breasts and buttocks. Besides being the provider of food, she is responsible for fertility in man, animals, and plant life. Through magical thinking, awe-inspiring ritual, and animal or human sacrifice, primitive peoples attempted to entreat the goddess to insure fertility everywhere.

The great mother goddess took on various names. In Mesopotamia, including Babylonia, she was called Ishtar; among the Semitic tribes, she was Astarte or Ashtoreth; in Greece, Gaea or Rhea; in Egypt, Isis; in Phrygia (Asia Minor), Cybele; and in Persia, Anaitis. When nature proved to be destructive, people could blame themselves as being punished by the goddess for being sinful. This self-blame was preferable to seeing nature as impersonal and to being helpless, since people could at least attempt to undo their sinful acts by some form of penance or sacrifice.

In paleolithic, neolithic, and Bronze Age cave paintings and artifacts, these goddesses are portrayed as being associated with a variety of animals, such as birds, dogs, snakes, sheep, spiders, deer, fish, pigs, cattle, and bears. The goddesses could be seen as a projection of how women were perceived as not only representatives of nature but also of the animal part of human life. They and their animals were the forerunners of the Phrygian goddess Cybele and her lions, the Syrian goddess Dea Syria and her serpent, Artemis and her deer, as well as Eve and the snake. Possibly the prohibition against eating pig in the Middle East arose because the pig was generally the sacrificial animal to the goddess.

The Myth of an Original Matriarchal Society

The controversial feminist archeologist Marija Gimbutas (1974, 1989) speculates that the goddess had a golden age with gender equality during the Stone Age in Europe.[1] She portrays a peaceful, art-loving, earth-bound, and agricultural society, where people built settlements instead of forts, and made ceramics instead of weapons. She claims the culture was matrilineal, unstratified hierarchically, and the tribes were headed by queen-priestesses. Gimbutas further speculates that this harmonious and egalitarian culture which centered around women was destroyed by Indo-European invaders from the Pontic steppe about six thousand years ago, and that it was then that a patriarchal warlike culture became dominant. According to Gimbutas, the Indo-Europeans were indifferent to art, their gods were male warriors, and they were oriented toward the sky and the sun.

However, there is evidence that the people of old Europe were not simply gentle and peace loving. David Anthony, an anthropologist at Hartwick College who studied this same period, found fortified sites and weapons indicating that warfare did exist during the Stone Age (Steinfels 1990). Also found were symbols of status, evidence of human sacrifice, hierarchy, and social inequality. Anthony concluded that there was no evidence that women played a central or powerful role in the social structure, despite the religious worship of the goddess. Most other archeologists and anthropologists also question the conclusions drawn by Gambutas. They do not see any direct connection between goddess worship and an elevation of female status in those societies.

According to Sally Binford (1982), what appears to be a current feminist fundamentalism, centering on the great mother goddess and a matriarchal culture, cannot be supported by scientific evidence. She states that when anthropologists did serious fieldwork, "the simplistic notion of a matriarchal stage in the human past had to be discarded." The anthropologist James Preston considered that there may even have been an inverse relationship between goddess worship and women's social status; that is, the more goddess worship existed in a culture, the lower the status of women (Rabuzzi 1989). Women were feared and needed

---

1. Gimbutas's speculations of a golden age in old Europe, a time when women were socially empowered, serves as a rationale in certain feminist literature for rejecting the patriarchal aspects of Judeo-Christian religion and returning to worshipping the goddess (Spretnak 1982). Often this feminist theology is tied to an ecological movement that seeks harmony with mother earth. Another group that worships the goddess today is based on witchcraft, the Wiccan (old English for witch) movement, a remnant of pagan nature worship. In both the feminist and Wiccan groups, worship of the great mother goddess may include dance, art, meditation, herbal medicine, ritual, and magic. Unger (1990) estimates that more than 100,000 people currently worship the goddess in the United States.

to be controlled because of their mysterious magical powers that were connected to nature.[2]

Nature was (and still is) personified as a mother, who could be either beneficent and nurturant or terrifying, destructive, and able to inflict pain or death. The great mother goddess was not only the giver of life and fertility, but she was also the spinner or weaver of human destiny. Her life-giving aspects were associated with pigs, bulls, and goats, while her death-giving aspects were connected to images of vultures and owls. In Mesopotamia, Ishtar (who was the same as the Semitic goddess Astarte) was both the cruel goddess of war and the kindly sympathetic helper of the diseased and unfortunate. In the Hindu religion, there was the powerful goddess Kali, who was both loving and creative as well as terrifying and destructive. In Greek mythology, Athena was the goddess of war as well as of wisdom and handicrafts. However, the most dramatic split demonstrating the power of women was in the myth of the ancient Greek goddess Persephone and her mother, Demeter. The change in seasons was considered to be due to Demeter (the great mother goddess), who withheld the fertility of crops and created winter in retaliation for Pluto's abduction of Persephone to the underworld. Persephone was cherished by the Greeks as the harbinger of new life in spring, when she returned to her mother each year; and she was feared as the cruel goddess who punished the dead while in Hades.

Women alone, like the goddess Demeter, were felt to possess the magical powers of fertility, since at that time the role of the father in procreation was unknown. For example, Hesiod, the eighth- century B.C. Greek poet, recounted the earliest Greek mythology of the creation of the earth and its gods and goddesses. He told of Gaea, the great mother goddess, giving birth, through parthenogenesis, of her son-husband Uranus. The female body was seen as similar to the earth, which could spontaneously produce new life from itself. This great power of procreation that only women possess was considered to come from their contact with natural forces, ancestral spirits, and the goddesses.

De Beauvoir (1961) noted that historically women have been assigned agricultural tasks, since they could obtain supernatural help with the

2. Sprengnether (1990) comments that this same conflict concerning an original matriarchal society existed between Jung and Freud. Jung, who was influenced by J. J. Bachofen's book on mother-right, considered that historically there was a primary matriarchy. Rejecting Bachofen's ideas as inadequate, Freud, in *Totem and Taboo* (1912), felt society was always patriarchal, with perhaps a brief interval of matriarchy after the sons in the primal horde killed the primal father.

fertility of crops. Human fertility and rebirth were connected and also tied in with the supernatural forces that regenerated plants. Children were thought to be the reincarnated souls of dead ancestors that entered the mother's body through some mysterious spiritual visitation. In this way, female procreation was related to rebirth after death.

Social Control of Women

Paradoxically, even though women were feared for their mysterious powers in the fertility of crops, birth, and in rebirth after death, they did not have actual social power and were at the mercy of men. As a protection against abduction and rape by men, women stayed in their own clans, with authority over them vested in their father, maternal uncle, or brother. Although society was patriarchal, property was descended along matrilineal lines, since the father's role in procreation was unknown. In these early primitive societies, there was probably no concept of a permanent tie such as husband and wife, let alone any expectation of privacy, constancy, or fidelity. A man would stay with the woman's clan during specified and contracted periods of time (Smith 1952). Thus the price that women paid for physical protection was the reduction of their status to that of chattel (Brownmiller 1975).

Lévi-Strauss (1968) has made interpretations that link this use of women by men as chattel with the establishment of incest taboos and the development of early kinship systems. The prohibition of incestuous relations forced the family in primitive societies to give up its females to another family. This served as the basis for social organization in tribal societies. Women became the medium of exchange, or the equivalent of a sign being communicated between men to sustain the society. Women were exchanged for something considered of equal value in the marital contract. The formalized marriage regulations and the rules of kinship thereby cemented the society. The strongest incest taboo existed between brothers and sisters and parents and children, who were biologically the closest. The incest taboo served as a social necessity that guaranteed exogamy, and thereby protected the kinship structure of these primitive tribal societies.

Lévi-Strauss notes that only women, never men, have been used as a medium of exchange throughout the history of all human societies. In these primitive societies, the basic relationship of power was between the father and son-in-law or the brother and brother-in-law. A patriarchal power structure in marital institutions thus existed in matrilineal and later patrilineal societies.

In modern society, the incest taboo no longer serves this kinship function, but has become internalized as the Oedipus complex. This explanation of the origin of the incest taboo is different than that proposed by Freud in *Totem and Taboo* (1912). Freud had speculated that in prehistory, a group of brothers banded together to kill their father. Freud considered that the guilt for this action has persisted over thousands of years in the collective mind and resulted in the incest taboo. This formulation is similar to Jung's concepts of the collective unconscious. It is an example of Lamarckian evolutionary theory, in which occurrences during the life of an organism are passed on genetically to the offspring. Lamarckian theory was contemporary with and opposed to Darwinian theory, and is now generally discredited. Anthropological evidence has also not substantiated Freud's view, but has supported that of Lévi-Strauss concerning the incest taboo in society.

Malinowski (1929) discovered a primitive society similar to a Stone Age one existing among the Trobriand Islanders off the east coast of New Guinea. A woman was considered as an economic pawn for her family. When her brother surrendered her to a man to become his wife, the brother had to be compensated for her surrender by a dowry from the husband. The father's role in paternity was unknown and the husband remained an outsider, even though his wife lived with him and his clan. Property, kinship, totemic allegiance, and social status were still passed on matrilineally. The father had no authority to discipline the children, this role being exercised by the maternal uncle. Since the father did not impose restrictions and sexual relations between children occurred freely on the paternal side of the family, no Oedipus complex developed toward the father. Instead, hatred was directed toward the maternal relatives. There was a fear of sorcery from the *maternal* family, and all illnesses and misfortunes were seen as coming from their "wizards" and "flying witches."

Another example of the paradox between the fear of women's magical powers and their inferior social position in primitive societies is presented in *Oedipus in the Stone Age* (1988) by Theodore and Ruth Lidz. In investigating tribal societies in Papua New Guinea, the Lidzes found that men in these primitive societies were fearful of women's powerful and "magical" vaginal emanations. Because of this fear, adult men lived in a separate hut, apart from women and children. Young boys lived with their mothers until seven to fifteen years of age and were categorized with this feminine sector. At puberty, the boys went through initiation rituals to disidentify with their mothers and identify with the men. They were bled in the ritual to get rid of the mother's blood that created them. Then they were induced to vomit, or their skin was scarified to remove contamination caused by the mother's menstrual blood, physical contact, and food. The boy was symbolically reborn through men to become a male; this was accomplished through repeated homosexual inseminations, the drinking of semen, or the rubbing of semen into his skin. In some areas of New Guinea, the fear of the women's vagina was so great that homosexual anal intercourse was the preferred form of sex. The Lidzes found no evidence of an Oedipus complex between the ages of three to six. The main castration threat for boys came from the mother and not the father. All these New Guinea societies related a myth that the rituals and ritual objects used in these magical ceremonies were first created by women, then the objects were taken away by men through force or guile. The Lidzes posited that the men's aggressive masculinity and demeaning of women socially represented the defense of reaction formation against their envy of the creative power of women, that is, womb envy.

Some Native American tribes have also shown a fear of women's bodies and of their sexuality while they also deprive women of social power. Women's menstrual cycles are perceived as mysteriously being tied to the cycles of the moon. When a woman is menstruating, she is "in her moon," and her spiritual powers are considered to be so great that she is not allowed to touch the tribal drums. If she touched them, she would deprive them of their spiritual powers when used in rituals. Despite being feared for their sexual powers, women were denied a voice in tribal governing councils until very recently.

Thus throughout early history and in investigations of primitive and currently existing societies, substantial evidence indicates that women have been feared, demeaned, and controlled. Despite speculations, there is *no evidence of any golden age of matriarchy* that consisted of peaceful, art-loving societies with gender equality and headed by queen-priestesses. Woman's ability to create and nurture new life intimately tied her to the mystery of nature. Instead of viewing nature as indifferent and uncontrollable, nature was personified as a woman, the great mother goddess. Both women and nature needed to be controlled to insure survival, by trying to enhance the protective and minimizing the feared destructive forces. This control was accomplished through primitive religious myths and rituals, as well as by diminishing women's place in the fabric of society. Women thus appear to have been controlled, demeaned, and dehumanized in patriarchal societies from the Stone Age through the Victorian period.

What may have given rise to the myth of the golden age of matriarchy could be due to the fact that infants are reared by their mothers, who have power over them during early childhood. Thus individuals' early childhood experiences, when their mothers are dominant, may have been projected onto ancient societies. This projection is facilitated by the similar ways that primitive societies deal with their helplessness and survival—through fantasy and magical thinking. These are the same mechanisms used by infants during the preoedipal period of development.

3. Preoedipal Development and Social Attitudes toward Women

The Interaction of Ontogeny and Phylogeny

Ernst Haeckel (1834–1919) proposed the biogenetic law in evolutionary Darwinism that *ontogeny recapitulates phylogeny*, that is, that individual embryological and behavioral development repeats the history of a group or species. Freud, in *Civilization and Its Discontents* (1930), insightfully proposed that the reverse is also true in terms of behavioral development: "At this point we cannot fail to be struck by the similarity between the process of civilization and the libidinal development of the individual." Thus, *phylogeny also recapitulates ontogeny.* The history of a group can be compared to a repetition of individual personality development. Freud's insight can be expanded to trace the adaptation of societies through history that parallel and reflect the stages of object relations and symbolic development of the infant. Besides being reversible, there is a dynamic back-and-forth interaction between individual and group development. Individual functioning determines the way the group functions, and the group in turn influences the individual.

To cope with its helplessness in very early childhood, the infant needs to empower the mother by projecting a fantasy of omnipotence and merging with her. We could hypothesize that this merged symbiotic relationship with the preoedipal mother, which occurs during each person's childhood, was externalized onto the goddess in early societies to provide a sense of security. Like the omnipotent preoedipal mother, the great mother goddess was perceived as all powerful over life and death. Just as the infant deals with its helplessness and insecurity by the fantasy of fusion with the omnipotent preoedipal mother, primitive peoples attempted to establish a similar connection with the great mother goddess. During normal child development, the infant attempts, through fantasy and magical thinking, to obtain control over the all powerful mother upon whom its survival depends.

Malignant Transitional Objects and Idols

In the process of growth and separation from the mother, the infant employs a transitional object, such as a teddy bear or blanket. This object can be physically manipulated and controlled to maintain a sense of safety and security. Winnicott (1965) termed this object the first "not me" possession. The transitional object serves as an external symbol that maintains the internal fantasy of fusion with the omnipotent good mother. It is a form of symbolic activity that sustains the child's dependency and avoids the dreaded feelings of annihilation associated with separation anxiety and helplessness. Later, the emotional investment in the transitional object is given up when the child internalizes the mother's function and can comfort itself.

Freud (1927) considered that later in life, religion serves to provide a powerful and protective father and mother, as we had in childhood. It has been noted that pagan idols functioned for adults much like an infant's transitional objects (Slipp 1986). The idols served as a symbolic connection to the omnipotent goddess, so that anxiety and helplessness could be contained. However, the idols were unlike normal transitional objects, which are given up when the infant internalizes the parental figures to become self-empowering and self-comforting. The idol can be considered a pathological or malignant transitional object. It does not lead us to self-growth and independence, but permanently retains the omnipotent power projected into it. This symbolic process to deal with helplessness in turn only perpetuates that the idol remains empowered and continues the individual's dependency and helplessness.

How Magic Works

Primitive peoples believed that goddesses and gods, onto whom omnipotent power was projected, could be influenced magically—through sacrifices, rituals, and prayers—to exert their power benevolently. Why would these ritualistic actions be thought to propitiate the deity? Piaget's (1954, 1963) research into the infant's ability to symbolize sheds some light here. Initially, infants cannot retain a mental image of an object when it is concealed or removed. To the infant, when an object is out of sight it ceases to exist. Later the infant evolves what Piaget terms "sensori-motor" intelligence, which considers that *objects come and go as a result of the infant's actions*. This mental "schema of action" is felt to control the object. Thus the infant feels its actions are omnipotent, since the object is not considered to have a permanent and separate existence of its own.

In psychoanalytic theory, this is the type of primary-process thinking that occurs in early infancy before ego boundaries and secondary-process thinking are established. During the early part of the preoedipal period, fantasy and action are not differentiated from reality, but are seen as causally connected. For example, the infant may fantasize that crying for the mother's breast magically controls the breast's appearance. This omnipotent thinking that *one's fantasy and actions can influence external events is the fundamental basis for magic and ritual.*

This sensori-motor intelligence found in infancy by Piaget or the primary-process thinking described in psychoanalysis is demonstrated in primitive cultures. Sir James Frazer, in *The Golden Bough* (1922), studied the magical rituals found among primitive peoples. He identified this type of omnipotent thinking, which he termed an "imitative" form of "sympathetic magic." By performing a prescribed form of action, often similar to what they expect to happen, individuals believe they exert magical control over an external object. For example, if they pour water out of a pan, it is supposed to bring on rain. The fantasy world of the primitive is not differentiated from the real physical world, but is seen as merged and causally connected. One's fantasies and actions are felt magically to control external events and become the basis for rituals.

From the ages of four to seven, Piaget noted a period of symbolizing activity he termed "assimilation." Schemata of environmental objects are incorporated into patterns of behavior that connect the past with the present. The child judges its world in a moralistic, authoritarian fashion, in which rules are sacred and immutable. Much like the primitive individual, the child egocentrically feels its actions have produced certain environmental effects as a reward or punishment for its past behavior. In psychoanalytic terms, the child views the world from a narcissistic position. It feels it is to blame for whatever happens, since it does not yet experience others as wholly separate and independently motivated. This forms the basis for the magical belief that one is responsible for the good or bad fortune that occurs. Freud discussed this phenomenon in *The Future of an Illusion* (1927), seeing the motivation for religious ritual as an attempt to propitiate or manipulate the forces that are experienced as a judgment of one's behavior.

In another form of "sympathetic magic" that Frazer (1922) terms "contagious," a *symbol* is incompletely separated from its external object and is still considered as having control over it. The symbol may be a total representation of the external object, or else a part that is equated with the whole. For example, a voodoo doll, a symbol of a person, is used magically to inflict injury on that person. If the magician puts needles into the doll, he or she believes injury will occur to the person. A part of a person, such as a bit of hair or nails, a photograph, or even a name, may also be used by the magician to exert control over that person magically. Freud (1912) mentions an example of this form of magic in the cannibalism of primitive peoples. By eating a part of a person, individuals believe they can magically possess the other's qualities. Freud also noted that in neurotic fetishism, a piece of clothing can symbolize the entire object. These are also related to the first symbol during infancy, the transitional object. By manipulating the transitional object, which symbolizes the mother, the small child feels able to exert magical control over the mother to deal with separation anxiety.

As noted earlier, in primitive societies women were seen as symbolically connected to nature, which was personalized as the great mother goddess. The projection of an ambivalent mother image onto nature, which can be nurturant or destructive, formed the basis for the symbolic connection of women to nature. By controlling women, a sense of control over nature is established and maintained.

Enhancing Magic through Ritual Merging

Magic is usually shared with others to enhance its effectiveness. Ritual represents the communal form of magic. It is expressed by an institutionalized series of movements, songs, and words, which often have a rhythmic and repetitive quality to *promote psychological merging or bonding*. Susan Langer, in *Philosophy in a New Key* (1942), comments on the power of musical rhythm to sympathetically evoke similar feelings of happiness, sadness, courage, and the like, or to influence actions in people. Thus musical and rhythmic rituals serve to create a shared emotional climate, facilitate mutual identification, and foster group bonding. This nonverbal communication is a remnant of an infantile or egocentric form of symbolic activity that persists alongside the later social development of language. In the nonverbal, which Langer terms "nondiscursive," the *form or context* of the communication is what is essential and is used to express *feelings and imagery*. In the verbal type of symbolic thought, which she calls "discursive," the *content* of language is used to express *ideas and describe events*. Language tends to shape the communication into being more discrete and linear, which is shared socially so that thoughts and facts can be expressed. Nondiscursive symbolic thought tends to be more fluid and global, metaphorical and imagistic, and is likely to be more personal, emotional, and intimate. As we will see later, men tend to focus more on the content, the discursive form, while women tend to be more sensitive to the context, the nondiscursive form.

In rituals, the sound of words and not their actual meaning is important. Langer points out that the very lack of comprehension of meaning to words adds to the magical power of the rhythm when performed in unison. During early childhood the first symbolic value of words does not have a specific external meaning but is personal, expressive, and has magical significance. It is the meter, alliteration, assonance, and the rhythm of these words that are important. Examples are "fee, fi, fo, fum" or "eeni, meeni, myni, mo." These words are more closely related to visual imagery, dreams, and fantasy and can include a multitude of meanings. Primitive peoples, like very young children, therefore feel they are able magically to influence and control their environment through ritual and magical thinking.

Langer's nondiscursive and discursive forms of symbolism thus represent two different forms of symbolic communication, which express emotions and imagery as well as cognitive thought. She provides us with an understanding of how the interaction of these two symbolic activities can be found in poetry, literature, dance, art, and religion. However, when the nondiscursive overshadows the discursive, magical causality supersedes more objective and socially accepted reality.

In contemporary society, we see a similar temporary loss of ego boundaries and regression to the symbiotic phase of merging in the group mind of mob psychology. However, in primitive societies this nondiscursive form of thinking may facilitate the primary form of adaptation that is shared socially. This rhythmic repetition of words and actions in ritual stimulates merging with others and enhances the magical appeal to influence an omnipotent deity. When ritual merging with the group occurs, the group's power and protection are enlisted as well. Just as merging with the preoedipal mother had occurred during childhood, merging with an external force or group larger than oneself in adult life diminishes the individual's sense of isolation and helplessness.

The Preoedipal Period and Social Domination of Women

The preoedipal period has been highlighted by the feminists—Simone de Beauvoir (1961) and Dorothy Dinnerstein (1976)—as an explanation for the dehumanization and domination of women since primitive times. The basis for their argument is that women dominate early child rearing and are not only a source of bodily pleasure but also of pain. Dinnerstein speculates that both sexes need to control and retaliate against having to submit to the powerful preoedipal mother. She feels that people never outgrow their vindictiveness for having to submit to Mother's power, and later need to vent their rage at her. According to her, men need to dominate women as a compensation for being controlled by their mothers during infancy. Women may also share these vindictive feelings against other women. Men express it by degrading everything female, and some women may live vicariously through men by offering themselves up to male tyranny. Dinnerstein states that because of these early preoedipal and oedipal attitudes, women in adult life are still seen as semihuman, being primarily sources of emotional sustenance and regarded as sexual objects.

Dinnerstein also speculates that the mother is perceived as the embodiment of all that is carnal and mortal, the prototype of death, which needs to be confined and denied. That this experience of the mother is destructive and connected to death stems from the preoedipal fear of engulfment and annihilation. The child also fears death when it is frustrated by loss of maternal nurturance and support. The mother becomes the "dirty goddess," "the scapegoat-idol."

Dinnerstein's solution is for both parents to partake equally in early child rearing. Indeed, the father's greater involvement in child care is becoming more and more acceptable in middle-class American families. Attachment to the father facilitates the child's separation from the mother, and boys achieving a masculine gender identity, and girls developing a positive self-image as a woman. Dinnerstein's insight is especially valid for boys, who need to disengage from the powerful preoedipal mother to establish gender identity as well as autonomy. Although infants may fear being engulfed by their powerful mothers, at the same time they need to idealize and merge with her as an omnipotent object for their own security. Thus they need and fear the omnipotent mother. When mothering is responsive and nurturant, that is, "good enough," and the mother is not intrusive and can contain the infant's aggression without retaliation or abandonment, it is unlikely that all infants will grow up to display persistent rage and vindictiveness. Under normal conditions, children gradually differentiate themselves to become independent and competent individuals, and process and integrate their ambivalence toward their mothers.

It is more likely that persistent rage toward the mother is carried from childhood into adulthood not only because of her preoedipal powerful position but her continued dominance later on. The postoedipal mother may be intrusive, exert excessive control, be overly protective, or interfere with separation and the establishment of the child's autonomy. Thus the infant's own need to experience the preoedipal mother as dominant is not resolved but reinforced throughout childhood by her continued controlling behavior. It is more likely the reality of an excessively controlling and intrusive mother in the postoedipal period of development that perpetuates the child's rage and interferes with the normal integration of ambivalence. When the mother is not excessively controlling, the child generally resolves its fantasies that perceive the mother as a dominant, frustrating, and controlling object around three years of age. The need for the mother to continue to be controlling, exploitative, and to prevent separation may in large part be due to her constricted role in a patriarchal society.

Another scenario that is perhaps even more devastating to a child's development is the *weakness* of the mother, not her dominance. The weak mother may provide insufficient or inadequate nurturance and security, which produces deprivation and rage when the child's needs are ignored. In addition, the child may be forced to be sensitive to the mother's needs, with a reversal of generational boundaries occurring and the child functioning as a "good mother." Instead of being nurtured and protected by the mother, the child must perform these functions for her. In addition, the child must suppress its rage for being deprived, since it has experienced the mother as vulnerable. The end result is that self-assertion and anger are felt as destructive of the mother, and not integrated and resolved as is normal. The repressed rage may then be displaced onto other women. (These family patterns, where the child feels responsible for the self-esteem and personal integrity and survival of the parent(s), will be discussed at length in chapters 9 and 12.)

Finally, Dinnerstein does not give sufficient import to the influence of culture. In ancient societies attitudes toward women and nature were originally derived from an infant's magical way of coping with its help-lessness and ambivalence toward the mother. However, these attitudes achieved a life of their own and were passed down through the generations. These cultural attitudes were psychologically adaptive to a hostile and indifferent environment. The myths and attitudes were accepted by both genders, otherwise all individuals would have felt totally vulnerable and unprotected against the forces of nature. These cultural myths and attitudes influenced how women were perceived and how they perceived themselves. Only in recent years have women felt entitled to own their own bodies and to enjoy their sexuality. The myths of primitive societies have persisted to the present and are only now slowly changing.

What may have also created rage toward the mother up to Victorian times is the birth of so many children. This situation was due to the lack of birth control and to compensate for the high death rate during child-hood. The result was often insufficient mothering and neglect of individual children's developmental needs. In addition, women's role in a patriarchal society was markedly constricted, and the source of their identity rested on their functioning as a mother. In order to retain the role of mother and sustain their self-esteem, they may have interfered with the emanci-pation of their children. Lack of power *outside* the home may also have made some mothers more dominant and controlling toward their children *within* the home. Finally, the emotional needs of children were not known prior to Freud, who was a pioneer in exploring child development. Knowl-edge of child development is changing modern society in terms of the relationships of parents to their children.

4. Dethroning the Goddess and Phallocentrism

Cultural Advance to the Oedipal Period

In this chapter we will further develop the hypothesis that phylogeny also recapitulates ontogeny—the history of a culture parallels individual psychological development. In the previous chapter we examined mythology in primitive cultures as an externalization of the adaptation used in the early preoedipal period of child development. In this chapter we will explore the outward expressions of the phallic and genital periods of child development in later cultures.

As already noted, Gimbutas (1974) speculated that the great mother goddess was dethroned and replaced by male warrior gods about six thousand years ago, when waves of Indo-Europeans on horseback invaded Europe. However, it appears that dethroning of the goddess was a much more gradual process than Gimbutas envisions. At some unknown time in prehistory, people figured out the role of the father in procreation. As a result, the great mother goddess was at first supplemented with a male god, and only later was she totally supplanted in importance by a masculine god of fecundity. Male phallic symbols now became more important than female symbols of the womb. A phallocentric society gradually evolved and in time became the most common form of social organization throughout the world.

In ancient agricultural societies, the human sexual experience was projected onto nature, which was personified. To deal with one's helplessness against natural forces and the trauma of death, human life was considered to be similar to plant life. An analogy was made between men inseminating women to produce human life and the need for seeds to be sown in the earth to yield plant life. Campbell (1988) points out that analogies were also made between humans and plants concerning rebirth or life after death. The dead body was buried in the earth, believed to be Mother Nature's womb. Like a seed, the dead body would then be reborn magically later in women. Phallic symbols were placed on tombstones in the hope of rebirth after death. Out of death came life.

Examples of Phallic Worship

Direct reproductions were made of the male genitalia, or in their symbolic form by erect stones and trees, which represented the male generative power. Stones were worshiped by the ancient Greeks, Romans, Germans, Gauls, and Britons. Greeks wore phallic amulets made of wood (especially from the fig tree), stone, or metal, which were associated with Dionysos, the male god of generation and the harbinger of spring. Cakes shaped like a phallus were popular sacramental foods in Greece and Rome (Briffault 1929). The circle of large stones at Stonehenge, on Salisbury Plain in England, was probably another phallic symbol. The axis of these stones was arranged to point toward the sun on summer solstice, which probably means that a male sun god was worshiped. Early Christian clergy attempted to stamp out phallic worship, but the Christmas tree bedecked with lights remains a carryover of this pagan mythology. Man identified himself with his penis as a symbol of strength and worshiped its generative power.

A mythology about the change of seasons also arose in Europe and the Middle East, which replaced the one solely associated with the female deity. A male deity was now also introduced into the mythology alongside the female deity. It was thought that a male god died before each winter, as a scapegoat for man's sins, and was reborn each spring. However, he was brought back to life by his wife-mother, and his generative power gave new life to plants and animals. The Maypole celebration is a remnant of this annual rebirth of male generativity.

Beyond the Preoedipal Period in Culture

One can hypothesize from this new mythology that the development of culture had progressed beyond the preoedipal period and into the phallic period of child development. The great mother goddess, the externalization of the preoedipal mother, remained strong but was no longer the only powerful deity. The Oedipus complex occurring during the phallic period of male child development now appeared to be externalized in this new mythology. As evidence of this hypothesis, the female goddess was depicted as the wife-mother of the male god. Thus the relationship of the male god seemed to be the fulfillment of an oedipal wish, to be the husband-son of his mother. The seasonal cycle could also be explained in phallocentric terms. One might speculate that the death of the male god each winter, because of man's sins, could represent punishment for oedipal desires toward the mother. The names for the male god and his wife-mother varied in different mythologies. In Egypt it was Osiris and Isis; in Phoenicia, Adonis and Astarte; in Babylonia, Tammuz and Ishtar; in Phrygia, Attis and Cybele; and in Greece, Zeus and Rhea or Adonis and Aphrodite.

While the great mother goddess still represented the earth, the new male god was associated with the phallic power of the sun or sky. The dominant great mother goddess was later dethroned in Egypt by Ra, the sun god of light and virility; in Babylonia, it was Bel-Marduk; in Phoenicia, Baal; among the Celtic Druids, Be al; and in Greece, it was Zeus (Bulfinch 1964).

Along with the establishment of the magical power of the phallus, there appeared an accompanying change in social organization. Although a patriarchal society still persisted, a patrilineal descent of property was instituted. Women were owned by their husbands, similar to other private property, and they joined the husband's clan instead of remaining in their maternal clan. This meant that children were now under the authority of the father. In order to insure the passing down of status and possessions, paternity had to be assured. Therefore, the wife was expected to be a virgin at marriage, and adultery became a crime. A man's claim for immortality was now through his seed, which would be passed on only by his male heirs. The family's survival, through his son's generative power, meant personal survival.

Phallic-Sexual Mythology

The central feature of primitive pagan religions was its sexual mythology. It was through imitative sympathetic magic that sexual relations between men and women were thought to influence nature's fertility; many of these primitive religions therefore had open sexual intercourse, often ending in orgies, as part of their magical ritual to insure fertility of plants, animals, and people. Smith (1952) notes that men, while seeking the embraces of the priestesses of Ishtar, also considered this sexual union to be with the fruitful goddess herself, who was the female mother fertility goddess. In this way men became blessed with fertility. Other gods and goddesses of sex were the Babylonian Mylitta, the Greeks Aphrodite and Dionysos, and the Roman Priapus. In India, copulation as a religious experience was connected with the Hindu god of love, Kama (Klaf 1964). An Indian manual on the art and technique of love, the *Kama Sutra*, was compiled by the poet Vatsyayana Mallanaga. It was based on earlier Sanskrit texts devoted to Kama.

An example of the use of ritual sexual orgy as a form of imitative sympathetic magic to insure nature's fertility has been described by Goldberg (1930). The followers of the god Baal in the Middle East believed Baal was the sun who kissed Mother Earth and made her fruitful. Each winter Baal died and his worshippers mourned and begged the powerful goddess Ishtar to bring him back to life, and each spring sacrificial animal offerings were made. This was followed by the mystic union in physical sex between male worshipers and priestesses in a frenzied, drunken, sexual orgy. These sacrificial and sexual rituals were believed magically to insure the fertility of plants, animals, and men.

In many societies of the Near East and Europe, all women had to be married to the male god of fertility, or a surrogate priest, at some time. After this marriage, women were obliged to serve as sacred prostitutes in their temples (Briffault 1929). According to Herodotus, the Greek historian who lived around 450 B.C., nearly all men had intercourse with these women prostitute/priestesses inside their temples.

A remnant of this imitative form of sympathetic magic was also seen in India, where girls were deflowered before marriage by using a lingam or phallus made of stone, ivory, or metal, which was the emblem of the god Siva. And in Rome, brides were also required to lose their virginity before marriage by sitting on the lap of the phallic god Mutunus Tutunus. This fertility ritual continued symbolically through the Middle Ages through the practice of *jus primae noctis*, whereby a priest or secular lord had the right to sleep with the bride on the wedding night.

The Judeo-Christian Religion

The Hebrews considered pagan idol worship, especially its practice of sacred prostitution and licentious sexual fertility rituals to Baal with the priestesses of Ishtar, as an abomination. The biblical land of Eden is thought to have been located in the Mesopotamian valley, and its city of Ur was the birthplace of the patriarch Abraham. The valley was important in the worshiping of the great mother goddess. However, in the Old Testament story of Adam and Eve, men were considered to be closer to God than women, and the magical ability to produce life was taken away from women and given to men. Not only was Adam created by God and Eve created from his rib, but Eve's weakness to temptation led Adam into sin and the expulsion of both from Eden. In other words, women's erotic sexuality was to blame. Both parts of this biblical story neutralized the power of women that had existed in the pagan fertility rituals to Baal, where priestesses of Ishtar and their sexuality had been intermediary in the great mother goddess's power of fertility and new life.

The biblical story of men replacing women as the source of creativity and closeness to God is not limited to the Jewish religion. It is reflected in religions throughout the world, where women became the second sex and men controlled spirituality. The story in the Bible of Noah and the flood is viewed by Dundes (1988) to be a universal reflection of patriarchal society usurping the procreative powers of women. There are over one thousand similar stories in Europe, Asia, Africa, Australia, and America recounting the destruction of life by a flood and a second re-creation of life. "Amniotic fluid is the flood of creation," speculates Dundes. "A man must use whatever means he has to create a flood." The global flood stories are myths that may unconsciously represent a urinary flood and symbolize male envy of women's original procreative powers, that is, womb envy. Men destroy the first creation of women and, after a flood created by men, substitute a second creation of their own making.

The ancient Israelites, by advocating a monotheistic religion of a non-corporeal God, made a leap forward that permitted a greater degree of personal independence and individual identity to evolve (Slipp 1986). They banned idol worship in the belief that idols perpetuated an external dependency on a pantheon of female and male gods and the associated sexual licentiousness. The earliest Israelites lived in the twelfth century B.C. in the hill country around Canaan. Unlike any other culture, they left no evidence of any divine imagery or votive figures in archaeological excavations. The first mention of the male Israelite God, Yahweh, is in ancient Hebrew inscriptions found in the ninth century B.C. Most important of all, the Hebrew religion practiced by the Israelites was no longer a magical way of manipulating and controlling the whims of capricious gods and goddesses to insure fertility. God's presence could be experienced as ever present, even when he is not seen.

Resolution of the Oedipal Conflict in Culture

This cultural advance of giving up the worship of idols is similar to the child's relinquishment of its transitional objects and separation from the mother. During normal development, the child no longer needs to manipulate and control the mother simply as a need-satisfying object, but recognizes her as a separate whole individual. The mother becomes internalized and her memory can be evoked without her physical presence. This allows the child to acknowledge the separateness and constancy of the self as well as the internalized maternal object. The child can then comfort and direct itself, and is less dependent for its self-esteem and identity on the reactions of the mother and others.

This same process of individual development was thus replicated on a larger social scale. Idols of capricious pagan gods and goddesses had functioned as external transitional objects that needed to be manipulated to satisfy one's needs. By internalizing God and being guided by his laws—the ten commandments and the Bible—the Israelites contributed to a leap forward in superego and personality development. In the Hebrew religion, God was separate, invisible, yet ever present within each individual. People experienced greater individuation as well as personal guilt. They could be guided by internal values instead of by shame or fear of external punishment.[1]

According to classical psychoanalytic theory, this process occurs after the oedipal period. The child resolves the Oedipus complex and passes from the phallic to the genital stage of development. For boys, this turning from the mother and identification with an idealized father consolidates male gender identity. Internalization of the father occurs, and concern and empathy for others as separate individuals becomes consolidated. Freud maintained that this process occurs in children during the genital period of development, representing the sublimation of sexuality into tenderness and love. In addition, having an all-powerful God with whom one could identify served as a source of strength and reinforced the law of the father in society.

Regarding religion, Freud (1939) recognized that God and his laws become a permanent and constant part of one's personality. However, Freud's conceptions regarding internalization of the father as responsible

---

1. Bergmann (1989) notes that Freud misinterpreted the story of Oedipus Rex, who felt responsible for the external vengeance of the Greek gods but did not suffer internal Jewish guilt.

for superego development would seem to have a closer similarity to the internalization of the Hebrew God in religion than what occurs during child development.

Religion now became a way of understanding and internalizing the values connected with people's relation to God, parents, society, and each other. Ethical and spiritual issues that governed relationships became important, with justice and consideration for others as well as altruistic love becoming paramount. Christ continued to advocate these ethical and spiritual concepts in his sayings that the kingdom of God is within us, and that we should treat others as we wished to be treated by them.

Campbell (1988) pointed out that in the evolution of Christianity, goddess worship continued, but at a more symbolic level. Many churches were called Notre Dame (Our Lady), and symbolized that we are spiritually, not literally, reborn by a female divinity upon entering and leaving the church. Campbell noted that the worship of Mary, mother of Christ, occupied the place of the female goddess and became integrated into Christianity. He commented that the main reference to the immaculate conception and the virgin birth was only mentioned by the later Christian writer, Luke, who was a Greek. Neither Matthew, Mark, nor John mentioned the virgin birth in their gospels. Campbell interprets Luke's writings as a further perpetuation of pre-Christian Greek and Egyptian goddess mythology, some of which made references to childbirths that were not preceded by sexual relations with a male.

Female Sexuality Continued to Be Feared and Condemned

Because the early Christians took upon themselves the difficult task of converting people from participating in erotic pagan rituals, the sexual instinct was often considered to be the essence of evil and thus condemned. For example, Clement of Alexandria denounced the citizens of Rome thus: "You believe in your idols because you crave after their licentiousness" (Briffault 1929). Since most heathen religions involved women as sacred prostitute/priestesses in their sexual rituals, feminine sexuality was considered especially impure and was suppressed.

A number of early Christian leaders were so uncompromising in their denunciation of sex—because of its association with heathen religions—that they condemned marriage, idealized celibacy, and considered women to be the gateway to hell. In the New Testament (Corinthians 11–14) women were undermined in their relation to men: "Man . . . is the image and glory of God, but the woman is the glory of the man. Neither was the man created for the woman, but the woman for the man. Let your women keep silence in churches. . . . And if they will learn anything, let them ask their husbands at home."

Saint Augustine in the fifth century and Thomas Aquinas in the thirteenth believed that good women were submissive to their husbands and their major function was to bear children (Matlin 1987). Western religion became sharply opposed to sexual relations, with women being put down and again split along an all good or an all bad dimension. Good women repressed their sexuality, while sinful women were erotic and sensual.

Remnants of pagan nature worship, which had existed in the forests throughout Europe, continued alongside Christianity until the seventeenth century. In the Middle Ages these pagan meetings were considered to be witchcraft and were greatly feared. In these pagan rituals, a male priest would dress in the skin of a goat or bull, with its horns and tail simulating the phallic god of fertility, Dionysos. The priest became the image used to depict the devil, who was part man and part goat. The women, who were considered witches, had made a pact with the devil: in exchange for their bodies and souls, he enabled these women to practice black art, to fly, and to transform themselves into animals.

Four nights a year until the cock crowed, these witches engaged in nude, sensual meetings that were called witches' Sabbaths. The most famous ones were October 31 (Hallowe'en), and the eve of May Day (Walpurgis Night), which occurred at the changes of seasons. On Hallowe'en, the barriers between the living and the dead were supposedly lifted, and witches were able to cast spells to contact the dead. This mythology stemmed from the belief that the change of seasons from summer to winter was related to death and rebirth. The witches were the overt manifestations of a long line of pagan great mother goddesses, from Ishtar and Isis to Persephone. Like them, the witches were thought to have power over death and rebirth, as well as over the fertility of humans and plants.

During the Middle Ages in Europe, people feared the power of the witches to cast spells that could make others sick or cause death— or even to bring the dead back to life. Dominican monks, who wrote "Malleus Maleficarum" (The Witches' Hammer) in 1494, denounced all women as sexual temptresses, as evils of nature, and as potential witches (Summers 1951). Women accused of being witches were tortured, tried, convicted, and burned at the stake. From 1484, when the Inquisition took over the investigation of witchcraft, to 1782, when the last servant girl was executed in Switzerland, it is estimated that over 300,000 women were killed in Europe. In the United States in the late seventeenth century, fifty-five people were tortured and twenty were executed as witches in Salem, Massachusetts.

Views of Women in Philosophy

Among philosophers, Plato (427–347 B.C.) viewed women as less competent than men, but he conceded that some women had qualities that overlapped with those of men. These male qualities were intelligence, courage, and the ability to resist temptation, which enabled them to rule. Aristotle (Plato's pupil, 384–322 B.C.), noted that women were one of nature's deformities, an unfinished man who never developed rationally and needed to be ruled by men. Woman's best condition in life was to have a quiet home life. Rousseau (1712–1778) wrote that nature dictated the submission of women to men. Women's role was to please men, to be useful, and to make men's lives pleasant. Nietzsche (1844–1900) was profoundly antifeminist and phallocentric, stating that a man "must conceive of woman as a possession, as property that can be locked, as something predestined for service and achieving her perfection in that" (Matlin 1987).

To summarize, like the helpless infant who attempts to control its mother, societies too have controlled women and their bodies in an attempt to solve the existential dilemma. In time, a patriarchal society evolved that had control over women and their sexuality. Women were viewed as *split* into all good or all bad. This is similar to the way the infant experiences the mother. Like the omnipotent preoedipal mother, the great mother goddesses were seen as both nurturant and destructive. With the knowledge of male generative power, patriarchal society also became phallocentric. Men attempted to gain greater control over nature and women in order to master their existence. Women were thus not only controlled socially but their sexuality was demeaned. To eliminate sacred prostitution existing in pagan religions, early Judeo-Christian leaders considered women and sexuality as sinful. Female sexuality was split into good asexual women and bad sexual women. This split was later expressed in Victorian society as the madonna/whore complex. Women were chaste and all good or seductive and all bad. Probably Freud's greatest contribution to modern culture was to be the Moses who liberated women from the slavery imposed upon them by a sexually repressive society that had existed for thousands of years.

5. *Projective Identification and Misogyny*

Even though misogyny, the hatred of women, is based on irrational magical thinking, it persisted in Europe into and beyond the Enlightenment, when rationality and science were emphasized. In Charles Darwin's evolutionary theory of natural selection and Herbert Spencer's philosophy of the survival of the fittest, women were seen as emotional, less rational, and passive, as well as physically weaker and hence inferior to men. Women's skulls and brains were smaller than men's, and this was taken as proof that women were less intelligent. Evolutionary theory was used to justify the cultural bias against women.

As in prescientific days, women continued to be suppressed by men. Men's reliance on science and rationality now fueled a renewed effort to master their environment. Every major thinker during the Enlightenment assumed religion would disappear, because they thought it was based on animistic superstition and magic. Man's cognitive ability was the new source of power, in effect becoming a new form of religion. This new subtle phallic worship was not expressed in overt images of the penis, but symbolically. The penis was sublimated and displaced upward to the mind, being manifested through the masculine preoccupations of rationalism, individualism, realism, and materialism. Now it would not be traditional religion but objective scientific technology that would conquer Mother Nature and her earthly sisters, women. Nature was like a machine, and discovering her universal laws through mathematics would lead to control of her. The laboratory and the factory now became the monastery and cathedral for this new materialistic religion. Pilgrimages were made to expositions held in the United States, England, and throughout Europe that exalted man's achievements in technology and science. The paternalistic phallocentric Victorian society that evolved in Europe during the eighteenth and nineteenth centuries not only stressed control over nature through "objective" science, but also suppressed women, emotions, pleasure, and other subjective experiences.

A pervasive male orientation and misogyny existed in the scientific community. This bias against women ranged from the work of Paul Broca, who discovered the area of the brain responsible for speech, to Havelock Ellis, who introduced an "objective" approach to the study of sex. In literature, even John Stuart Mill, the early champion of feminism, made no mention of his mother at all in his *Autobiography*. Samuel Butler, in *The Way of All Flesh*, ignored his mother and was obsessed with the father-son relationship (Roazen 1984).

Blaming Freud for his male orientation and for the derogation of the importance of women in psychoanalysis is too simplistic, since it was a universal cultural phenomenon. Even though Freud did surmount his bias toward women in some areas, elsewhere his ideas directly mirrored the culture in which he lived.

Phallocentrism had existed as the predominant thread that ran from ancient times to the present. Freud similarly idealized the male phallus and its sublimated expression in the male mind. The penis became central to psychoanalytic theory, duplicating its importance in a phallocentric society. In Freud's theory, during the *phallic* phase, *castration anxiety* over possible loss of the penis for the male and *penis envy* for the female were the major motivations for personality development. The female genitals had no important role in psychoanalytic theory, and a woman's mind was considered inferior to a man's. There was no mention of womb or breast envy in the male, only penis envy in the female. Psychoanalytic theory placed women's generative powers secondary to that of men. Freud stated that because of penis envy and a desire to compensate for the lack of this appendage, women turn from the mother to the father, become feminine, and want to bear children. Thus, femininity and women's procreative ability were seen as the end result of not having a penis. The mother's role in child development was generally ignored in psychoanalysis until the 1920s. According to Freud, it was only the father who was internalized, after the resolution of the Oedipus complex, to form the core of the superego in the personality of the child.

Projective Identification in the Culture

In order to feel powerful and in control of nature, men unconsciously project unacceptable aspects of themselves onto women. However, this cultural process has its psychological underpinnings in the early mother-child relationship of male infants. The primitive defense mechanisms used in early child development find expression in the culture. In turn, the culture reinforces these psychological defenses.

The initial identification of all infants is considered by modern psychoanalytic theory to occur during the symbiotic stage of development, when merging with the all-powerful preoedipal mother occurs. Using the primitive defense of *splitting*, the mother is seen as being either all good or all bad. The all-bad mother is projected and evacuated, while the all-good mother image is internalized further to form the core of the ego for both sexes. For a boy to achieve a masculine gender identity, he needs to distance himself from this initial feminine internalization of the mother and to identify with the father and other male figures. The boy needs to deny aspects of himself considered as feminine, in order to differentiate and protect himself from engulfment by the all-powerful preoedipal mother. This is accomplished through the use of the primitive defense of *projective identification*. Those aspects of himself that are unacceptable to his masculine identity are repressed and projected onto women. These include feelings of dependency, helplessness, and emotionality.

Projective identification is the interpersonal equivalent of the intrapsychic mechanism of repression. Projective identification is an earlier and primitive defense mechanism, occurring before adequate boundaries between the self and others are established. In repression, unacceptable aspects of oneself are pushed down into one's own unconscious part of the mind. In projective identification, another person serves as a container into which unacceptable parts of oneself are unconsciously placed. These unacceptable aspects are projected into another person and, like material repressed into one's own unconscious, need not be owned consciously. The other is unconsciously or consciously manipulated to fit the projection placed into them. The projector can then identify with the unacceptable aspects that the other is expressing, without taking conscious responsibility for them. Even though induced into this role, the other can be controlled and demeaned for seeming to possess or express these unacceptable aspects.

By constricting the feminine role in society and fostering dependency, helplessness, and emotionality, women were unconsciously induced into expressing these unacceptable feelings for men. In turn, men could condemn women as being inferior for having these undesirable qualities. Because this process occurred at an unconscious level, men did not have to take responsibility for having placed women into a position of dependency in society. Although women could be demeaned for being weak, men could live vicariously through women and avoid taking responsibility for their own vulnerabilities.

This need to bolster man's sense of strength and masculinity in the culture by dissociating unacceptable aspects and projecting them on others was not limited to women, but was evident in European nationalism, imperialism, racism, and religious bigotry. Efforts to change this state of social inequality for women and other minorities emerged around the turn of the century.

The Early Feminist Movement

The social emancipation of women began with the early feminist movement during the latter part of the eighteenth century in Europe and the United States. Unlike the current feminist movement, which emphasizes organizations for social action, the early feminists relied on the power of the written word to bring about social change (Rossi 1973). The early feminists were also heirs of the Enlightenment. They trusted reason and believed that open discussion and education would cure ignorance and bring about social equality.

Although their trust in the power of rationality may have been naive, they wrote with deep passion and conviction. These feminists viewed male domination of women as analogous to political tyranny, and advocated a number of ideological positions. William Godwin, the husband of Mary Wollstonecraft, recommended such radical measures as disregard of marriage, the state, and the church. Mary Wollstonecraft wrote on the rights of women and advocated that child rearing be similar for girls and boys. Fanny Wright advocated a separate community, Nashoba, where a perfect society could be created that did not cripple women psychologically. Abigail Adams sent the famous "Remember the Ladies" letter to her husband, President John Adams, recommending that the Second Continental Congress attend to the political rights of women. John Stuart Mill wrote one of the classics of feminist literature, *The Subjugation of Women*, in 1869. In this work he advocated equality of the sexes in marriage, and considered customs and institutions opposed to equality as "relics of primitive barbarism." Marriage was to be based on a complementarity of skills, with leadership alternating back and forth according to these skills, in a context of shared values and goals. Mill was also a member of the English House of Commons and sponsored the first bill to enfranchise women.

Freud translated four essays from Mill's collected works from English into German when he was twenty-four years old (Gay 1988). He sharply disagreed with Mill's thesis concerning the equality of women. In a letter to his fiancée Martha, Freud wrote: "The position of women cannot be other than what it is; to be an adored sweetheart in youth, and a beloved wife in maturity." These opinions expressed by Freud were clearly the values prevalent in the culture.

In the world of literature, Henrik Ibsen, in *A Doll's House*, opposed this prevailing view and advocated equal rights for women. Female writers began to make an impact in the literary field, such as Louisa May Alcott, Jane Austen, the Brontë sisters, George Eliot, Mary Shelley (Wollstonecraft's daughter), and George Sand. However, for the majority of women in nineteenth-century America and Europe, life was constricted to the prescribed stereotyped roles. In Germany, for example, women were controlled and limited to three spheres of existence—*Kinder, Kirche,* and *Küche* (children, church, and kitchen). To these three K's, a fourth was added facetiously for Austrian women—*Kaffeeklatsch*.

In general, women's roles were split into the good and the bad. The good were the selfless, suffering martyrs who were chaste, undemanding, compliant, and passive: the virgin-madonna. The ultimate was the consumptive heroine as depicted in novels, operas, and art, for example, Mimi in the opera *La Bohème*. The bad were the sensual, assertive, manipulative, castrating, or engulfing femmes fatales: the virago-vampire-whore, for example Musetta in *La Bohème*. In the opera *La Traviata*, the powerful and sensual femme fatale is transformed into the selfless and consumptive woman who dies. These sensuous femmes fatales were portrayed as erotic and menacing in some of the paintings of fin-de-siècle Viennese artists such as Gustav Klimt, Oskar Kokoschka, and Egon Schiele.

The social bias against women and sexuality was most clearly epitomized in a book by Otto Weininger called *Sex and Character*, published in Vienna in 1903 (Janik and Toulmin 1973). The idea for the book was developed by Freud's friend, Wilhelm Fliess, who had speculated about an inborn bisexuality in all people. Freud had revealed Fliess's ideas about bisexuality to one of his patients, Hermann Swoboda. Swoboda then passed it on to Weininger. When Fliess later found out, he felt betrayed by Freud. Even though Freud offered to delay publication of his own book, *Three Essays on the Theory of Sexuality* (1905b) until after Fliess published, this conflict eventually contributed to ending the Freud-Fliess relationship (Gay 1988).

Weininger had already published first. He claimed that his idea that each individual's character is made up of both masculine and feminine components was drawn from Plato, Aristotle, Kant, and Schopenhauer. The masculine component represented rationality, creativity, and order, while the feminine one was sexual, irrational, emotional, and chaotic. All positive achievements in history were thought to be due to the masculine principle, while all feminine aspects were responsible for destructive and nihilistic tendencies. Aryans were considered innately to embody the male principle, and Jews the female principle. It is of some interest that Weininger himself was born Jewish, and had converted to Protestantism; but his intense self-hatred for being Jewish led to his suicide at the age of twenty-four, in the same house where Beethoven had died. Weininger's book was more widely read than Freud's because of its support by Karl Kraus, editor of the witty and satirical periodical, *Die Fackel* (The Torch). Kraus vehemently opposed the feminist movement and women generally, Zionism, and psychoanalysis.

Misogyny and Anti-Semitism

Since anti-Semitism is based on the same psychodynamics as misogyny and played a significant role in shaping Freud's life and work, a deeper understanding of this attitude is essential. As part of the popular European ethos of the time, Jews were equated with women, and both were denigrated. It was Freud's wish to have his work in psychoanalysis accepted in the scientific community, and thus he needed to distinguish himself as a "manly" Jew apart from "feminine" ideals.

A direct link was created between anti-Semitism and misogyny in Europe because both Jews and women simultaneously became visible at the turn of the century by their demands for social equality. In the backlash against feminist and Jewish efforts for social emancipation, many influential writers stressed the connection between women and Jews. Walter Rathenau, in his 1897 essay, described the discourse of Jews as similar to that of women, which was different than that of men (Gilman 1986). Immanuel Kant, in his *Anthology from a Pragmatic Point of View*, emphasized the "loquacity and passionate eloquence" of woman, by which she became "the ruler of men through modesty and eloquence in speech and expression." Arthur Schopenhauer considered women to be less intelligent and weaker than men, and therefore resorted to cunning and treachery. He believed that women and Jews misused language and resorted to lying and manipulation.

According to Otto Weininger's *Sex and Character*, women did not use logic, but thought by association. They are influenced by immediate sensations and perceptions of the moment, which prevent their memory from being continuous. The result is that women speak, but they misuse language and lie. Weininger considered women as "logically insane," a condition that becomes overtly manifested in hysteria. He also believed that Jews used the same faulty logic as women and were unable to think scientifically: both are unable to use language to express themselves aesthetically; both lack a sense of humor and use satire. However, Weininger considered Jews to be even worse than women, since they had no center: Jews did not believe in themselves or in anything else. They stood outside reality and did not enter it. At least women had their man at the center of their lives, and they could believe in their husbands, lovers, or children. Weininger then considered that this undesirable quality of femaleness was part of the bisexual nature of all human beings, and more pronounced in Jews.

Freud read Weininger's *Sex and Character* and was probably influenced by it. Although he did not suffer self-hatred to the extent Weininger did, he experienced conflict about his identity as a scientist and a Jew. Freud needed to draw a sharp distinction between the language of science he used, and the language Weininger attributed to Jews. To solve this problem Freud created a new language for himself, one that was used by neither women nor Jews (Gilman 1986). He hoped that the new language of psychoanalysis would be universally applicable and achieve scientific credibility, without being contaminated by sexual or religious prejudice. He feared that he would be considered the outsider Jew, still speaking the language of the Jews, and his work would not be accepted by the scientific community. The threat that psychoanalysis would be denigrated and dismissed as a Jewish-feminine-sexual science persisted, and, ironically, by the 1930s it was indeed labeled by European anti-Semites as the new language of the Jews.

Possibly to keep psychoanalysis from being viewed as a feminine science, Freud worked to dissociate it from women and stressed the characteristics of men. The libido needed to be a masculine drive, and the child development of boys became the standard by which to judge girls' development. This need may also have contributed to the importance Freud gave to fathers and the oedipal period, while he neglected mothers and the preoedipal period. How strongly did anti-Semitism in fin-de-siècle Europe influence Freud to unconsciously attempt to make psychoanalysis a masculine science?

It was not until 1848 that Jewish religious services were legalized in the Austro-Hungarian empire, and that humiliating special taxes against Jews were eliminated. Jews could now own property like Christians, and could enter professions or assume public office (Gay 1988). Jewish households could employ Christian servants, and gentile households could use Jewish midwives. In 1848, after having lived for ten years as a tolerated Jew in Freiberg, Moravia, Freud's father, Jacob, was granted official domicile (Krull 1986). In 1860 the liberal political party won the election in Vienna, which included several ministers who were Jewish. At this time Freud's parents met a fortuneteller in a Prater restaurant. She prophesied that their four-year-old son Sigmund was destined to become a governmental minister, which the family now hoped could become a reality.

In keeping with the ideas of the Enlightenment concerning the rights of men, the liberal government that came into power in Austria brought in a constitutional democracy based on reason and law to replace the older aristocratic absolutism. Under this liberal government, Jews and all other citizens were provided with an opportunity for social advancement. In 1870 Jews were no longer required to convert to Christianity before they could enter the universities. (For example, the great German lyrical poet Heinrich Heine was obliged to convert from Judaism to Christianity before he could enter the university about forty years earlier.) In 1873, only three years later, Freud passed his *matura* exam and matriculated in the medical faculty of the University of Vienna.

This liberalization resulted in an influx of Jews from provincial parts of the Austro-Hungarian empire into Vienna. Jews were now able to achieve positions in the arts and professions—opportunities that gentiles envied and resented. Jews were seen as parvenus and outsiders; they were marked by their speech, which was either Yiddish or German with an accent. Because they were enfranchised and now able to be full members of society, Jews supported, and were closely associated by others, with this liberal government. Around this same time, the liberation of women both sexually and politically was also advocated by such liberal parties as the Young Germany movement. Thus there was a popular triad of associations of Jew-liberal-woman (Gilman 1986). Schorske (1981) also considers that when the emperor and the liberal government offered equal status to Jews without demanding their nationality, Jews became viewed as supernational, as if they had stepped into the shoes of the earlier aristocracy.

The stock market crash of 1873 was the beginning of the end for the liberal government in the empire. When Emperor Franz Joseph introduced modern industrial production, the new factories destroyed the guilds. In

1880 these artisans formed the first anti-Semitic group in Vienna, the Society for the Defense of the Handworker. Political anti-Semitism was then used by Georg von Schönerer in his election to the Reichsrat in 1873, and Karl Lueger in his bid for mayor of Vienna in 1895. A two-year period of deadlock occurred before Emperor Franz Joseph ratified Lueger's election, which ended Viennese liberalism.

Influence of Anti-Semitism on Freud's Theories

A world of virulent anti-Semitism came into existence in Europe during the time Freud developed his theories and techniques. The Dreyfus affair occurred in France in 1894, where a Jewish officer on the general staff was falsely convicted of spying for the Germans; he was defended by Emile Zola. In 1899 the Hilsner affair occurred in Czechoslovakia, with a Jewish shoemaker unjustly convicted of ritual murder; he was defended by Thomas Garrigue Masaryk, who was an ardent feminist and later became the father of his country.

As he formulated psychoanalysis in this ethos, Freud tried to make his theory as scientific and universally valid as possible; he did not want to be influenced by feminist or Jewish views. Paradoxically, Freud's first theory (Freud and Breuer 1895) evolved out of treating eighteen young women who suffered from hysteria and reported having been sexually seduced during childhood. Freud must have been aware of the implications of his being Jewish and boldly presenting a sexual theory of the etiology of neurosis. Because sex was repressed in Victorian society, sexuality was seen as bad and attributed to Jews and seductive women. Presenting a sexual theory was like mounting a frontal military attack against an anti-Semitic enemy. Unlike his father who had been intimidated by anti-Semitism, Freud probably needed to assert his manliness by publicly presenting his findings. He proudly reported his seduction theory before the prestigious Vienna Society for Psychiatry and Neurology in April 1896, with Baron Richard von Krafft-Ebbing, professor of psychiatry at the University of Vienna, presiding. Freud delivered his lecture in a flowing poetic style without notes, boldly comparing himself to an explorer who had discovered the head of the Nile, the root cause of hysteria. Freud stated that the traumatic memories and associated feelings of a childhood seduction were repressed into the unconscious, where they exerted power and were converted into physical symptoms. Freud believed that the hysterical women suffered from "reminiscences," and that treatment consisted of recovering the traumatic memory from the unconscious and releasing the associated feelings. Writing to his friend Wilhelm Fliess (Bonaparte, Freud, and Kris 1954), Freud commented on the "icy reception" he received and the remark of Krafft-Ebbing that his work sounded "like a scientific fairy tale." Freud became scorned and isolated in the medical community and was referred to as a Jewish pornographer (Jones 1953).

In October 1896 Freud's father died, which was another blow he suffered. Freud considered resigning from the University of Vienna in January 1897, since he had not been promoted from instructor, the lowest academic rank, for twelve years. Even though Professor Hermann Nothnagel, chief of internal medicine, recommended his promotion, it was blocked by anti-Semitic laws limiting Jewish appointments. Freud's seduction theory appeared to blame mostly fathers for being seducers. Freud, and apparently his brother and several sisters, also experienced hysterical symptoms. In May 1897, Freud dreamed of feeling overly affectionate toward his daughter Mathilde. On May 31, he wrote to his friend Fliess, interpreting this dream as his wanting to "pin down a father as the originator of neurosis."

On August 18, 1897, Freud sent a letter to Fliess giving his itinerary for an intended trip to Italy. Freud avoided visiting Rome, and then he became aware that he was following in Hannibal's footsteps against the Romans. Freud then remembered an incident he was told as a young boy by his father. His father had been insulted for being Jewish and his fur cap was knocked off. Freud became aware that he resented his father for submitting meekly to this humiliation, which he saw as cowardly, making it difficult for Freud to identify with his father as a model of masculinity. Freud's solution was to turn to military heroes, especially Semitic and Jewish ones, and later to medical colleagues as father figures whom he could idealize. Some of the military leaders who fought tyranny whom Freud admired were Alexander the Great (after whom Freud named his younger brother), Oliver Cromwell (after whom Freud named his second son), Garibaldi (who was associated with his father), and Hannibal (who, like Freud, was Semitic and had vowed to avenge his father's humiliation by Rome).

McGrath (1986) feels that the precipitating incident that brought back the issue of a cowardly father and the need to follow in Hannibal's footsteps in Italy was the submission of Emperor Franz Joseph to Rome in ratifying the election of the anti-Semitic mayor of Vienna, Karl Lueger. Again a father figure had groveled to anti-Semitic pressure and not behaved in a manly fashion. Only several days later, Freud planned his trip to Italy.

In *The Interpretation of Dreams* (1900), Freud mentions that besides reenacting his Hannibal fantasy, he associated Rome with Winckelmann, an eighteenth-century archeologist and art historian who loved Rome as the *mother* of European culture and who *converted from Judaism*. Freud became aware of the *power of fantasy* in shaping behavior while it remained unconscious. Freud connected the Winckelmann association with his own unconscious sexual fantasies for his mother, and the need to triumph over his father, which he later formulated as the Oedipus complex.

On September 21, 1897, the day after returning from Italy, Freud wrote to Fliess that he no longer believed in his seduction theory. Eight days later, Freud decided to join the Jewish fraternal organization, B'nai Brith, where he continued to present his scientific work. McGrath considers that Freud's joining a Jewish group represented an act of reconciliation with the memory of his father. Instead of the vain unsuccessful heroics of directly conquering anti-Semitism, as in the Hannibal fantasy, Freud accepted the same dignified response of enlightened humanism practiced by his father. Freud lessened his harsh judgment against his father, identified with him, and was brought into closer touch with the traditions of his forefathers.

Freud discontinued teaching at the university until 1904. He set up his own Wednesday night circle of professionals in 1902, who were also mostly Jewish. Freud was thus able to create a support network for himself, and to continue his work courageously in the face of anti-Semitism. The Wednesday night group developed eventually into the Vienna Psychoanalytic Society. Thus, in response to anti-Semitism, the psychoanalytic movement arose.

However, Freud's accommodation to this antagonistic culture still left him open to criticism by himself and others. He, like other Jews, was forced to use the means employed by women to sustain autonomy. Women did not have the power to directly confront misogyny in society, and needed to band together or use indirect means for self-assertion. Freud's change from the seduction theory to the Oedipus theory may have lessened the risk of psychoanalysis being labeled a Jewish-feminine-sexual science. Freud's seduction theory of hysteria rested on the patient feeling *shame* about being seduced, which resulted in repression. According to Victorian stereotypes, this passive experience of seduction would have been considered feminine. By Freud emphasizing the child's experiencing *guilt* for its instinctual strivings, a more active position was emphasized reflecting a more masculine connotation. If this motivation to have his theory appear more manly did exist in Freud, it would certainly have been unconscious.

The change from being a passive object to an active subject made psychoanalytic theory less vulnerable to being labeled as a feminine-Jewish-sexual science. Freud's seduction theory was the first attempt to understand what we today call a post-traumatic stress disorder. We now know that both of Freud's theories were correct.

PART TWO

Freud and Feminine Psychology

6. Freud and His Mother

Freud's Parents

A detailed picture of Sigmund Freud's earliest years is provided by his biographers Ernest Jones (1953, 1955, 1957), Paul Roazen (1984), and Peter Gay (1978, 1988). Freud's father, Jacob, had come from an Orthodox Jewish background. A widower, married once or possibly twice before, Jacob was twenty years older than Freud's mother, Amalie. He lived in a small town in Moravia, which became part of Czechoslovakia following the collapse of the Austro-Hungarian empire after World War I. Jacob's oldest son, Emanuel, was married and lived nearby with his wife and child. His younger son, Philipp, nineteen years old and only a year younger than Amalie, still lived at home.

Amalie, Freud's mother, was a vital, strong, bright, and attractive young women, from a middle-class Viennese family that could afford a good dowry. The marriage seemed fraught with potential difficulties from its inception. Why Amalie Nathansohn would make such an unsuitable choice for a husband is a mystery. Jacob was old enough to be her father, was a grandfather, and had a son still living in his house. The marriage required her to move from cosmopolitan and exciting Vienna to Freiberg, a small sleepy provincial town in Moravia. On the positive side of the ledger, Jacob had an established business as a wool trader, and could provide economic security. This marriage, like others in middle-class bourgeois families, was not based on love but on material security. But most important, Jacob was a tall, good-looking, benign, and kindly man.

The marriage of Amalie and Jacob was consecrated in a Reform Jewish ceremony. Later the family did not observe religious practices, except for the Jewish holidays of Purim and Passover (Krull 1986). This probably reflected Amalie's preference, since she was more assimilated into the Christian culture than her husband. Freud's father had been religious in his previous marriage, and continued to read the Philippson Bible in this one. Freud was born one year after the marriage. As he got older, his father would often read to him from this Bible, and Sigmund was fascinated by the many illustrations. Freud recalled that his very early childhood was a happy time. He remembered having a good relationship with his mother, and being his mother's favorite, which he said instilled in him "self-reliance and an unshakeable optimism" (Freud 1900).

Psychoanalysis was a creation of Freud's self-analysis. Although his writings about his self-analysis stem from his childhood memories and can be subject to retroactive distortion, he provides us with considerable information about his early life. Foremost is Freud's selection of his oedipal period of development to formulate psychoanalytic theory. However, we will examine his earlier preoedipal period, since it seems far more significant (Slipp 1988a). The preoedipal period, from birth to about three years of age when the relationship to the mother is crucial, is generally ignored in Freud's writings. On the other hand, during the oedipal period, from four to six years of age, for a boy the father becomes more prominent. Even though Freud idealized his early childhood in his conscious memory, his preoedipal period was fraught with emotional trauma centering around his mother. He provided a good deal of information about her in his writings, yet he never analyzed their relationship. She remained idealized, and he denied his intense ambivalence toward her. It appears that the trauma of their early relationship was so overwhelming that it remained repressed and blocked out of his conscious awareness. Consequently, the mother was not included as a significant figure when Freud formulated a general psychoanalytic theory of child development. He ignored the importance of the mother during the first four years of a child's life, a time when attachment and dependency on her are of utmost significance. In his self-analysis, Freud had no problems dealing with later oedipal issues of competition with his father and analyzing his ambivalence toward him.

When Freud was one and a half years old, his brother Julius was born. Freud recognized and admitted that he had guilt about entertaining death wishes toward his baby brother. Six months later, in April 1858, when Freud was almost two, little Julius died. It was a calamitous time for the family. A series of traumatic events were closely following one upon another. In March, the previous month, Amalie's brother Julius had died in Vienna of pulmonary tuberculosis. At that time, Amalie was already pregnant with her third child, Anna. She was not able to mourn the deaths of her child and brother in the security of her home, since Jacob's wool business went bankrupt. Jones (1953) blames this failure on an economic depression, inflation, and the fact that the northern railroad bypassed Freiberg. To make matters worse, Jewish businesses were boycotted because of an outbreak of anti-Semitism following the Czech nationalist revolution of 1848.

Amalie may have felt trapped in this marriage to an older man who could no longer provide her and her children with the economic security, status, and protection she had expected. Her marriage, like many others in Europe, had been arranged like a business contract based primarily on economic concerns about dowry, inheritance, and social status. No doubt she was in a state of despair over Jacob's business failure and the deaths of her brother and baby. Her deep personal tragedies in all likelihood influenced her inability to be emotionally available to Sigmund.[1]

Freud's Preoedipal Trauma

Freud was only two years old when these events occurred, which is during the *rapprochement* subphase of the separation-individuation phase of preoedipal development described by Mahler (Mahler and Furer 1968). This is a time when omnipotent fantasies are normally differentiated from reality and impulse control is established. It is also the time for further differentiation of self from the object, and of consolidating male or female gender identity. This phase is especially characterized by a high degree of anxiety as the small child becomes aware of its separateness and helplessness. The child is also fearful of regressing, being engulfed, and losing its sense of differentiation.

The two-year-old child still uses the primitive defenses of *splitting and projective identification*. In splitting, the ego begins to primitively differentiate the self and other persons as entirely all good or all bad. However, the establishment of real boundaries between oneself and others remains incomplete at this stage. In projective identification, the ego experiences a magical (omnipotent) fantasy of placing an unwanted aspect of oneself

1. In John Bowlby's (1969–80, vol. 2) research, separation anxiety experienced by a small child may not only result from physical loss of the mother, but also from her emotional unresponsiveness or threats of abandonment.

into another person. The aim is to control and take possession of that person. Empathic connection is maintained with what has been projected, so that the ego can vicariously experience its unacceptable aspects through the other person. (When seen in adult patients, unconscious efforts may be made to induce feelings, thoughts, or behavior in the other person to correspond to what has been projected.)

After the rapprochement subphase of development is completed successfully, the child is able to achieve what is termed *object constancy*. In object constancy the child can maintain an enduring and stable internalized image of the mother. The child can then evoke the memory of the mother even when she is not there. This further allows the child to separate and differentiate without the constant fear of loss of the mother, which is experienced as a threat to self-esteem, integration of the self, and even physical survival. Along with the formation of object constancy, there develops a constancy of the self.

Because of the tragic real circumstances existing at the time of Freud's early childhood, many of these early developmental tasks do not seem to have been surmounted successfully. The theme of fear of abandonment by his mother and annihilation anxiety runs through much of Freud's life. This was expressed during his adulthood in fears concerning his health, phobias about riding trains and visiting Rome, and his addiction to smoking. In addition, this early childhood fear influenced his relationship with his wife, daughter, and female professional associates, as we will see later.

Jones (1953) noted that because of the emotional trauma Freud suffered during his preoedipal period, he did not differentiate psychologically from his mother. According to Jones, Freud sought continued fusion with her rather than sexual union. This fused identification of his self and his mother persisted, rather than the differentiation and separation that occur normally. As already noted, differentiation from the mother is particularly significant for the attainment of a masculine identity. In the instances where development is arrested, the boundaries between the mother and self remain vague. Therefore, the individual may alternate back and forth between these two identifications in relationship to others. The person may experience him/herself as the child and the other as the mother, or experience him/herself as the mother in relation to the other as the child. For example, in Freud's relationship to his daughter Anna, she seemed to function as his good preoedipal mother, who sensitively was attuned to and unconditionally cared for his needs. On the other hand, Freud was just as protective and nurturant a parent to her.

Freud's identification with his mother may have been revealed in another way as well. His relation to Anna was very similar to his mother's toward her own daughter, Dolfie. Each of these daughters, Anna and Dolfie, sacrificed an independent life and devoted themselves to care for their parent. We will discuss this preoedipal fused identity of mother/self later, especially how it probably influenced Freud's theories of infantile sexuality, bisexuality, and his ideas on gender identity in men and women. As we will see in chapters 13 and 14, it is also possible that Freud's early identification with his mother/self resulted in his surrounding himself with career-oriented women. These women seem to have functioned as good preoedipal mothers for him. At the same time, he was a powerful parental figure to them and they competed for his favor.

If the birth of another child occurs during the rapprochement phase of development, the child's relationship to the mother is more vulnerable to disruption. The child has not internalized the mother enough to achieve object constancy, and displacement of her attention to the newborn baby may be experienced as an abandonment. As a result, it may be difficult to integrate ambivalence toward the mother. The child may continue to use splitting to protect the internalized good-mother image from destruction by its rage. Then the mother remains idealized as all good, and all the rage toward her tends to be displaced onto the newborn or turned on the self. As a small child, Freud probably displaced his rage for his mother onto his baby brother, Julius. Freud admitted experiencing destructive fantasies of killing and eliminating his rival for his idealized, good mother. Unfortunately, these fantasies could not be differentiated from reality, since his baby brother Julius actually did die. This occurrence probably disrupted the normal developmental tasks of differentiating fantasy from reality, establishing impulse control, and integrating ambivalence into the personality. Julius's sudden disappearance due to death became a central issue in Freud's life. In all likelihood, his baby brother's death left Freud fearful of the power of his own aggressive fantasies. What appeared to become deeply etched into Freud's unconscious mind was that his death wishes toward his baby brother had magically killed him.

In view of his suppressed rage at his mother, Freud was probably also fearful that his aggression might magically kill her as well. Because his aggressive fantasy seemed to become a reality with Julius, Freud probably felt his mother was also vulnerable to the power of his rage, and that she would disappear as well. It is interesting that even in later life, Freud's immediate colleagues were fearful of his anger, as if he indeed had the power of life and death over them (Roazen, pers. com.). This inability to integrate his aggression and establish appropriate impulse control probably perpetuated Freud's vulnerability to the loss of his mother. As a consequence, Freud continued to idealize her, repressed his anger, and had difficulty through most of his life dealing with his ambivalence toward her. Repression of his aggression toward his mother can be seen as his way of protecting her and himself against her loss.

In a letter to his friend Fliess (Bonaparte et al. 1954), Freud admitted his feelings of guilt for experiencing jealousy and death wishes toward Julius. Freud recounted that shortly after Julius died, he fell from a stool and cut his jaw. The fall left Freud with a scar for life. This incident can also be looked at symbolically. I suggest that Sigmund's fall from a high place and being scarred may represent the loss of his mother's emotional availability and his suffering a lifelong narcissistic injury. The scarring could also have represented little Sigmund's self-injury as a penance for guilt over death wishes toward Julius.

Schur (1972), Freud's personal physician, describes that during Sigmund's first two years of life the Freud family lived in a small house in Freiberg. Therefore, sexual relations, birth, and death all occurred in the same room. Freud must have been witness to his parents' sexual intercourse (the primal scene), which stimulated strong sexual feelings in him. Because life events followed one another sequentially in this single room, there was a natural association in Freud's mind between sex, birth, and death.

Freud's mother then became pregnant for the third time. This situation presented the new fear that not only would Freud lose his favored position with his mother, but that he might lose her altogether. Freud's sister Anna was born eight months later, and it would be entirely consistent if she were the sibling he liked the least. The loss of Julius, the potential loss of his mother, and later the loss of a number of important attachment figures resulted in Freud's suffering lifelong separation anxiety.

Freud's Two Mothers

An added confusion beclouded young Sigmund's first two years of life. He was raised by two mother figures. Besides his biological mother, Amalie, he was cared for by an elderly Czech nanny named Resi Wittek (also called Monika Zajic by other writers). To add to the confusion, Resi, who was Catholic, was allowed to take little Sigmund to church with her. At Catholic church he learned about sin, heaven, and hell. Amalie was clearly aware that the nanny was taking Sigmund to church with her, but she expressed a cavalier attitude about it. Amalie related with amusement how Sigmund would come home from church and preach to the family. Why was this Jewish mother amused that her son was attending church? Was she encouraging Christian assimilation as her way of dealing with anti-Semitism? Assimilation was not an uncommon path followed by many Austrian and German Jews. Was she angry at her religious Jewish husband who had become bankrupt? Allowing Sigmund to go to church might have been her way of acting out her defiance and her anger against her husband. Or, was Amalie so preoccupied with her pregnancies and losses that she was not emotionally invested in her oldest son at that time? It is impossible to discern whether one, two, or all of these issues were a factor in Amalie's decision to let Sigmund go to church. The fact that she was amused might add some weight to the assimilation or anger-at-her-husband hypotheses.

Jones (1953) reported that as a small child, Freud was very confused about these two women to whom he was so strongly bonded. He thought that his father, Jacob, was married to his nanny, Resi. They were his grandparents, since they were both elderly authority figures. This assumption was confirmed by his nephew John, who was one year older, and his niece Pauline, who was one year younger, since they called Jacob "Grandfather." John and Pauline were the children of Jacob's older son Emanuel and his wife Maria. Freud then jumped to the conclusion that Jacob's younger son, Philipp, was married to his mother. Philipp and Amalie were about the same age, in their twenties. According to Jones (1953), to Sigmund this conclusion appeared "tidy and logical, but still there was the awkward fact that Jacob, not Philipp, slept in the same bed as Amalie. It was all very puzzling."

In January 1859, a month after his sister Anna's birth, Philipp caught Freud's nanny stealing money and had her arrested. Forty years later, in a painful recollection during his self-analysis, Freud recalled that he suspected Philipp was involved in his nanny's disappearance. He remembered fearfully asking the "naughty" Philipp where his nanny was. Philipp replied jokingly, "Sie ist eingekastelt." Literally, this means that she was put into a chest, but colloquially it was an expression for being imprisoned. Freud remembered crying bitterly and begging Philipp to open up the chest, since he feared his mother was also lost. It was a natural assumption that if his surrogate mother disappeared, then his real mother might also be gone permanently. He had assumed that his naughty brother had placed his mother into the chest as well. Fortunately at that point, his mother walked into the room, which reassured Sigmund. On continuing his analysis of this memory, Freud associated the chest to the womb. Since he connected Philipp with putting people in "chests," he entertained the fantasy that his half-brother and mother had been together sexually and another unwelcomed brother, like Julius, would be born. Thus sex seems to have been associated with abandonment. This abandonment might be his mother's emotional unavailability or her physical disappearance in death with the birth of another brother.

Why was sex associated with the disappearance of his mother surrogate or his real mother? I suggest it was partly because of his observing sex, births, and Julius's death in the same room in which the family lived. In all likelihood, Freud even saw his dead brother's body in a chest, the coffin.

However, another reason could be the close and seductive relationship that Freud had with Resi. In a letter to Fliess on October 3, 1897 (Bonaparte et al. 1954), concerning seduction, Freud wrote: "In my case my father played no active role . . . my primary originator of neurosis was an ugly, elderly but clever woman [his nanny] who told me a great deal about God and hell, and gave me a high opinion of my capabilities. . . . I shall have to thank the memory of the old woman who provided me at such an early age with the means for living and surviving" (219–20).

Here Freud made the sequential connections of seduction and hell. I suggest that he might have attributed Resi's loss as her banishment to hell, as punishment for their illicit sexual activity. As further evidence, Freud described his relationship to his nanny in this same letter to Fliess: "She was my instructress in sexual matters, and chided me for being clumsy and not being able to do anything. . . . Also she washed me in reddish water in which she had previously washed herself . . . and she encouraged me to steal 'Zehners' to give to her" (220–21).

Resi apparently had fondled his genitals, and he also experienced as seductive being washed in the water she had already used. After recounting this seductive experience, Freud's next association was Resi's encouraging him to steal money (the "Zehners"). Freud probably connected that sexual activity, like stealing money, was wrong and punishable. We know that Freud feared that, like his brother Julius, people might magically disappear as a result of his aggressive fantasies. A similar fear that loss would occur because of his sexual fantasies or activities is very likely. This is the kind of magical thinking entertained by a two-year-old during the rapprochement subphase of development, when fantasy and reality are not differentiated. Instead, fantasy and reality are seen by a two-year-old child as causally connected.

This type of magical thinking probably persisted in Freud's unconscious, making him feel overly responsible for the loss of others. The fantasy connecting the disappearance of Resi with sexuality was also further reinforced by outside reality. Resi had been seductive with him, and then she suddenly and permanently disappeared. She had informed him of punishment in hell for sins, and thus it would be natural for Freud to assume that because of their sexual sin she was sent to hell.

In August 1859, out of economic necessity, Jacob, Amalie, and the children left the city of Freiberg for Leipzig to resettle. Freud recalled that when the train arrived at Breslau, he saw a number of giant gas jets aflame, which he associated with souls burning in hell. Thus Freud was thinking about people being punished for their sins and burning in the fires of hell. This is yet another piece of evidence that Resi's disappearance might have been connected with her banishment to hell because she had been sexual with him.

The other evidence for the connection of loss as punishment for sexuality was that Sigmund, before he was two and a half years old, had sexual feelings toward his niece, Pauline. This is described in his screen memory of the botanical monograph I will describe later (Freud 1899). Then Pauline was also permanently lost to him: Freud's two half-brothers, Philipp and Emanuel, his nephew John, and Emanuel's wife Maria moved to England and took Pauline with them. These events occurred when Freud was less than three years old, before object constancy is established and before fantasy is differentiated from outside reality. Freud suffered a series of losses of important attachment figures before he was three that etched themselves into his personality and haunted him throughout his life.

At the International Psychoanalytic Congress in Wiesbaden, Sandor Ferenczi (1932), who had been Freud's closest psychoanalytic colleague, read his last paper, entitled the "Confusion of Tongues between Adults and the Child." In it he noted that after an adult is seductive to a child, the adult may deal with his or her guilt by projecting it onto the child, who is then punished. Was Freud's guilt and fear of punishment for sexuality not only derived from his own fantasy, but due to Resi's blame as well?

Ferenczi was also one of the first to note that after seduction, a child may become sexually precocious. In Freud's "Screen Memories" (1899) he recounted a dream in which he had written a botanical monograph on a certain plant. In associating to this dream, Freud recalled the childhood memory that he and his nephew, John, had behaved seductively toward his niece, Pauline. They were all picking yellow dandelions on a meadow when they fell on Pauline and took away her flowers. She ran crying to a peasant woman who gave her a piece of black bread. Then the boys also ran to the peasant woman who gave them each a piece of black bread as well. This memory involved deflowering a girl, Pauline, and the black bread offered by the peasant woman "was delicious." Deflowering Pauline indicated to Freud that he had wished to be sexual with her. It can be hypothesized that the peasant woman in the dream was Resi, who had introduced Freud to the delights of sexuality earlier. Had Resi's petting his genitals stimulated his precocious wish to seduce Pauline? The association of sex and loss was a recurrent theme for Freud, and will be explored further in the next chapter.

7. Sex, Death, and Abandonment

The Train Trip to Vienna

One of the most significant events that shaped Freud's emotional life occurred when he was almost four years old. After living a year in Leipzig, his entire family left by train for Vienna in March 1860. In the same October 3, 1897, letter to Fliess, Freud also wrote:

> Between the ages of two and two-and-a-half, libido towards *matrem* was aroused; the occasion must have been the journey with her from Leipzig to Vienna, during which we spent a night together and I must have had the opportunity of seeing her *nudam* ... and that I welcomed my one-year younger brother (who died within a few months) with ill wishes and real infantile jealousy, and that his death left the germ of guilt in me. I have long known that my companion in crime between the ages of one and two was a nephew of mine who is a year older than I am. . . . We seem occasionally to have treated my niece, who was a year younger, shockingly. My nephew and younger brother (Philipp) determined, not only the neurotic side of all my friendships, but also their depth. My anxiety over travel you have seen yourself in full bloom. (Bonaparte et al. 1954, 221–22)

This letter provides a number of revelations concerning the sources of Freud's neurosis. The letter contains an error in time, since the train trip from Leipzig to Vienna took place when Freud was almost four years old and not two and a half, as he states. He was two and a half during the train trip from Freiberg to Leipzig and had recently lost his nanny. During this earlier train trip, Freud saw the gas jets and thought of souls burning in hell. According to Jones (1953), Freud had telescoped the memories of these two train experiences into one. In the earlier memory, it was his mother surrogate, Resi, who was seductive, while in the later memory it was his mother, Amalie. Did Freud telescope these two train trips because he was fearful that he would lose his mother like he lost his nanny? Would his mother disappear like his nanny and also be sent to hell as punishment for being sexual?

As evidence for the powerful impact of seeing his mother nude, Freud used the Latin terms *matrem* and *nudam*. Niederland (1965), in a psychobiography of Heinrich Schliemann, noted that memories of experiences that are terrifying often can be expressed intellectually only when transposed into a foreign language. Ego distance is gained, so the person can deal with an experience that is overwhelming. This may explain Freud's use of Latin terms for "mother" and "nude" to depict a traumatic event that his biographer, Jones, described as "awesome."

The theme of this letter to Fliess concerns the arousal of sexual feelings for his mother and Resi. It is then followed by his discussing guilt over his aggressive feelings toward Julius and sexual behavior toward Pauline. I would link these associations together into the hypothesis that as a small child Freud experienced both his sexual and aggressive feelings as omnipotent, and he felt responsible for the loss of these people. As noted, he felt guilty for the loss of his brother Julius because of aggressive feelings. He felt responsible for the loss of Resi, his niece Pauline, as well as the potential loss of his mother because of sexual feelings. Sigmund, when he was about two years old, did not comprehend that Resi's disappearance was due to her being sent to prison for theft. He could not understand that Pauline had left because her family was moving to England for economic reasons. He attributed their disappearance to his sexual or aggressive feelings. This is the typical egocentric, magical way of thinking used by two-year-olds.

Ferenczi on Nakedness to Inspire Terror

In connection with this memory of seeing his mother nude on the train trip, I would like to offer some speculations about Freud's early relationship with his mother. Sandor Ferenczi became Freud's closest friend after Freud broke off his relationship with Fliess. Freud and Ferenczi may have shared their inner secrets with each other. Often the case materials they published were biographical, though presented in a disguised form. I have speculated (Slipp 1988b) that in "Nakedness as a Means of Inspiring Terror," Ferenczi (1919a) might have included material revealed to him by Freud. Even if this is not the case, the reports bear similarities to Freud's experience with his mother on the train. In this case report, Ferenczi discussed two mothers who exposed themselves physically to their son out of sadistic motives. Therefore, sexuality was used as a form of abuse and tied in with aggression and rejection.[1]

The first case described a mother who had unexpectedly lost her eldest boy and was depressed and preoccupied with suicide. She had been sexually frustrated with her husband, and had transferred her love and tenderness to this elder boy. She knew that if she undressed and washed herself naked in front of her remaining son, "the child will have an imperishable memory that might harm him or even prove his complete undoing." She then went ahead and inspired terror by her nakedness, being consciously aware of her hostile feelings toward her younger son. She also "had a fantasy in which the tragic fate of the elder was transferred to the younger," and he would also die. Sexuality was used as a hostile assault on her son, and was associated with doing damage or killing.

Could Ferenczi have been reporting Freud's experience with his mother's nakedness on the train, and disguising it by reversing the sibling order? When the Freud family moved from Leipzig, Jacob had been unsuccessful again in reestablishing himself economically. Did Amalie have suicidal ideas, because she was returning to her home in Vienna, humiliated at her life circumstances? She was married to an older man, who for the second time had failed in business. In addition, Jacob himself must have been depressed over his failed economic circumstances. It is possible that Jacob's depression also diminished his sexual libido and emotional availability toward Amalie. Amalie may have felt enraged at her fate. And now she was pregnant with her fourth child, which further trapped her in the marriage.

In the second case mentioned by Ferenczi, a mother is described who exposed herself nude to her son in order to frighten him away. This exposure "cured" the boy of clinging to her and refusing to go to sleep without her. Was this insecure little boy Sigmund, whose basic security had been disrupted by the two moves of the family and by the loss of important attachment figures? Was Sigmund the little boy who feared losing his mother and demanded that she sleep with him on the train trip

---

1. Niederland (1958) notes that linguistically, sexuality is often tied in with aggression. Often the same word is used for both, especially in slang, such as "to knock up a woman."

from Leipzig? I suggest that this was close to the facts. In the letter to Fliess that Freud wrote about seeing his mother nude, the very next thought is of his dead brother and his guilt. Did Amalie wish that Sigmund was also dead like his brother, Julius? Did Amalie evacuate her own guilt into him through projective identification?

In both of these cases, Ferenczi mentions that the child's immature ego was flooded with sexual libido and overwhelmed. The traumatic experience was repressed and expressed symptomatically through phobias. Ferenczi states in his diary that Freud needed to see women as asexual, since he felt Freud could not deal with his mother's sexuality. (We will explore this topic more fully in later chapters.) For Freud, the experience of observing his mother's nakedness was probably overwhelming on several accounts. First, he was sexually overstimulated. Second, his mother's sexuality may have been used to express her hidden aggression, either to get rid of her son's clinging behavior or wishing him dead also as a way out of her unhappy marriage. The traumatic experience of seeing his mother naked on the train trip probably resulted in the development of a train phobia that Freud suffered for the rest of his life.

Other Evidence Associating Sex with Loss

This same theme of associating sex with the loss of his mother occurred in the earliest dream that Freud (1900) could remember, when he was between seven and eight years old. In the dream he saw his mother, with a peaceful sleeping expression on her face, being carried into her room by people who had birds' beaks for heads, and was laid onto her bed. Freud recalled that he awoke in terror, and he ran into his parents' bedroom to see his mother and reassure himself that she was not dead. He recalled seeing such figures with birds' beaks for heads in the Philippson Bible his father had used to teach him to read. They were Egyptian gods, with falcon heads, carrying on a bier a dead body with a peaceful expression on its face. Freud's next association was to "vögeln" a word that suggests birds but is also a German colloquial expression for sexual intercourse. Here again, Freud brings up this same association of sexuality with death and abandonment by his mother.

What effect did these traumatic experiences of early childhood have upon Freud later in life? He had a deep desire to visit Rome, yet he suffered from a phobia about traveling there that prevented him from visiting the Eternal City for many years. I suggest that this phobia was related to his early abandonment by his Catholic nanny and the loss of his brother Julius. In Freud's (1901) discussion of his forgetting the name of the Italian painter Signorelli, who had done the fresco of the Last Judgment in Orvieto, he could think only of Botticelli and Boltraffio. Through a series of associations, Freud thought of the Bosnian worship of sexuality, "Herr" which is German for "signor," and the memory that one of his homosexual patients had committed suicide. He then concluded his schematic diagram of this parapraxis with the association of sexuality and death. The painting of Signorelli was also of the *last judgment*, in which those guilty of sins are consigned to *hell*. Freud seemed to be concerned about hell again, just as he had been as a small child when he saw the gas jets from the train at Breslau. Was Freud unconsciously experiencing guilt over aggressive fantasies toward Julius and sexual fantasies toward Resi and his mother? Was he fearful that he also would be condemned to hell and disappear? (See Freud-Fliess letter of December 3, 1897.)

Some writers consider that since Rome was the center of Catholicism, entering Rome was symbolically associated with Freud's oedipal desire for his mother. Swales (1982) notes in the prophecy of Tarquins that the conquest of Rome would be by the man who would first "kiss" his mother. Indeed, there had been a seductive relationship with his surrogate mother Resi, who was Catholic, as well as with his mother in the train incident. These experiences of sexuality, however, were associated with the fear of loss of the mother out of punishment. It was not out of fear that the father would be castrating, which would be part of an oedipal conflict. It seems clearly that the preoedipal issue of loss of his mother was primary here, even though it confounded Freud's later oedipal conflict. Thus entering Rome, I suggest, was more likely to be associated with the loss of the mother, or by Freud himself being punished by death for his sins and sent to hell.

Rome, according to Blum (1983), represented the pre-Catholic city of Julius Caesar as well. As a young boy, Freud played the role of Brutus with his nephew John, who played Julius Caesar. Freud's identification with Brutus, Blum speculates, comes from his fantasy that he slew his brother Julius. In Freud's (1900) *non vixit* dream of October 1898, John is a screen memory for his brother Julius. Freud writes: "All my friends have in a certain sense been reincarnations of this first figure . . . they have been revenants. My nephew himself reappeared in my boyhood, and at that time we acted the parts of Caesar and Brutus together. My emotional life has always insisted that I should have an intimate friend and hated enemy" (421–25).

The Latin inscription *non vixit* means "he didn't live," which referred to Julius. Freud mentions his self-reproach of turning his aggression against himself out of guilt for his death wishes for his brother. In addition, he seems to have punished himself by being concerned about his own death every day of his life, and fearing that he also would die young. There is evidence that entering Rome was associated with guilt over sexual feelings toward his nanny and mother as well as aggressive feelings for his baby brother. Freud had learned about sin, heaven, and hell from his Catholic nanny, and Rome was the center of Catholicism. Freud may have felt responsible for their loss and was also fearful of his own death as a punishment for having sinned.[2]

Rome had other significances for Freud as well. One of them could be traced to his father's humiliation and emotional defeat due to anti-Semitic prejudice. Freud's father had been cowed by anti-Semitism, as Freud (1900) related in an incident reported in *The Interpretation of Dreams*. As we already noted in chapter 5, his father recounted that as a young man he went for a walk on a Saturday. A Christian man came up to him, knocked off his new fur cap into the mud, and shouted, "Jew, get off the pavement!" Freud asked what his father did in response to this humiliating incident. According to Freud, his father did the following: "I went into the roadway and picked up my cap was his quiet reply. This struck me as unheroic conduct on the part of the big, strong man who was holding the little boy by the hand."

When his father died in 1896, Freud thought he looked like Garibaldi, the Italian hero who had militarily united the small kingdoms of Italy into one nation. This was clearly wishful thinking—of wanting his father to be an idealized heroic figure with whom he could identify.

Freud had a dream concerning Hannibal in 1897, the day after Karl Lueger was sworn in as mayor of Vienna. Hannibal had failed to conquer Rome, even though this Semitic general swore to avenge his father for the Roman destruction of Carthage. Similarly, Rome had destroyed Jerusalem and defeated Freud's father. Karl Lueger had run on the ticket of the Christian Social Party, using political anti-Semitism as a tactic to become elected. Emperor Franz Joseph, who had been protective of Jewish interests, opposed the confirmation of Lueger a number of times. However, pressure from Rome forced the emperor to appoint Lueger to office. Thus Rome, which supported the confirmation of Lueger, an enemy of

2. Grosskurth (1991) notes that when Freud referred to sex in his letters, he frequently added three crosses, which was the anti-hex symbol used by peasants to ward off witches and their feared powers derived from the devil.

the Jews, must have been the manifest content stimulating the Hannibal dream of Freud (D. Klein 1981).

Several years later this same theme appeared in Freud's *The Psychopathology of Everyday Life* (1901). Freud analyzed the forgetting of words, in particular the word *aliquis*. The quote from Virgil is, "Exoriare aliquis nostris ex ossibus ultor," meaning, "Let *someone* arise from my bones as an avenger." He then associated to Garibaldi, and to his father looking like Garibaldi on his deathbed. Thus one can interpret his need to avenge his father with Rome.

Another speculation was that Rome may also have represented his powerful matriarchal mother, who subjugated his father and threatened to engulf and destroy Freud himself. Even though the stereotype of women was one of passivity and submission in the Viennese culture, his mother's personality was more aggressive and dominant than his father's. Did Freud also need to act as an avenger for his father toward his mother, Rome, to strengthen his masculine identification?

The association of the mother with birth, sexuality, and death is made by Freud in his paper, "The Theme of the Three Caskets" (1913). As mentioned earlier, women in ancient cultures were associated with the great mother goddess, who through sexuality had the power of birth and death as well. Examples were Ishtar, who was both the cruel goddess of war and healer of the sick and unfortunate; the Greek goddess Persephone, who was the bringer of spring and rebirth as well as the cruel goddess of death; and the Hindu goddess Kali, who was both loving and creative as well as terrifying and destructive. Freud was aware of these ambivalent mother figures, since in his collection of antiquities he had statues of the Mesopotamian great mother goddess as well as Isis and Demeter. The significance of Freud's art collection of antiquities will be more fully covered in chapter 14.

In fin-de-siècle Europe, sexuality was also closely associated with death for other reasons. Not based on myth and magic but on harsh realities, sexuality was related to disease and death. Since sex was considered as sinful, good women denied their sexual appetites and remained chaste when they were unmarried. When they married, women often were frigid or unresponsive sexually. The result was that many unmarried and married men frequented prostitutes and thereby large numbers contracted venereal diseases. Syphilis was the most dangerous, since there was no treatment at the time. At least 25 percent of people infected with this disease wound up severely crippled or died of its complications. It was not until 1905 that the organism responsible for syphilis, *treponema pallidum*, was isolated and discovered by Schaudinn and Hoffman. The first treatment that was at all partially effective against the disease, "the magic bullet" salvarsan, was not introduced until 1910 by Paul Ehrlich. If the disease was not fatal by destroying the aorta or the nervous system, it could cause blindness, arthritis, skin and mucous membrane lesions, and insanity.

Sexuality was also associated with death among women for other reasons. Good women who became pregnant out of wedlock were ostracized. As a consequence, many women committed suicide if they became pregnant or died from poorly performed abortions. In addition, childbirth fever and the complications of delivery took a large toll. Sex and death remained closely associated.[3]

Expressions of the Theme of Two Mothers

Freud had no conscious insight into his conflictual relationship with his mother and nanny. Instead, he unconsciously proceeded to recapitulate his early childhood by having two mothers in his marital life as well. In this way he could prevent a repetition of his preoedipal trauma, of loss of his mother and nanny, by living through his children. Freud invited his sister-in-law, Minna, to help Martha with the family. Freud proudly referred to his own children as having two mothers. Thus I would speculate that Minna was a replacement for his lost nanny, Resi. By identifying with his children, he would not suffer the same loss or the threat of loss of either mother, as had occurred in his own childhood. It was an unconscious insurance policy.

Freud's concern about his childhood trauma with his two mothers is also brought up in his psychohistory of Leonardo da Vinci. Freud (1910) interpreted da Vinci's painting of "The Virgin, Saint Anne, and the Christ Child" to indicate that Leonardo was raised by two mothers. In fact, Jones (1955) considered that Freud's work on Leonardo da Vinci to be autobiographical. Freud (1939) also identified himself with Moses when he wrote his book, *Moses and Monotheism*. Moses also had two mothers, one Jewish, who gave birth to him, and one non-Jewish, who reared him.

Freud's major identification, however, seems to have been with Oedipus, who also had two mothers. Oedipus's real mother gave him up, and

3. Another association of sex and death was the apparent love death of Crown Prince Rudolph, the heir to the Habsburg throne, and his mistress, Baroness Mary Vetsera, in his hunting lodge at Mayerling in January 30, 1889. In what seems to have been part of a mutual pact, Rudolph shot his teenage lover and then committed suicide.

his adoptive mother reared him. The Greek myth of Oedipus concerned the Delphic oracle's prophecy that he would kill his father Laius, King of Thebes, and marry his mother, Jocasta. To prevent the prophecy from coming true, Laius ordered the baby's feet pierced and cast him out to die. The baby was found by a herdsman, taken to Corinth, and reared by King Polybus and his queen. He was called Oedipus, which means swollen foot in Greek. On the road to Thebes, the adult Oedipus entered into an argument with an old man and killed him. Unknowingly, the old man was his father, Laius. At Thebes, Oedipus was confronted by the Sphinx, a monster that was half lion and half woman. The Sphinx asked each passerby a riddle, and killed them if they did not answer correctly. The Sphinx asked what animal goes on four feet in the morning, two in the afternoon, and three in the evening. Oedipus answered the riddle correctly. It was man. The Sphinx then killed herself, and in gratitude Oedipus was made king of Thebes and married to his mother, Queen Jocasta. On discovering the truth later, Jocasta committed suicide and Oedipus blinded himself.

Freud's answer to the psychological Sphinx was that every child between three to six years of age had sexual feelings for the parent of the opposite sex and wished to kill the parent of the same sex. The oedipal conflict was the cornerstone of Freud's theory, which he felt was responsible for neuroses. As evidence of his identification with Oedipus, Freud had a picture of Oedipus at the foot of his analytic couch. Just as Oedipus's mother had done, Freud's mother had also given him up to be reared by another woman. Significantly, Freud called his youngest daughter, Anna, his Antigone, after the faithful daughter who cared for her blind father Oedipus.

8. Freud's Family Dynamics

The Depressive Family Constellation

The first three years of Freud's life were characterized by loss or threat of loss of his mother. This situation appears to have resulted in his problems of separating and individuating. Not only did Freud have difficulty establishing firm boundaries between himself and his mother, but he had difficulty dealing with his ambivalence toward her for fear of further loss. In addition, the ongoing postoedipal relationship with her probably continued to bind him to her and fuel his anger. As mentioned earlier, Freud (1900) felt that being his mother's favorite child had instilled in him "self-reliance and an unshakeable optimism." Sigmund was indeed his mother's "golden son" (Gay 1988), and Amalie preferred both her sons over all her daughters. However, Freud paid a price for being his mother's favorite, since he felt bound to achieve for her throughout his life.

The descriptions of Amalie by Judith Bernays Heller (1956) and Martin Freud (1983) picture her as a great beauty but impetuous, moody, narcissistic, and a controlling tyrant in the family. Martin, Freud's son, described his grandmother, Amalie, as an example of Galician Jews, who would seem like "untamed barbarians to more civilized people." He described her as belligerent and like a "tornado." Jacob, Freud's father, was described as a good-natured, passive man, warm and engaging, but an impractical dreamer. After leaving Freiberg, he was never able to reestablish himself economically. He saw himself as a failure, and the family lived in poverty. To add to his disgrace, Jacob needed financial help from his sons in England and from Amalie's family. Amalie saw him as a failure as well, and attempted to regain her social status by living vicariously through her son Sigmund's achievements.

This is the specific form of family constellation I have already described in which a child develops a depressive disorder later in life (Slipp 1976, 1984, 1988a). In these families, one of the parents (Jacob) is perceived by others and oneself as a failure. This parent loses stature and power in the family, while the other parent becomes more dominant and controlling (Amalie). In the Freud family, Amalie, like other Victorian bourgeois wives, depended on the economic success of her husband for identity and self-esteem. Despite a few exceptions, women were deprived of a separate identity by the culture, and gained prestige and self-esteem only by identification with their husbands.

Social prestige in the middle class depended on the *achieved* status of the husband. This was unlike the nobility, who could rely on *ascribed* status by virtue of birth. Jacob's failure meant Amalie suffered diminished social prestige—a blow to her narcissism. Since she was unable to achieve success on her own, she blamed and demeaned her husband.

In our study of families, we have found that the failed parent may suffer further rejection when the dominant parent turns toward and shows preference for a gifted child (Slipp 1976). This child is then expected to make up for the other parent's failure and to feed the self-esteem of the dominant parent. The dominant parent remains dependent on the success of this child, who is overtly pressured to achieve socially. For identification, the dominant parent can then substitute a child for the spouse and live vicariously through the child's success. The child feels compelled to achieve and function as the family *savior*, in order to enhance the dominant parent's self-esteem. Failure to perform and succeed will bring rejection by the dominant parent, just as it did the failed parent.

However, the child is unable to own its success, since the dominant parent does not directly gratify or mirror the achievement to the child. The child's success is never good enough, taken for granted, or attributed to luck or circumstance. This lack of external validation occurs, first of all, because of the dominant parent's unconscious envy. This parent feels personally deprived and trapped and envies the opportunities open to the child. Second, the parent needs to control and safeguard this source of narcissistic supply by preventing the child from emancipating and becoming independent. The child is used as an extension of the parent, who takes over the child's achievement as his or her own. Even though these parents do not compliment the child for its success, they often brag about the achievement to relatives, neighbors, and others. In this way the dominant parent feeds his or her narcissism.

The child cannot gain strength and a healthy sense of confidence from its achievements so it can separate and become independent. The child remains symbiotically bound to this dominant parent, constantly hoping to get the needed approval. Besides the overt message to succeed, there is a covert message to remain weak and dependent. I have termed this interactional conflict "the double bind on achievement." The child feels helpless and cannot win, either through success or failure. Failure results in rejection, but success brings no reward, only further pressure to achieve even more. Even though the child resents this exploitation and lack of gratification, he or she represses aggression for fear of abandonment.

The fear of abandonment and annihilation anxiety was probably already a core issue for Freud, in view of his early childhood experiences. His later experiences with his mother extended and reinforced this core unconscious conflict into his adulthood. Freud had been unable to deal with his ambivalent fantasies and unable to differentiate and separate himself from his mother. His mother's persistence in using him as an extension of herself only perpetuated this conflict.

The continuing relationships in the family from childhood into adulthood have not been sufficiently recognized in traditional psychoanalytic theory as contributors to emotional problems. Instead, psychoanalytic theory has generally limited itself to the first six years of life. Even though there is normally a fear of abandonment during very early childhood, this ongoing conditional acceptance based on performance further reinforces the original threat of rejection and annihilation. It keeps the individual dependent, and serves further to repress the expression of anger or self-assertion. The child continues to place the needs of the parent ahead of its own needs.

The pressuring, nongratifying parent is incorporated into the superego to form the ego ideal. As an adult, this ego ideal of the depressive person continues to be pressuring and perfectionistic vis-à-vis others. Depressives cannot live up to this ideal and are therefore unable to find gratification in an achievement. The superego now does to the ego internally what the parents previously did to the child externally. No matter what the person achieves, it is never good enough, so that he or she does not develop confidence and autonomy. Failure to achieve is now replaced by self-reproach and loss of self-esteem. Depressives are harsh and unforgiving of themselves if they fail. Just as they expected rejection when they did not succeed, they cannot comfort themselves but reject themselves intrapsychically.

Arieti (1962) pointed out that depressives continue to remain dependent as adults on an external person, a dominant other, for approval and the maintenance of their self-esteem. Bonime (1959) has also noted that depressives engage in an oppositional game with others. They initially comply to others' needs, then rebel to frustrate the wishes and expectations of these others. They may even stimulate others to have expectations of them, and then frustrate them by not meeting these expectations. They reenact the relationship with their dominant parent, and passive-aggressively act out their rage at feeling exploited without having conscious awareness of their anger. This is a compromise solution, since the depressive can avoid taking responsibility for unconscious hostility, and thereby avoid the risk of rejection.

Freud's Denial of Ambivalence for His Mother

Freud's fear of abandonment by his mother was a significant factor in view of his childhood experiences, when there was disruption of familiar surroundings and the loss of important attachment figures. His fear that the expression of aggressive feelings would magically result in loss was reinforced quite early by the death of his younger brother, Julius. Freud himself mentioned that he suffered from neurasthenia and depression (Schur 1972). Freud also acknowledges that mothers (including his) lived vicariously through their sons' achievements. However, since this phenomenon was so much a part of the culture, he accepted this as normal and denied any anger over it. In his *New Introductory Lectures* (1933) Freud wrote: "A mother is only brought unlimited satisfaction by her relation to a son; this is altogether the most perfect, the most free from ambivalence of all human relationships. A mother can transfer to her son the ambition which she has been obliged to suppress in herself, and she can expect from him the satisfaction of all that has been left over in her of her masculinity complex."

Freud's comments indicated that living vicariously through a son gave the mother pleasure, but he denied that he felt pressured or exploited. There is evidence that he had some conscious awareness of his repressed anger toward his mother. According to Jones (1953), Freud said to his wife Martha Bernays after his occasional outbursts: "Since I am violent and passionate, with all sorts of devils pent up that cannot emerge, they rumble about inside or else are released against you, you dear one." In his letter to Breuer, Freud states ironically: "Even if I become a Docent, lecturing will not come my way, and my Martha, a born German Frau Professor, will have to do without her fine position" (Jones 1953).

Even though Freud considered it normal for a mother to live vicariously off a son's success, there seems to be a hint of sarcasm at Martha's living vicariously through his achievement. Possibly, Freud's resentment against his mother was unconsciously displaced and expressed toward his wife. This may also have been the case in Freud's decision to cease regular sexual relations with his wife from the age of forty-one onward, as mentioned in his letter to Fliess on October 31, 1897 (Bonaparte et al. 1954). However, his motivation is uncertain, since Freud's effort to be sexually abstinent may have been related to a possible heart attack in 1894 or served as a birth control measure (Schur 1972).

There is, however, more evidence concerning Freud's expression of anger toward his mother, even though it probably remained out of his conscious awareness. Jones (1955) and Roazen (1984) report that Freud had attacks of indigestion before visiting his mother on Sundays. Did Freud have difficulty stomaching the pressure from his mother, and therefore expressed it somatically? Freud's son Martin also recalled that Amalie had family gatherings at her flat on Christmas Day and New Year's Eve each year: "My father always came to these gatherings—I know of no occasion when he disappointed her—but his working day was a long one and he always came much later than any one else" (M. Freud 1983). This frustrated Amalie, who would run repeatedly to the staircase landing, anxiously asking if he is coming, where is he, and is it not getting very late? Freud always came late, but somehow never arrived when Amalie was at the landing looking for him. Since Freud knew how important these two gatherings were to his mother, and how upset she would become at his lateness, his action seems an unconscious way of passive-aggressively expressing his hostility toward her.

Paul Roazen (pers. com.) has stated that when Freud's mother came to his seventieth birthday party, she brought a basket of eggs and introduced herself to everyone as Freud's mother. It is unclear what significance the eggs had, except as a symbol of life and renewal. Freud had been a source of life and renewal for her, adding to her sense of pride and joy. She had failed with her husband, but succeeded with her son in gaining narcissistic supplies. Perhaps Sigmund was one of her eggs, which she proudly wanted to display and proclaim.

When Amalie died at the age of ninety-five in 1930, Jones (1957) reported that Freud wrote him that he felt a great increase in his sense of personal freedom and did not suffer any grief. However, his younger brother, Alexander, did mourn Amalie's loss deeply. Freud did not attend her funeral—which was unusual even though Freud himself was quite ill at the time with cancer. Instead, he sent his daughter Anna to represent him. In his letter to Jones, Freud wrote that his lack of grief or pain after her death could be explained by his mother's great age, and by her release from the suffering of gangrene of the leg, which had required morphine. He wrote, "I was not allowed to die as long as she was alive and now I may. Somehow the values of life have notably changed in the deeper layers." I interpret Freud's statement that he was not *allowed* to die as an expression of his continued compliance to a demand for performance from his mother. Attachment to his mother, while she was alive, had meant that he was unable to function autonomously. Apparently, her death served as a liberation from her control and demands. Freud's ambivalent relationship to his mother, which remained unconscious, influenced psychoanalytic theory and the therapy of women.

Freud's View of Male Homosexuality as Pathology

Freud considered that a particular form of family constellation prevented the young boy from resolving the Oedipus complex and was the cause of homosexuality. His view, which has persisted until recently in psychoanalysis, was that homosexuality was pathological and resulted from this developmental arrest that interfered with identification with the father. In Freud's (1910) essay on Leonardo da Vinci, which Jones (1955) considers to be autobiographical, Leonardo was depicted as becoming a homosexual because of a pathological relationship with his mother. The mother was described as overinvolved, close-binding, and aggressively pushing a passive father out of his "proper place": "So like all unsatisfied mothers, she took her little son in place of her husband, and by the too early maturing of his erotism robbed him of a part of his masculinity" (Freud 1910, 117).

The Bieber et al. study (1962) of homosexually oriented male patients who came for psychoanalytic treatment replicated Freud's findings about this family constellation. However, they used a biased sample, since these patients came for treatment because of emotional difficulties. A control group of homosexually oriented males who were functioning normally was not studied. Although this family constellation does interfere with the differentiation of the son from the mother and his identification with the father, it is not now seen as causing homosexuality, as Freud and Bieber speculated. Instead, this type of family was found, in my own research, to be correlated with the development of a depressive personality, no matter what the sexual orientation of the child. If seduction is also prominent in the family constellation, borderline features may develop as well. The depressive family constellation is intrusive and contributes to the child's difficulty in separating and individuating. As in Freud's own life, these children remain dependent as adults; but they maintain some autonomy by becoming oppositional.

The etiology of Freud's own sexual difficulties are probably related to the following circumstances. First, he felt emotionally abandoned by his mother at two years of age and feared to differentiate because of annihilation anxiety. Second, Freud's fear of sexual women may have been caused by his feeling overpowered by the seductive experience he described of his mother's nudity on the train trip from Leipzig. Third, his ambivalence and distance toward women who were mothers probably resulted from the continual exploitation by his mother, who fed her narcissism off his success—the depressive family constellation.

The current widely held view of homosexuality in psychiatry is that it is generally a normal variant of sexual orientation, which is inborn and is not itself pathological. Male homosexuality itself does not stem from family relations, but pathology can be inflicted by how the family and society relates to the gay youngster. If his father and peers are hostile and rejecting because the boy is too sensitive and less competitive and aggressive than others, the homosexually oriented boy may suffer low self-esteem and have difficulty relating to other men intimately. Since society tends to be homophobic, this attitude may be internalized by the boy. This can create self-hatred and conflict concerning homoerotic feelings and fantasies that often start in early childhood. In turn, a gay boy may distance himself from his father, who may be warm and accepting, in order to repress unacceptable homoerotic feelings. Under the best of circumstances, homosexuality can be associated with little or no apparent emotional difficulty.

In summary, it is not the passive or hostile father and the overinvolved exploitative mother in the family that causes homosexuality. However, these family dynamics *can* be pathogenic and contribute to depressive problems and other difficulties. What Freud seemed to be describing as homosexuality was not related to sexual orientation but to gender identity disorder, which Freud himself probably suffered from. He was emotionally abandoned by his mother at two years of age, when gender identity is first established. Core gender identity is a learned psychological phenomenon that determines attitudes toward masculinity and femininity and becomes fixed around two and a half years of age (Stoller 1968). Freud's theory reflects his own personal issues, since he considered activity as masculine and passivity as feminine, which he learned by the culture's definition of each gender. These cultural definitions influenced his erroneous ideas about bisexuality in female development as well as his belief that passivity can be ascribed to latent homosexuality in men.

Because of the depressive constellation in his family, Freud had further difficulty identifying with his father as an idealized model of masculinity. Instead, he seems to have turned to his father as a mother surrogate for nurturance. This helps us understand why later in life Freud mourned his father's but not his mother's death. It also would explain why Freud equated the penis with the breast, and fellatio with sucking milk from the mother, and that these were part of homosexuality. However, since Freud's basic sexual orientation was heterosexual, this compensatory adaptation of turning to the father for mothering probably was experienced with intense homophobic anxiety. This conflict would explain why Freud fainted at several encounters with Jung, which he himself recognized as due to what he called homosexual cathexis. This entire issue will be discussed in further detail in chapter II.

9. Omitting the Mother and Preoedipal Period in Freud's Theory

Freud's Preoedipal Trauma

Psychoanalysis arose from Freud's self-analysis during the time he was mourning the death of his father. Jacob died in October 1896, and Freud started analyzing himself in July 1897, nine months later, after buying a tombstone for his father's grave (Jones 1953). The theory sprung from the insights of this self-analysis, which dealt primarily with Freud's oedipal relationship to his father. Freud did not analyze his preoedipal relationship to his mother until the end of his life, and even then it was incomplete. Since Freud's traumatic early relationship to his nanny and mother remained repressed, he did not include the preoedipal period into the body of psychoanalysis. The effect was that Freud's theory focused on a male child's relation to the father and not the mother. Current psychoanalysis has reversed Freud's theory. Now the preoedipal period is considered more significant than the oedipal period, and the child's relationship to the mother is more important than to the father.

Freud considered his major discovery in psychoanalysis to be *infantile sexuality*, which started at about four years of age. He found that sexuality was not only manifested in adult life but existed during childhood as well. Freud noted that all small children had sexual feelings directed at the parent of the opposite sex during the oedipal period. The main threat to the little boy in the oedipal period was physical castration by the father. With little girls, the same theme of castration and resultant penis envy was paramount in Freud's theoretical formulations. It was as if girls were little boys who already had suffered castration. Freud did not give recognition to the uniqueness of femininity, that feminine sexuality was as much inborn in the female as masculinity is in the male.

Currently it is accepted that the preoedipal danger to the child, from birth to three years of age, is of either abandonment or engulfment by the mother. We now know that if an infant suffers emotional or physical abandonment by the mother, the child ceases to thrive and may die. The relationship to the mother serves to protect the child's physical and emotional survival. The other preoedipal danger is engulfment, where merging continues and a separate differentiated sense of self from the mother is lost. Freud defended himself against awareness of his own repressed preoedipal issues, and therefore omitted them from his theoretical formulations. However, even when Freud later in life did recognize the preoedipal period, he felt it was more significant for girls than for boys. Although not more significant in girls, the preoedipal period is considered to be more repressed in boys than girls. To develop a masculine identity, boys need to distance themselves to differentiate from their preoedipal mothers and identify with their fathers.

Problems Differentiating from Mother

Freud had difficulty differentiating from his mother because of the traumatic separations from his mother and nanny as a small child, and it probably continued throughout the rest of his adult life because of the depressive constellation in his family of origin. Freud's mother was intrusive and used him as an extension of herself, further interfering with the establishment of boundaries. She exploited his successes for her own narcissistic enhancement.

Hardin (1988a) provides a good deal of evidence to substantiate that Amalie appeared to be a rather narcissistic person, unable to be truly nurturant and emotionally available to Freud. The most convincing piece of evidence is from a letter written by Freud himself at sixteen years of age while visiting the Fluss family in his hometown of Freiberg (Clark 1980). In the letter, Freud praised Frau Fluss for her nurturant qualities and ability to look after her children's spiritual needs. Freud wrote she was unlike his own mother, who restricted herself to looking after only his physical needs. As further evidence, Judith Bernays Heller, writing about the time her grandmother, Amalie, went to Freud's seventieth birthday party, recalls that "she had to be carried . . . but she did not mind so long as she could be present to be honored and feted as the *mother* of her 'golden son' as she called *her* Sigmund" (1956, 420).

Amalie defined herself as the mother of her golden Sigi. He was an extension of her and not a separate person. This relationship also had been emotionally seductive and was strongly oedipally tinged, since Amalie preferred her son to her husband. However, this was a hollow victory for Freud, since the relationship served Amalie's narcissistic needs primarily, and not his own. Freud said he freely accepted the burden of the exploitative relationship his mother had with him. He could rationalize it as a consequence of a mother's "masculinity complex," since this statement fit the stereotyped role prescribed for women in patriarchal society. Achieving social success or recognition on their own was seen as a masculine trait in women. As part of the cultural pattern in nineteenth-century Europe, feminine women were constricted from achieving an identity of their own but had to live vicariously through their husbands or sons.

Even though this cultural Victorian stereotype is normative, Freud was consciously aware of some of his ambivalence regarding the close-binding and exploitative relationship he had with his mother. However, he generally blamed his ambivalence on his own sibling rivalry and not on anything that his mother did or failed to do. Freud's repressed anger toward his mother found expression in his train phobia, his fear of going to Rome, his dread of dying young, and in his states of depression. As previously noted, Freud's behavior also communicated his resentment toward her. He suffered attacks of nervous indigestion before visiting his mother every Sunday, kept her waiting at holiday gatherings, did not attend her funeral, and after her death experienced a great increase in his sense of personal freedom (Jones 1957).

In all of the correspondence he had with his friend Wilhelm Fliess, Freud mentioned his mother only once in depth. When Amalie was visiting Berlin, where Fliess lived, Freud mentions that she would be an obstacle. Freud would be forced "to devote a part of the already short time to her," instead of being able to spend it all with his friend, Fliess (Masson 1985). Max Schur, Freud's personal physician, stated that Freud as an adult spoke very little of his mother. He noted that it was not a close and warm relationship. Instead, Freud's relationship with Amalie later in life was "one of cordial filial duty" (Schur 1972).

The Dark Continent

Because Freud repressed his ambivalence toward his mother, feminine psychology remained veiled in what Freud termed an "impenetrable obscurity." His inability to consciously work through his emotions toward his mother limited Freud's capacity to observe women and to give them a significant place in his theories. This remained so even until late in his life. In 1928 he informed Ernest Jones that "everything we know of feminine early development appears to me unsatisfactory and uncertain." He had tried his best to comprehend the "sexual life of adult women," but it remained a mysterious "dark continent" (Gay 1988).

Besides femininity, music and religion posed difficult problems, since Freud could not understand them on a rational basis. Certainly Freud was the proper Victorian gentleman, influenced by the ideals of the Enlightenment that emphasized rationality, individualism, realism, and materialism. However, Freud's emphasis on rationality was probably also derived from his repressing and distancing himself from what he considered feminine. This may have been his unconscious effort to differentiate himself from the fused relationship with his mother, so he would not feel emasculated.

Even though Freud did provide some factual material about his mother in his letters to Fliess, he scarcely mentioned mothers in his clinical works. In his case histories, such as Dora, Little Hans, the Rat Man, the Schreber case, and the Wolf Man, mothers played an important role, yet they received little or no attention from Freud.

One example is the case of Little Hans, who was a small boy with a phobia about horses. Freud treated the boy through the father, who was told how to interpret Hans's conflict. The father acknowledged the boy's fear of castration by him, because of Hans's oedipal desires for his mother. However, Little Hans's mother played a very significant role in the development of the phobia. His mother had seductively invited the small boy into bed with her. After he became excited sexually, she threatened that his penis would be cut off (Freud 1909). Yet while he studied the case, Freud ignored the mother's active seduction and threat of castration, and focused only on the little boy's oedipal fear of his father.

Freud's repression of his anger and distancing himself from his mother seems to have extended to his sisters as well. Freud mentions almost nothing about any sibling rivalry for his five sisters, who were born sequentially after him. The one exception is his conscious dislike for his next-born sister, Anna. Anna was born in Freiberg eight months after his brother Julius died. This resentment of Anna persisted even later into life, since when Anna married his brother-in-law, Eli Bernays, Freud did not attend the wedding. His biographer, Jones, says Freud did not attend for reasons that could not be divulged. Anna was probably the recipient of Freud's displaced unconscious rage at his mother. He probably blamed Anna for his mother's abandonment of him during her pregnancy.

An article by Anna's granddaughter, Anne Bernays, shows that this ambivalence was not one-sided. Anna resented that she was obliged to hire herself out as a governess to help finance her brother's medical education: "I believe that even at her advanced age [she lived into her 90s] she still harbored what he no doubt would have called conflicted feelings towards him" (Bernays 1988).

The Freudian Preoedipal Period

Freud denied that, in the early development of the child's personality, the child made any significant attachments. Instead of seeking to bond to the mother, Freud saw the infant as desiring only to satisfy inner instinctual drives. The mother is seen only as a distant *object*, used to gratify the child's needs. The child is described as autoerotic, mainly interested in stimulating its own mouth, then its anus, and finally the penis, all of which he termed erogenous zones.

The first two *preoedipal* stages of psychosexual development, the oral and anal phases, Freud considered to be similar for boys and girls. During the oral phase, from birth to about one and a half years of age, the baby is dependent and seeks stimulation of its mouth as well as satisfaction of its hunger. Aggression is expressed by biting. During the anal stage, from about one and a half to three years of age, the child is concerned with sphincter and impulse control, with withholding or loss of its stools, and with dealing with sadistic feelings.

At the next stage, the phallic phase, from about three to five years of age, the developmental sequences for boys and girls diverge. For the boy, the mother becomes the object of his sexual drive and the father the target of his aggressive drive. The role of the mother, as a person actively influencing and affecting the infant of either gender, was ignored by Freud. The preoedipal issues of attachment and the fears of engulfment or abandonment were not dealt with. Instead, to Freud the mother remained a passive detached *object* of the child's oral, anal, and sexual drives.

Freud's consideration of the mother as a passive object was in tune with the patriarchal Victorian stereotype. However, on a personal level, if the mother were only the object of instinctual drives and the child made no significant attachment, the painful threat of her loss or her engulfment could be denied. Freud's theory gives the illusion that the infant is narcissistically self-sufficient and denies its deeply dependent relationship to the mother.

Therefore, one can speculate that Freud's theory of child development represented a defensive maneuver, which he himself employed for his own protection. If the infant were not dependently attached, it could not suffer the traumatic loss of the mother. The infant would not experience murderous rage against a mother who is experienced as bad and abandoning. By making the mother a distant object, Freud may also have attempted to differentiate himself from his close-binding relationship and to protect her from his rage.

Freud was fearful not only of the destructive effects of his own rage but that a sexual relationship with a motherly woman would also magically result in her loss. Therefore, if the mother were not an active participant but only a passive object of the child's sexual drive, the mother's seductive influence could be denied. Making the mother into a passive object prevented her loss, and denied the danger of abandonment or engulfment.

Another reason that Freud focused on the oedipal and ignored the preoedipal period of child development may be that he found guilt preferable to helplessness. If the child is bad or sinful, guilt is easier to deal with intrapsychically than helplessness. For example, when the little boy wishes to eliminate the father and possess the mother, he experiences guilt and feels threatened with castration by the father. However, this can be managed internally. All the little boy needs to do is to renounce his sexual desire for his mother, resolve his guilt, and then he can identify with his father. The threat of castration by the father is thereby magically eliminated. The oedipal boy can change *himself* to influence the environment. This gives the oedipal child the illusion of magical control over its environment. However, the threat of abandonment by the preoedipal mother is a much greater threat, one that cannot be controlled by intrapsychic maneuvers. Even if the infant were able to renounce its dependency on the mother, which it cannot do, this would only result in death. Under these circumstances the child would experience itself as totally powerless to change its destiny. I suggest that Freud also defended himself from experiencing himself as a passive and helpless person by focusing on the oedipal period and not the preoedipal period. Instead, he made his mother the passive one.

When Freud originally formulated his so-called seduction theory, it applied to both men and women. He considered that adult neurosis resulted from childhood sexual seduction, usually by the father. This was not the case for Freud, since he clearly mentioned in his letter to Fliess that it was his nanny who was his temptress. Only two months after starting his self-analysis, in his letter of September 21, 1897, to Fliess (Bonaparte et al. 1954), Freud stated he had abandoned his seduction theory. This rejection denied that a parent or other adult played a significant or active role in the genesis of neurosis. This is a position he held until the time of his death. Freud considered the child's inborn instincts to be responsible for fantasies that affected how the child perceived its world. The tales of sexual seduction he heard from his patients were discounted as only fantasies. The adult was not responsible for being seductive, and the child was not the helpless passive victim. The implication was that the child's own instincts had actively warped its perception. The parent's actual emotional neglect or sexual temptation and overstimulation were thus largely denied and ignored.

Preoedipal Influence on the Oedipal Period

The death of his father enabled Freud to regress to his childhood and reexperience patricidal wishes that were associated with his oedipal conflict. The guilt over his father's death probably also brought back Freud's preoedipal guilt concerning anger toward his father for making his mother pregnant and thus unavailable to him. At the age of two, Freud protected his father from his anger by displacing the blame onto his "naughty" half-brother Philipp. He thought it was Philipp who was Amalie's husband and responsible for her pregnancy. The mother's pregnancy and Anna's birth were experienced as maternal abandonment and fueled little Sigmund's disappointment and rage at her, and at his father as well.

The traumatic loss of his nanny and his mother's emotional unavailability when Freud was two years old also probably prevented the normal process of differentiation and separation from the mother and the establishment of firm ego boundaries. One can assume that these preoedipal issues affected Freud's later oedipal conflict with his father. Anger toward the father for the preoedipal loss of the mother was added to the anger at the father as a competitor for the mother oedipally. Because Freud's fantasies were probably not differentiated from reality due to arrested development, the unconscious anger during the oedipal period may have become even more frightening. Preoedipal issues shape how the later Oedipus complex will be experienced and resolved.

10. Female Sexual Development in Freudian Theory

Oedipal Development in Girls

Two important factors contributed to Freud's formulation of a theory about female sexual development. One was his fear of seeing women as sexually active, and the other was the fear of his own aggression. Freud did not acknowledge that women have their own sexual desires and seek gratification. In his unconscious mind, seeing his preoedipal mother as a temptress would probably mean to him that she would be sent to hell as a sinner, and he would be abandoned. A reason for Freud's subsequent rejection of the seduction theory may have been a denial of the seductive sexuality of his mother. The rejection of the theory occurred after his father's death, when Freud dreamed that he closed one eye: the blind spot could possibly have been the denial of his mother's influence, particularly her aggressive sexuality.

Nowhere in the Standard Edition of his collected works does Freud discuss matricide. However, patricide is a prominent theme. The omission of death wishes toward the mother is most likely due to the denial of his ambivalence toward his own mother. Protecting his mother against loss was an important dynamic in Freud's early childhood. Consciously, Freud idealized his mother and denied anger. To deal with his dread of maternal abandonment, he embarked on a circuitous route to explain femininity. He denied the basic feminine nature of women and attempted to make them into diminished men. In female development during the phallic phase, Freud considered that little girls observe the male penis and feel castrated and inferior. He believed that girls then suffer from "envy of the penis which will leave ineradicable traces on their development and the formation of their character and which will not be surmounted in even the most favourable cases without a severe expenditure of psychical energy" (1933, 125).

During this oedipal period, girls turn to their fathers to give them a gift of a penis. This desire for a penis is then sublimated into the hope to have a child by the father. Girls become interested in playing with dolls, which represent a symbolic penis. With the resolution of the oedipal phase, the girls give up their sexual desire for the father and identify with the mother. However, Freud made no mention that girls might enjoy their own sexuality. Nor did he consider that boys might envy girls of their physical endowments or their ability to create new life.

The first internalization of a parent, according to Freud, is after the child resolves the Oedipus complex. For the boy it is resolved after he gives up his desire for his mother and identifies with his father. The boy relinquishes his desire for the mother only because of the threat of castration by the father. The boy then internalizes the father. Freud saw the father, and not the mother, as the first parent internalized by both boys and girls. The father forms the core of the superego. Because women do not have a penis, they do not suffer castration anxiety. Therefore, Freud considered the resolution of the Oedipus complex less complete and superego formation less differentiated than in males. Since Freud originally presumed that internalization of the father forms the superego, women never develop as complete a superego as men. This argument for the inferiority of women began with erroneous assumptions that the penis is all-important and that the superego is derived only from the father. Modern infant research has shown that the first attachment and internalization during infancy is with the mother.

The next phase of development described by Freud was the latency period, from about five to seven years of age. During this time an apparent diminution of the sexual drive occurs for both sexes. This is followed by the genital phase, from six years of age onward, when sexuality is sublimated and integrated with affectionate feelings. It is at the genital stage that the capacity for love develops.

In his developmental theory, Freud dealt with the issues of individuation and autonomy. These are issues of greater concern for boys, because of their need to differentiate from the mother to achieve a masculine gender identity. Freud did not focus on empathy or relationships, which are more characteristic of women's interests. These more masculine or phallocentric issues were also reinforced by the patriarchal Victorian culture.

A year after his mother died, Freud published "Female Sexuality." He wrote: "The phase of exclusive attachment to the mother, which may be called the preoedipus phase, possesses a far greater importance in women than it can have in men" (1931, 230). For girls there is a strong preoedipal attachment to the mother that is "intense" and "passionate." He minimized the importance of the preoedipal period in boys, though he did acknowledge the work of psychoanalyst Jeanne Lampl-de Groot, who recognized the importance of the preoedipal phase for boys as well as for girls. Freud's attitude toward accepting that preoedipal issues existed in boys now seemed to have softened.

In "Female Sexuality," Freud also referred to Otto Fenichel, who noted that it is often difficult to recognize preoedipal material in analysis since it might be unchanged or distorted by repression. This apparently provided an explanation for Freud's lack of recognition of preoedipal material in psychoanalytic theory. Freud openly admitted this to be the case: "Everything in the sphere of this first attachment to the mother seemed to me so difficult to grasp in analysis—so grey with age and shadowy and almost impossible to revivify—that it was as if it had succumbed to an especially inexorable repression" (1931, 226).

In Freud's *New Introductory Lectures on Psychoanalysis* (1933), he indicated that in religions the creator is usually a male deity endowed with "power, wisdom, and the strength of his passions—an idealized superman." Furthermore, "Our further path is made easy to recognize, for this god-creator is undisguisedly called 'father.' Psychoanalysis infers that he really is the father, with all the magnificence in which he once appeared to the small child. A religious man pictures the creation of the universe just as he pictures his own origin" (1933, 163).

Although Freud acknowledges the importance of the father as the creator in religion, this same bias had been inadvertently introduced into his theory of early child development. As in patriarchal religion, the father also assumed the central role in Freud's ideas of personality development. It was as if women were like a sexually tempting Eve, who would bring down punishment by God and loss of the garden of Eden. In psychoanalytic theory it was the father, like God, who was the threatening and external subject.

However, in his *New Introductory Lectures*, Freud also acknowledged that some mythologies claim that creation began "with a male god getting rid of a female deity, who is degraded into being a monster." Freud does acknowledge the replacement of the mother by the father in religion, and that her importance was demeaned. It can be speculated that this was a beginning recognition, although externalized onto the culture, of how his own personal conflicts had influenced his thinking to minimize the earlier role of the mother in personality development of the child. Freud proceeded to correct his statement that the child owed its existence to the father's protection by a parenthetical, "or more correctly, no doubt, the parental agency compounded by the father *and mother*" (Freud 1933).

It is worth noting that in "Analysis Terminable and Interminable" (1937a), Freud mentioned that Ferenczi pointed out the importance of the analyst's countertransference feelings. This was one of the topics Ferenczi mentioned in his last paper, "The Confusion of Tongues between Adults and the Child," delivered before the International Psychoanalytic Congress at Wiesbaden in 1932. His main point was that external traumatic factors had been "undeservedly neglected of late in the pathogenesis of the neurosis" by the exclusive attention to the child's inner drives.

Ferenczi had not rejected Freud's original seduction theory about the traumatic influence of important figures on the child. Ferenczi especially emphasized the mother-child relationship during the child's preoedipal stages of development. The trauma for the child did not have to be a sexual seduction but could be emotional deprivation or neglect. Ferenczi saw the mother as an active and influential person in the mother-child interaction. These issues had caused a rift in the close friendship between Freud and Ferenczi before Ferenczi's death a year later in 1933. However, in "Constructions in Analysis" (1937b), published four years later, Freud agreed with Ferenczi about the lack of attention given to the mother-child relationship in psychoanalysis.

Freud had already given up the seduction theory as the cause of neurosis in 1897, but he did not renounce it publicly until 1905, with the publication of his *Three Essays on the Theory of Sexuality* (1905b). Nevertheless, he did hold on to the traumatic effect of the "primal scene," where the young child witnesses the parents' sexual intercourse. But he denied this as preoedipal trauma. Instead, he considered the "primal scene" as a delayed trauma that did not become pathogenic until the phallic phase of development occurred. This was probably another example of Freud's denial of his own preoedipal trauma, which he preferred to place into the oedipal period.

Acknowledging the Preoedipal Period

In "Constructions in Analysis," Freud (1937b) discusses the analyst's reconstruction of the patient's very early life experiences. This reconstruction allows repressed memories and their affective feelings to be reexperienced, so that inhibitions and symptoms can be relieved. Freud openly acknowledged that "sufficient attention has not hitherto been paid" to early preoedipal experiences in the child. Freud recognized that these experiences were what the child really saw or heard even though they could seem hallucinatory, because the preoedipal child was also largely preverbal. Freud also acknowledged the importance of the early attachment to his mother, his loss and resultant ambivalence toward her, and why his father assumed such a position of importance for him:

Up to your *n*th year you regarded yourself as the sole and unlimited possessor of your mother; then came another baby and brought you grave disillusionment. Your mother left you for some time, and even after her reappearance she was never again devoted to you exclusively. Your feelings towards your mother became ambivalent, your father gained a new importance for you. (1937b, 261).

Near the end of his life, Freud did gradually give preoedipal issues more importance. He recognized a child's attachment to and ambivalence toward the mother. However, he continued to blame the child. He placed primary responsibility for the ambivalence onto the small child's sibling rivalry and "disillusionment." He did not question why his mother left him, but simply accepted this as fact. He did not feel that his mother could have been more sensitive to him during and after her pregnancy. Perhaps if her life circumstances had been different, his mother could have been more emotionally available to him to help him cope with the new arrival. As a small child Freud shifted his attachment from his mother to his father, because of his ambivalent feelings and as a rejection of his abandoning mother, which could explain why the father assumed prominence and the mother was neglected in psychoanalytic theory.

Effects of Freud's Preoedipal Trauma

Freud consciously acknowledges that his attachment to his father became more significant because of his mother's unavailability. His father became, in a sense, another mother surrogate, which would also explain why his father's death, but not his mother's, was so profoundly moving for Freud—his father had become both mother and father for him. Not only were there oedipal issues, but they were superimposed on earlier preoedipal conflicts as well.

Freud's ambivalence toward his mother became more obvious after her death in September 1930. Hardin (1988a) comments on the time Freud sent his daughter Anna to attend his mother's funeral. Earlier, in the summer of 1930, Freud had sent Anna to Frankfurt as his representative to receive the Goethe Prize for literature, and she accepted the 10,000 marks prize and a medallion for her father. In view of Freud's ill health, this solution was appropriate. However, Hardin questions why he later sent her as a surrogate to his mother's funeral in Vienna as well. Hardin offers several interpretations. First, Anna could be a mourner-by-proxy who would be able to express Freud's grief, which he himself could not do because of his own alienation from his mother. Second, Hardin considers that sending Anna was an acting-out of his ambivalence based on the talion principle: "Freud, in effect, had sent a surrogate son to his mother's funeral, just as his mother, during a significant period of his infancy, had given over a major part of his care to a surrogate—the Kinderfrau (nanny)" (85).

If this was the case, Freud had not done this deliberately. His acting-out of his vengeance was without any conscious awareness of his ambivalence toward his mother. Clearly, seven years after his mother's death he was more consciously aware of his ambivalence toward her, as shown in "Constructions in Analysis" (1937b). During those seven years, Freud must have continued some self-analysis of his preoedipal period and achieved further insight. However, this period was almost at the end of his life, and the great majority of his important work in developing psychoanalytic theory had already been written. Therefore, the importance of the preoedipal period, the role of the mother, and the psychology of female development were never fully developed by him.

Freud's colleagues who brought up the importance of the mother in psychoanalytic developmental theory, such as Ferenczi, Jung, and Rank, probably became the recipients of Freud's displaced unconscious rage against his mother, and the relationships were destroyed as a result. This was a repetition of what had happened with Julius, onto whom Freud displaced his anger at his mother. These male psychoanalysts unknowingly became revenants of his brother Julius and were symbolically killed off by Freud's cessation of his relationship with them. The most tragic disruption of a relationship was the lifelong friendship between Freud and Ferenczi.

In his *non vixit* dream, Freud suggested that

all my friends have in a certain sense been reincarnations of this first figure ... they have been revenants. My nephew (John) himself reappeared in my boyhood, at that time we acted the parts of Caesar and Brutus together. My emotional life has always insisted that I should have an intimate friend and a hated enemy. I have always been able to provide myself afresh with both, and it has not infrequently happened that the ideal situation of childhood has been so completely reproduced that friend and enemy have come together in a single individual—though not of course, both at once or with constant oscillations, as may have been the case in my early childhood. (1900, 421–25)

Blum (1983) and Grinstein (1968) say that Freud's nephew, John, was important as a childhood friend, but more likely he represented a screen object for his brother Julius. Freud's playing Brutus, who killed Julius Caesar, played by his nephew, provides the rationale for this interpretation.

But why did Freud not object when women stressed the importance of the mother in the psychoanalytic theory of child development? First, this may have been due to Freud's use of the defense of splitting. Aggression was displaced away from the mother and from female analysts, who remained idealized, and it was projected onto his brother Julius and male analysts. Second, the women who were admitted into psychoanalytic training were not primarily interested in mothering, which may have also contributed to making them immune to his anger at mothers. Third, these women analysts often limited their theory to female child development. For these and other reasons, Freud did not reject these women analysts even when they stressed the importance of the mother in child development.

Although she never developed a comprehensive theory of her own, Lou Andreas-Salomé emphasized the early preoedipal relationship between mother and child. She objected to the pseudo-physical constructs of the libido theory and favored an interpersonal perspective much like Karen Horney, Melanie Klein, and Clara Thompson. Similar to Klein and Thompson, Lou Andreas-Salomé studied with Sandor Ferenczi in Budapest and was influenced by him. She emphasized the "primary state" before and after birth, in which there exists a lack of differentiation between the infant and its mother (Leavy 1964). She believed that feminine sexuality was closer to reexperiencing this primary merged preoedipal union of mother and infant, and due less to aggressive drives as in the male. Thus her theoretical ideas are closer to modern psychoanalytic theory than those of Freud.

She compared conception, childbearing, and child rearing in women to the creative process, very similar to an artist's work. She emphasized that this preoedipal relationship, characterized by a lack of differentiation, was employed by the artist also in creative work. Concerning the artist, she maintained that "he lays hold of this sense experience out of primitive impressions in which world and man are for him undifferentiated reality, and it is this which he realizes in his work" (Leavy 1964, 24).

Lou Andreas-Salomé was the lover of the famous poet Rainer Maria Rilke, and they remained lifelong friends. Rilke had also expressed some of these ideas about creativity in his *Duino Elegies*. Lou was also an accomplished poet and novelist before becoming a psychoanalyst. In 1882, the philosopher Friedrich Nietzsche had fallen desperately in love with Andreas-Salomé and proposed marriage. But she refused because she felt he was too emotionally unstable, and besides, Nietzsche's mother and sister were jealous of her and violently opposed their marriage. In 1884 Nietzsche said of Lou, "I have never known a more gifted or more understanding creature." Freud himself was strongly attached to her because of her brilliance, and he continued an ongoing correspondence with her for twenty-five years until her death. In a letter he wrote her in May 1931, he recognized "your superiority over all of us— in accord with the heights from which you descended to us" (Jones 1953).

11. Preoedipal Development in Girls and Boys

The Preoedipal Timetable

The original observational research of preoedipal development in infants was conducted by the psychoanalyst Margaret Mahler and her colleagues (Mahler and Furer 1968; Mahler, Pine, and Bergman 1975). They believed the earliest preoedipal developmental phases were similar for both sexes. For the first few months after birth, the infant was supposedly autistic, or unconnected with its surroundings. However, modern infant observational research by Stern (1985) and others have found the infant begins relating almost from the moment of birth onward, and there is no autistic phase.

Mahler then noted that from four to six months of age, the infant proceeds through the symbiotic phase. There is a lack of differentiation between the self and object representations. To deal with its helpless dependency, the infant experiences itself as merged with the mother, as if possessing a common boundary. By merging with the mother, who is experienced as omnipotent, the infant achieves a sense of power. Here again Stern does not consider that there is a direct development of the infant to the symbiotic phase. The infant develops a sense of self *before* entertaining the fantasy of symbiotic fusion with the mother.

The next phase, according to Mahler, is that of separation-individuation, which lasts until three years of age. This stage is subdivided into the hatching, practicing, and rapprochement subphases. Mahler viewed individuation as the process of acquiring intrapsychic autonomy. Separation deals with differentiating of self from the mother, distancing, and structuring personality boundaries. During this time, the toddler acquires motor skills and ventures forth to explore the world. The mother needs to allow for this separation, but still has to be available as an anchor to cue the child to reality and as a refueling station to provide comfort when required. When this process is successful, the infant can internalize aspects of the mother. The child learns to trust that the mother's love will continue despite her absence.

Because the child's symbolic capacity begins to flourish, object constancy can now develop. The child is able to evoke an image of the mother in its memory when needed, just as if the actual mother were present to provide nurturance, comfort, and love. A separate and cohesive self apart from the mother can develop and becomes relatively more and more autonomous. The child can gradually take over its own personality-maintaining functions that were previously provided by the mother, such as soothing and maintaining a narcissistic equilibrium to sustain self-esteem and confidence. At this point, the child gives up using primarily the defenses of splitting and projective identification, and it learns to integrate and tolerate ambivalence. Others are now seen as whole and separate individuals, who are both good and bad.

If the mother is unresponsive or physically or emotionally unavailable, developmental arrest can result, and this normal process of differentiation and separation from the mother may not proceed. During the preoedipal period of early child development, the rapprochement subphase of separation-individuation, from eighteen to thirty-six months of age, is an especially vulnerable one. In the rapprochement subphase, the infant gives up its fusion with the mother and becomes aware of its own separateness and helplessness. The child also begins to give up its belief in its own and the mother's omnipotence, resulting in increased clinging and sleep disturbances. During this rapprochement crisis, the infant becomes fearful of the loss of the mother as a separate and whole object and is vulnerable to despair. (Melanie Klein [1948] noted a similar stage, which she termed the "depressive position.") The child's ego becomes structuralized, as it internalizes the mother's rules, ideals, and demands in order to form a superego. The mastery of speech enables the child to express itself verbally, and symbolic play helps it to master its developmental tasks.

If developmental arrest occurs, the child may not separate or be unable to regulate its own narcissistic equilibrium. The child continues to be excessively sensitive to the mother in order to relieve and contain its tension and/or modulate its self-esteem. If separation from the mother and a cohesive sense of self are not achieved, later losses of important others, who symbolically represent the preoedipal mother, may result in severe depression or psychotic decompensation. These symptoms are seen in borderline personality disorders and psychotic conditions. If separation but not individuation is accomplished, others are still experienced as need-satisfying objects that are required to sustain the child's confidence and self-esteem. This condition is manifested in persons suffering narcissistic personality disorders. Patients with this narcissistic problem retain a grandiose sense of self and feel entitled to make demands of others, opposing any limits to these demands. Both the borderline and narcissistic patients continue to use the primitive defenses of splitting and projective identification, and attempt to control others in order to obtain needed narcissistic supplies to sustain the survival of their self and self-esteem.

Gender Differentiation

Freud (1933) speculated that gender differentiation occurred late during childhood, on the basis of possession of a penis. During the oedipal phase, according to him the boy fears loss of the penis, and the girl, seeing herself as already castrated, experiences penis envy. Penis envy becomes a prime motivation, leading the girl to turn to her father and to desire a baby. Freud also considered all children to be bisexual, and that during prephallic development the clitoris serves as the equivalent of the phallus. The little girl is supposedly unaware of her vagina until puberty. According to Freud, when the girl gives up masturbating, turning her emotional investment from activity and the "masculine" clitoris to passivity and the vagina, she achieves femininity.

Beginning with Horney (1926, 1932) and Jones (1927), theoreticians have stressed the preoedipal period as crucial for gender development. Horney felt that boys had a greater dread of the all-powerful preoedipal mother than of their oedipal father. The fear of the father is less threatening to total survival, is more tangible and less uncanny than the fear of the mother.

Modern observational research by Galenson and Roiphe (1974) and Galenson (1980) have questioned Freud's assumptions about early feminine development. They noted that an early genital phase occurs in the latter half of the second year, much before the oedipal period. There is a heightened genital sensitivity leading to manual self-stimulation, rocking, thigh pressure, and so on. In girls, the labia, mons area, and clitoris, but not the vagina, are the main sites. After discovering genital differences, boys demonstrate heightened physical activity and girls show increased sucking, fears of separation, and concern over body imperfections. Galenson and Roiphe interpreted these reactions as a preoedipal castration complex. They felt this facilitated the girl's erotic shift to the father, while maintaining an identification with the mother. Similarly, a spurt in the boy's identification with the father occurs. Essentially, penis envy in girls did not represent a permanent narcissistic injury as Freud had postulated, but was limited to this specific preoedipal developmental phase.

Current research considers that during the rapprochement subphase of separation-individuation, the development of male and female gender identity occurs. Kleeman (1976) noted that before the age of two, little girls not only discover their external genitalia but their vagina as well. Because the male genitalia are prominent, girls develop a less clear mental image of their genitalia than boys between two and three years of age. However, girls are aware that their genitals are pleasurable and are valued. There is an inborn sense of femaleness, which was also noted by Ehrhardt and Baker (1974), who attributed it to hormonal and central nervous system patterning. Stoller (1968) notes that by two and a half years of age, the child has psychologically learned and permanently fixed its core gender identity.

Chodorow (1978) has contradicted Freud's statement that the route to femininity was circuitous and difficult. She believed that a girl's development is easier than the boy's. The girl does not need to reject her primary symbiotic identification with her mother, so that differentiation can be a slower and more gradual process. To differentiate and achieve a masculine identity, the male child needs to deny and repress the dependent attachment on the mother. She noted that boys consider anything feminine in oneself and others to be devalued and unacceptable. To compensate for the fear of the all-powerful preoedipal mother, women and their bodies have to be dominated. Boys need to erect distancing defenses, establish firm ego boundaries, and deny self-other connectedness. The boy's sense of self is more separate, and striving for autonomy becomes more paramount for him than for a girl.

Since girls maintain the mother as the primary internalized object, a more flexible ego boundary that does not need to deny relatedness to others can be established. The girl's oedipal love for her father diminishes the intense dependency on the mother and facilitates her heterosexual object choice. Chodorow stated that although women remain erotically heterosexual, they tend to look to other women to fulfill their relationship needs. Because women do not have to repress their inner self-object world as men do, their relational capacities are greater. Their sense of self is continuous with others, which enables them to reproduce the capacity for mothering more effectively.

Gender Issues for Freud

Because of the traumatic loss of his mother surrogate and the emotional withdrawal of his mother during the preoedipal period, Freud seems to have experienced difficulty in differentiating himself from his mother and developing a firm male gender identity. Consciously, Freud's theory about bisexuality was derived from the speculations of his friend Wilhelm Fliess. Fliess believed both sexes were innately bisexual, with feminine men attracted to masculine women and visa versa. However, Freud's lack of differentiation from his mother during the preoedipal period may have resulted in his inability to develop male gender constancy. Freud defended himself against his problem by generalizing that all men had a feminine side and all women had a masculine one. This idea subsequently found expression in his theory of bisexuality as a universal biological force. Freud erroneously used bisexuality as the underpinning for feminine development and to define what was feminine and masculine in each gender.

Voth (1972) noted that Freud remained symbiotically attached to his mother, feared her, and felt guilty over his unconscious hostility toward her. According to Voth, Freud's adherence to the concept of bisexuality served not only a defensive need but was also a symptomatic expression of his own basic identification with his mother. The theory that bisexuality was normal thus provided Freud with a rationalization for accepting the "feminine" side of his own personality.

Modern research in the field of child development by Stoller (1968) and Money and Ehrhardt (1972) have contributed to our differentiation of the biological determinants of sexual orientation from the psychological aspect of gender development. Stoller noted that the core gender identity of a child as a male or female is learned primarily from cultural sexual stereotypes and augmented by biological forces. This process occurs during the second year of life and becomes a permanent part of the self-image by two and a half years. It determines how one views masculinity and femininity, the body image, the sense of self, and life goals. Mahler et al. (1975) also observed that gender identity begins to differentiate during the rapprochement subphase and consolidates at the end of the separation-individuation phase, at the beginning of object constancy.

In an inclusive review of the etiology of childhood gender identity disorder, Coates and Friedman (1989) specifically related *gender identity disorder* to *early object loss* and the associated experience of helplessness and vulnerability in *two-year-old males*. This sequence was first found in the cases reported by Friend et al. (1954), who noted that traumatic events occurring in the first two years of life produced gender identity disorders in boys. Disruption of normal separation in these boys occurred because their mothers experienced emotional trauma and became depressed or unavailable. Coates (1985) found that the boys suffered severe separation anxiety, which threatened cohesion of the self and total annihilation. As a reparative maneuver, these boys maintained fusion with the lost mother instead of separating, mourning, and internalizing only aspects of her. The boys employed the primitive defense mechanism of splitting, with idealization of the mother. This preserved the internalized image of the mother as all good, and protected it from destruction by the child's rage. Most of these boys later became homosexual as adults, although they represented only a small subgroup of all homosexuals. The mothers also devalued their husbands and masculinity, and all pinned their hopes for achievement on their sons.

Freud's traumatic loss of his mother and nanny at two years of age may have similarly resulted in his not developing gender stability or constancy. His mother suffered a series of severe traumatic losses at that time, including the death of her brother, her baby Julius, and the failure of her husband's business. From Freud's own accounts, she was not emotionally available, and he recalled experiencing severe separation anxiety. Instead of individuating from his mother and establishing a separate identity, Freud seems to have remained fused and identified with her. He continued to use the internal defense mechanism of splitting, repressing his hostility, and consciously idealizing his mother. Furthermore, Amalie *prevented* Freud's separation postoedipally, since she lived vicariously through her son because her husband had failed to be an adequate provider. Thus the picture of Freud's preoedipal trauma closely fits the research findings and would explain Freud's problems with bisexual feelings.

Blum (1990) speculates that during Freud's relationship with Fliess from 1887 to 1902, he dealt with both oedipal and preoedipal issues. Freud not only worked through his differentiation from his father, but also his fusion with his mother. According to Blum, the birth of Freud's own six children from October 6, 1887, to December 3, 1895, reactivated Freud's preoedipal childhood conflicts with his own mother and siblings. Freud's mother had given birth to seven children between 1856 and 1866, all spaced very closely. Each birth of a sibling represented a traumatic loss of the mother for him. Blum considers that Freud felt deprived and betrayed by his mother as she displaced her love and attention each time to the newborn baby.

During his courtship to Martha Bernays, Freud wrote over nine hundred love letters, full of passion; in them he wanted to know every detail of Martha's life. He said Martha was everything to him, being a sweetheart, comrade, working companion, and confidante. He felt deprived by her absence, but alive, strong, and complete when he was with her. During their early years of marriage, Freud remained quite possessive of her, and resented her independence of mind. He attempted to mold her into being exactly what he wanted, instead of accepting her as a separate person; in his eyes, she needed to be an extension of him, to be almost merged with him. One suspects that Freud wanted Martha to be the idealized good mother he did not have, to be exclusively his and controlled by him. He experienced the abandonment by his mother as being due to her pregnancies and did not want to suffer her loss or share her with any siblings. In his marriage, Freud probably unconsciously hoped he would make up for the deprivation he had suffered with his mother as a child. He would transform Martha into a good, nurturant, preoedipal mother, who would always be there for him and restore his wounded narcissism.

According to Jones, Martha did put Freud's comfort and needs first, and never made demands on his time. Although she had a mind of her own, she was basically a quiet and gentle person. However, each time Martha became pregnant, her pregnancy symbolically represented another displacement from his mother, which Freud probably unconsciously resented. Just as Freud had idealized his wife before all her pregnancies, he now shifted his attachment and idealized Fliess as his important "other," who strengthened his self-esteem and restored his narcissistic equilibrium.

In a letter of July 14, 1894, Freud considered Fliess's praise to be like "nectar" and "ambrosia." In the June 30, 1896, letter to Fliess, Freud stated, "I bring nothing but two open ears and one *temporal lobe lubricated for reception.*" Blum notes that Freud demonstrated a feminine passive attitude. He seems to have identified himself with his pregnant wife (a transference figure for his mother) and experienced Fliess as the impregnator (a transference figure for his father). Blum claims that Freud was able to relive his own early childhood with its themes of loss of the mother, sibling rivalry, and death; by idealizing Fliess, he was able to separate from both parents and work through his identification with his mother and his oedipal guilt toward his father. Blum believes that Freud resolved his preoedipal separation and oedipal castration anxiety as he learned to differentiate his identity from both his parents.

Although this would have been the desirable outcome, Blum's speculations seem unlikely. Freud (1937b) specifically states in his "Constructions in Analysis" that when his mother became unavailable, he shifted his attachment from his mother to his father. This same occurrence was repeated when Martha became unavailable because of her pregnancies. Freud identified with Martha, as he had fused with his mother, and shifted his attachment to Fliess, as with his father: Freud saw Fliess as a transference figure for his father, to whom he came "lubricated for reception" as a female.

In all likelihood, Freud was indeed able to work through his castration anxiety with his father and furthered his identification with him. By being more able to identify with his father and his own fatherhood, Freud no longer needed to turn to idealized father figures, such as Brucke, Meynert, Charcot, and Breuer to consolidate his masculine gender identity. It is interesting that Freud had named each of his children after men, or their wives or daughters, whom he had idolized as father figures. Mathilde, his firstborn, was named after Breuer's wife; Martin after Jean Martin Charcot; Oliver after Oliver Cromwell; Ernst after Ernst Brucke; and Sophie and Anna after Professor Paul Hammerschlag's niece and daughter, respectively. However, to disagree with Blum, I find it questionable that in his self-analysis with Fliess, Freud analyzed and resolved his relationship to his preoedipal mother. In 1910 Freud wrote a letter to his close friend Ferenczi, commenting on the ending of his relationship with Fliess: "I no longer have any need to uncover my personality completely. . . . Since Fliess's case . . . that need has been extinguished. A part of homosexual cathexis has been withdrawn and made use of to enlarge my own ego. I have succeeded where the paranoic fails" (Jones 1955, 83).

However, Freud did not differentiate himself from his mother, and despite his claim that he had resolved his "homosexual cathexis," he continued to have latent homosexual conflicts. As stated earlier, this was reflected in his feminine theory of development, which emphasized bisexuality, and in his ideas about homosexuality. In addition, in a letter to Jones (1953) Freud describes that he again experienced "unruly homosexual feelings" when he fainted in front of Jung in 1912.

Blum (1983) also mentions that Fliess was born the same year as Freud's brother, Julius. He suggests that with Fliess, Freud was possibly able to work through some of his guilt about his dead brother as well. However, in Freud's continuing relationships to male colleagues, this was not the case. Freud needed to repeat his relationship with his brother Julius with male colleagues such as Ferenczi, Jung, and Rank, generally around issues of the mother's importance during child development and feminine psychology. The end result was a splintering of the psychoanalytic movement that persists to this day, even though the reason for its creation is no longer valid.

Freud had allowed Fliess to operate on one of his patients, Emma Eckstein, who suffered from hysterical symptoms. Fliess had constructed a theory connecting the turbinate bones of the nose with female sexuality, and he guessed that this operation would help relieve Emma's psychological symptoms. The surgery was performed in February 1895, and Fliess carelessly left gauze in Emma's nose. This error produced a hemorrhage that proved to be almost fatal to Emma.

In July 1895, following the poorly performed nasal surgery, Freud dreamed of Irma's injection, in which he recounted the nasal operation on Emma (Irma in the dream) and denounced Fliess (Otto in the dream) for his incompetence, carelessness, and irresponsibility. At the time, Freud still consciously continued to idealize Fliess, however he kept this dream a secret from Fliess. Blum considers that the dream of Irma's injection also represented a revival and working through of Freud's witnessing the primal scene of his parents, and its associated feelings of sexual creation and destruction. The dream was later published in the *Interpretation of Dreams* (1900), two years before the breakup of the friendship with Fliess. Freud was able to terminate their relationship while retaining fond memories of Fliess.

In his relationship to Fliess, Freud probably did experience a regression but was not able to achieve any significant resolution of his preoedipal conflicts. It was not until his mother's death that Freud was able to separate and individuate from her. His traumatic relationship with his mother was not simply an occurrence of his infancy, but an ongoing and fresh reality, and could not be analyzed away. Amalie continued to be intrusive and to exploit Sigmund during his entire life for her own narcissistic gain. She used him as a confidante and counselor even when he was a youngster, and later, as an adult, she vicariously lived through his achievements. Freud remained symbiotically bound to her through adulthood. Amalie pressured her "golden Sigi" to function as a savior to regain the family's social status that had been lost by the father. This maternal preference of the son over the father provided Freud with a symbolic oedipal triumph that was destructive for him.

Reality again added to Freud's oedipal guilt for entertaining patricidal fantasies toward his father, just as it had done in his feelings toward his brother Julius. His father's failure, weakness, and vulnerability made Freud's destructive fantasies seem more capable of being realized in actuality. It was only after his father's death that Freud was able to work through his oedipal conflict in his self-analysis and to identify with him more fully.

I further speculate that it was precisely because his father was now dead that the distinction between fantasy and reality became sharply delineated. Unconscious fantasy and external reality no longer corresponded to one another, and now each was distinct and unrelated. Freud did not seem to be able to work through his unconscious hostility toward his mother, either, until a number of years after her death. After both his parents were dead, there was no longer any threat that his omnipotent rage would destroy either of them. Fantasy could no longer become external reality, and the parents became sharply differentiated by reality itself. Reality, which had been an enemy to Freud's unconscious, now became its friend.

12. Maternal Merging in Society and the Family

The Group Mind

Freud (1921) totally ignored the importance of women in his writing on group psychology, emphasizing attachment to a powerful male leader. Therefore, in this chapter we will explore the importance of the infant's merged relationship with the preoedipal mother as the prototype for social and family organization.

The formation of the family group enhances the chances for a child's physical survival. In most primitive societies, gender roles in the family were strictly separated, rigidly defined, and encompassing. These roles were originally determined by biological differences. Since women gave birth and lactated, child rearing was generally assigned to them. Since men were usually physically stronger, they provided food and protection. In addition, by joining into a collective group, not only could their mutual protection be greater, but they could impose their will on others. The natural formation of this collective group rested on the basis of family kinship, resulting in the evolution of tribal societies.

Many theorists suggest that in a tribal society, each member's autonomy and individuality were submerged for group survival. Members also merged symbolically, as if to form one physical body. The leader was literally the head, and the followers were the arms, legs, and body that executed the leader's will. Deviations from the group roles and norms were severely punished, seen not only as a personal threat to the leader's power but to the physical survival of the entire group. (In sociology, this type of authoritarian system was termed a *gemeinschaft* society.) The individual's role within the group replaced his or her uniqueness, but the group provided social support and security for all. These groups functioned as if they were merged into a single anthropomorphic entity with a solitary *group mind*. This phenomenon has been studied by philosophers, psychologists, and sociologists such as Hobbes, Spencer, Hegel, Marx, Wundt, Durkheim, Weber, LeBon, and Freud.

In Egypt during the first century, the philosopher Philo believed that the group mind phenomenon was magical. In Spain during the twelfth century, the famous physician and philosopher Moses Maimonides equated all group leaders with spellbinders and dreamers who could exert their power and control over a group. Freud (1921) also compared the group leader to a powerful male hypnotist; he felt that the group members had a libidinal attachment to the leader. In all these theories, the basis for group functioning rested on a masculine leader, who possessed some form of unusual power over others.

The British psychoanalyst Wilfred Bion disagreed with many of Freud's formulations concerning group functioning (Bion 1961). Bion agreed with the psychologists LeBon and McDougall, who explained that the group mind is due to an inherited herd instinct, a notion rejected by Freud. Bion observed normal groups of individuals at the Tavistock Clinic in London after World War II. He noted that when individuals were placed into a group with a leader who was emotionally abstinent, the members experienced feelings of helplessness. To cope with what Kleinians called impending "psychotic anxiety" (what others term "annihilation anxiety"), all the members temporarily regressed, lost their individuality, and used the defense of projective identification. They demonstrated a group mind behavior that was based on an unconscious fantasy that was shared by all the members. The fantasy itself was founded on irrational and magical thinking.

Bion called these merged groups *basic assumption groups*, and he was able to differentiate three types: dependency, fight/flight, and pairing. In *dependency*, the members looked for an absolute leader or deity upon whom to depend; in *fight/flight*, there was an outside enemy that needed to be attacked or avoided; in *pairing*, there was the messianic hope that a couple would give birth to a child who would be a savior for the group and resolve the members' hatred and despair.

Bion noted that the leader was not a powerful spellbinder or hypnotist, as Freud and others had postulated. Instead, leaders relinquished as much of their individuality as the group members did. They unconsciously shared the same collective magical beliefs, because of a simultaneous process of projection and identification between the leader and the members. Thus the leaders' control of the group did not come from the strength of their personalities, but it was based on a shared unconscious fantasy in which the leader fulfilled a role assigned by the group. In addition, Bion noted that leaders with certain personalities were more suited for a particular form of basic assumption group. For example, in the fight/flight group, a leader with a paranoid personality could help focus on a target that the group could attack or escape.

Regression to the Preoedipal Stage

Although Bion contributed to the understanding of the group mind phenomenon by pointing out the use of projective identification, he still attributed it to an inherited herd instinct. We now hypothesize that projective identification and splitting are primitive defenses used during early infancy, when the child is less differentiated from the mother. Unlike the more mature defense of projection, in which ego boundaries are intact, in projective identification aspects of oneself can be projected onto another who expresses them. I suggest that the group mind phenomenon occurs when a group of people feel helpless and unable to cope in an adult fashion. Because of annihilation anxiety, they regress to a preoedipal form of adaptation—which had previously been used during infancy with their mothers—and use fantasy and magical thinking to deal with their helplessness. Instead of merging with the preoedipal mother, the group members now merge with one another and the leader, as if they were a single anthropomorphic body.

Mahler and Furer (1968) suggested that infants use projection of omnipotence and merging with their preoedipal mothers to deal with helplessness. This process occurs in the first year of life during the symbiotic phase of child development. One can consider that in basic assumption groups, there is a psychological regression of all the members, as well as the leader, to this symbiotic phase of development (Slipp 1988a). This regression occurs because group members experience themselves again as helpless to cope with their environment, just as they did as small children, and they unconsciously suffer annihilation anxiety. All the members as well as the leader revert to using this form of symbiotic adaptation, derived from the early preoedipal infant-mother relationship, as a magical way of dealing with their helplessness later in life. With the loss of individual boundaries, the resulting primal feelings are experienced by all the group members as a form of emotional contagion. The primitive defenses of splitting and projective identification are again resurrected and shared. The group members again use the defense of splitting, seeing the self and others in sharp dichotomies of good or bad, love or hate, all powerful or helpless. Through projective identification, the members project a sense of omnipotence into the idealized leader with whom they merge. Since ego boundaries are diffused and are not differentiated, the members can feel as if they are the leader and become vicariously empowered. This time it is not only one individual (the child) vicariously living through another (the preoedipal mother) during the symbiotic stage in order to feel empowered; it is all the group members and the leader. In a parallel way, the group leader also regresses to this symbiotic level, but identifies with the role of the all-powerful preoedipal mother.

I have termed this type of group functioning the "symbiotic survival pattern" (Slipp 1969, 1973, 1976, 1977). There is no need to employ any speculative inherited herd instinct, which also minimizes the importance of the mother. A simpler explanation can be drawn from early child development. The ability to use fantasy and merge with another into a state of oneness is part of our inborn heritage, first experienced with the preoedipal mother during normal infant development. It is demonstrated in Bion's basic assumption groups and socially in authoritarian and primitive societies.

I found a similar type of symbiotic group adaptation, with breakdown of individual boundaries, in my research of dysfunctional families containing an emotionally ill child (Slipp 1984, 1988a). In these families, individual autonomy was unconsciously restricted to preserve cohesion of the family as a group. This sacrifice of an independent identity appeared to be related to the development of emotional disorders in one or more children in the family. Specific forms of splitting and projective identification were found to be related to specific forms of emotional disorders in young adults. (See diagram on p. 117.)

Familial interaction alone is not the sole factor for the development of psychopathology in a child, but it appears to be contributory. For example, in twin adoption studies, a genetic predisposition was found in the development of schizophrenia (Kety et al. 1968). Although a genetic predisposition was necessary, it was not sufficient: it required a disturbed family interaction as well (Tienari et al. 1984). Genetically loaded children, reared in relatively normal families, were at no greater risk to develop schizophrenia than children without genetic loading.

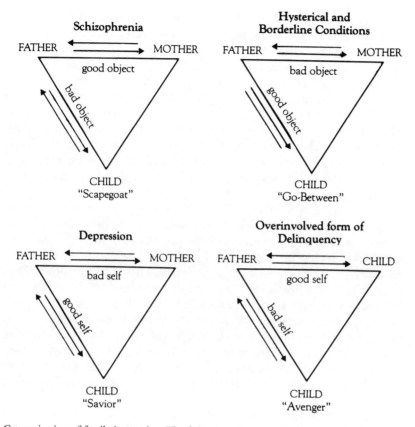

Categorization of family interaction. The father is indicated as the initiator of splitting and projective identification in all four patterns for purposes of simplicity. The mother may just as well be the initiator, except in hysterical and borderline conditions, in which the child is female. Projective identification is used as the intrapsychic and interpersonal defense mechanism that induces others to act out the internalized self or object image. The child serves as a container for the parent's projective identification, and a negative feedback cycle is thus established that (1) maintains the personality integrity of the parents, (2) maintains the family homeostasis, or balance defenses, and (3) sustains developmental fixation in the patient. In all these instances the child is made responsible for the self-esteem and, in schizophrenia and borderline conditions, the survival of the parent(s), thereby establishing a symbiotic survival pattern. In one type of delinquency, splitting and projective identification of the bad self into one child and the good self into another child occurs. (Reprinted from Samuel Slipp, *Object Relations: A Dynamic Bridge between Individual and Family Treatment*. Northvale, N.J.: Jason Aronson, 1984.)

In our own research of families containing an adolescent schizophrenic, the patient was found to be *scapegoated* (Slipp 1973). One or both of the parents had not adequately internalized their preoedipal mother in childhood, remained narcissistically vulnerable, and still unconsciously needed the spouse to function as a good maternal object to sustain self-esteem and personality integrity. Since anger was experienced as destructive to the parental relationship, it was split off and projected onto the child, who was demeaned or ignored, as if it was the bad mother. By projecting the anger onto the child, who became the container of the anger, the family cohesion was preserved. However, this "cohesion" was at the expense of the child, who developed a negative self-identity and was unable to integrate ambivalence into its own personality functioning.

In our study of families with a hysterical or borderline child (Slipp 1977), anger was not avoided in the parents' relationship but splitting still occurred. In most of our cases the patients were female. If the wife refused to give up her identity and be used by her husband as a need-satisfying good preoedipal mother, he devalued her as a bad mother. Then the child was idealized as the good mother and used by the husband to serve as a *go-between* or surrogate spouse. Even though the child had an oedipal victory, it required compliance to the father's needs at the expense of the child's developmental needs. The hysteric maintained this seductive alliance and did to others what was done to him or her, that is, used sexuality to get narcissistic nurturance. But the borderline youngster who was initially seduced into this alliance later suffered a lasting and traumatic rejection.

In researching families with a depressed young adult, we found that one spouse perceived the other spouse as a failure (Slipp 1986). This spouse assumed dominance, demeaning the failed spouse who represented the bad self, and lived vicariously through the child's social achievements, the good self. The child was pressured to achieve, and threatened with rejection if he or she failed. However, success was not validated by the dominant parent, which kept this child bound dependently for approval. The child could not own its success and build confidence, which interfered with its growth toward independence. The child felt itself to be in a no-win dilemma: there was no nurturance whether it succeeded or failed. I termed this "the double bind on achievement." (This no-win dilemma is similar to the experiments in learned helplessness that produce depression, where animals are punished no matter what choice they make [Seligman and Maier 1967].) This child's own needs were not met, but he or she was used as a *savior* to restore the self-esteem of the dominant parent.

Depressives internalize the nongratifying parental relationship, so they cannot gratify themselves for success and suffer severe narcissistic injury for failure. Because of the fear of rejection, they have difficulty in expressing anger directly; anger is instead either turned on the self or expressed in passive-aggressive oppositional behavior.

In one form of delinquency, a child may act out against society *for* a parent. The child may serve as an *avenger* for a parent, who lives vicariously through the child and expresses the rage of his or her negative self through the child. All these patterns were found in normal or mildly disturbed families as well. Several patterns could coexist simultaneously with different children, or even with the same child at different times. In these instances, the child fulfills a rigid encompassing role for others—to preserve the integrity of the family as a group—but the child's needs are not met.

In many respects, these dysfunctional families behave similarly to primitive tribal societies in their use of collusive magical fantasies. The fantasies are usually unconscious and not myths, as in tribal societies. However, in some dysfunctional families a conscious myth does exist, similar to a taboo in primitive societies. The family myth is that if a member openly expresses anger, it would upset a parent, who would become sick, have a nervous breakdown, or die. The rules and role structure of both the dysfunctional family and the tribal society severely constrict the autonomy of its members. The result is a diminution of each individual's identity in favor of the group's survival. In summary, the infant's symbiotic relationship to the mother forms the underlying basis for these primitive types of social groups, which include tribal societies, *gemeinschaft* societies, cults, totalitarian groups, the basic assumption groups of Bion, as well as dysfunctional families.

Laboratory Tachistoscopic Studies

Lloyd Silverman (1971) devised a laboratory technique that bypassed the conscious perceptual barrier and activated unconscious fantasies to influence affect, thought, behavior, level of self-differentiation, and psychopathology. Through the use of a two-channel tachistoscope, a picture and a message were flashed simultaneously at speeds too rapid to be perceived consciously. In moderately differentiated schizophrenic patients, the subliminal message of "MOMMY AND I ARE ONE" was temporarily ameliorative in reducing schizophrenic thought disorder. However, in schizophrenic patients with a low level of differentiation from the mother, as measured on psychological testing, the same symbiotic "MOMMY" message was ineffective. The lack of response was felt to occur because this message could lead to greater merging with the internalized mother and obliteration of the self. Schizophrenic patients exposed to the aggressive subliminal stimulation, "DESTROY MOTHER," experienced a loss of the internalized mother and an increase in thought disorder. A number of other studies (Silverman and Wolitzky 1982) showed that subliminal activation of the "MOMMY AND I ARE ONE" message increased the effectiveness of counseling treatment with phobic women, overweight women, cigarette smokers, and alcoholics. In group and individual psychotherapy, exposure to this maternal symbiotic gratification message fostered a safe holding environment that permitted greater trust and openness.

In our subliminal activation research, we studied forty-eight neurotically depressed women to validate my theory of a double bind on achievement in depression (Slipp and Nissenfeld 1981). The theory was operationalized and a Succeed-Fail questionnaire devised to measure parental pressure as well as self-pressure and gratification for achievement. It was administered prior to tachistoscopic exposure, along with the Beck Depression Inventory and Burdock and Hardesty's Structured Clinical Interview. Before and after tachistoscopic exposure, each woman was administered the Multiple Affect Adjective Checklist and Thematic Apperception Test to measure depression, hostility, and feelings of well-being. In addition, Silverman's Adjective Rating Scale was used to determine the level of self-object differentiation. The messages used included "MOMMY AND I ARE ONE," "DESTROY MOTHER," "SUCCEED FOR MOTHER OR FATHER," "SUCCEED FOR YOURSELF," and a control message of "PEOPLE ARE WALKING." A strict double-blind procedure was used so that neither the experimenter nor subject knew which message was being flashed.

Only the maternal symbiotic message of "MOMMY AND I ARE ONE" was effective in reducing depression among these women. However, if the relationship of these women to their mothers had been noted to be pressuring and nongratifying on our Succeed-Fail questionnaire, the maternal symbiotic message was not effective. The mother had not been experienced as a comforting and accepting person. This finding showed the importance of the quality of the internalized relationship to the mother. This result was in keeping with Silverman's general findings with other populations— that only when the mother was experienced as a good, gratifying object was the "MOMMY AND I ARE ONE" message ameliorative.

The "DESTROY MOTHER" message did not increase depression with this group of women who suffered neurosis as it did in subliminal studies with depressives who were psychotic. This fact probably indicated a greater degree of aggression in psychotic patients. It would validate the psychoanalytic finding of Karl Abraham (1911) that the psychotic depressive destroyed the internalized mother (as well as the self) intrapsychically. The neurotic depressive, on the other hand, preserved the internalized mother. The core of the self is related to the internalized good mother from early infancy. The effectiveness of this message, in activating the unconscious wish for fusion with the internalized good mother to preserve the self, supports the psychoanalytic theories of Jacobson (1971), Mahler and Furer (1968), and my own work (Slipp 1973).

In a study of underachievers, Greenberg (1980) and I (Slipp 1984) conducted a similar double-blind study of 108 high-school students of both sexes. We employed subliminal stimulation in a therapeutic fashion to see if it could improve their academic scores. In addition to the tests mentioned above, we used the Tennessee Self-Concept Scale and Cohen's Fear of Success Scale. We used the same maternal symbiotic message, "MOMMY AND I ARE ONE," as well as "MY SUCCESS IS OK." This latter message was substituted for "SUCCEED FOR YOURSELF," which was found not to work, probably because it stimulated autonomous functioning. In my theory of depression, success and autonomy are often equated with rejection. Therefore, autonomy was too threatening, and the message needed to be ignored. The new message sanctioned success while maintaining the needed dependent relationship with the good internalized parental object. We used the same control message, "PEOPLE ARE WALKING." The control and experimental groups were exposed to subliminal stimulation four times a week for six weeks, and the results were compared to one another. We found the "MOMMY AND I ARE ONE" message to be effective in improving school performance in boys, but not in girls. In boys, this message was most effective when the mother was experienced as gratifying. When the mothers were seen as gratifying, subliminal stimulation also resulted in a reduction of anxiety, hostility, and depression, as well as in an increase in the need to achieve. However, this message was not effective in boys who saw their mothers as pressuring for achievement but nongratifying. This latter group of boys had a high fear of success, a lower self-concept, and a lower self-mother and self-father differentiation on tests.

The "MOMMY AND I ARE ONE" message did not improve the girls' school performance at all. Instead, it caused higher anxiety, hostility, and depression, as well as lowering the need to achieve. When girls saw their relationship to their mothers as less gratifying and more conflictual, their need to achieve was even lower. These girls demonstrated lower differentiation of themselves from their mothers. The MOMMY message may not have been effective because it increased the girls' identification with their mothers. It is the mothers who usually contain or transmit the cultural values that do not reinforce achievement in women. A lessening of differentiation of the self from the mother would only increase the conflict over achievement. The girls demonstrated evidence of this conflict by an increase in anxiety, hostility, and depression. As further evidence for this conclusion, the "MOMMY AND I ARE ONE" message was found to be the least effective in boys as well as in girls who were the least differentiated from their mothers.

Both girls and boys who scored high on the fear of success scales responded poorly to the MOMMY message and also showed a lower self-concept and further loss of self-mother differentiation after stimulation. The fear of success has been attributed by Canovan-Gumpert, Garner, and Gumpert (1978), Cohen (1974), and J. R. Miller (1978) to negative reinforcement by one or both parents of movement by the child toward self-expression and mastery. Separation from the family and individuation are experienced by the child as threatening to the parent(s), and independent success is avoided to prevent rejection.

The "MY SUCCESS IS OK" message was the only one effective in gaining higher grade scores for girls. However, even though their achievement improved, these girls experienced higher levels of anxiety, hostility, and depression. This message was most effective when the girls saw their mothers as nongratifying but experienced their fathers as less conflicted about achievement. Following testing, these girls showed a lowering of differentiation of the self from their fathers. Thus the message sanctioning success seemed to be associated with being closer to and identifying with a gratifying message from their fathers.

In conclusion, the SUCCESS message served as a support for these girls for achievement from their fathers; it seemed to neutralize the fear of success and autonomy they derived from their mothers. Bolstering an identification with the father's achievement tended to diminish the dependency on the mother. Even though they had good intentions, the mothers probably personified the values of a culture that constrict and block women's achievement.

The "MY SUCCESS IS OK" message worked only to improve grades with boys who had a high fear of success and autonomy, and also resulted in a reduction of anxiety, hostility, and depression. As with the girls, this SUCCESS message reduced differentiation of the self from the father. All these success-fearing boys reported experiencing their mothers as nongratifying of achievement. After subliminal stimulation, they felt less differentiated and closer to their fathers, who served as a good object for sanctioning success and autonomy.

This experimental laboratory evidence seemed to validate aspects of my theory of the double bind on achievement in depression. Even though there is pressure by the parents for success, the achievement is not gratified. In this way, the success is not validated and the child remains tied to the parent, hoping for approval. The child cannot own its own success to gain strength, and strivings for autonomy are blocked. This is a pattern especially found in girls, who are placed into a position of competition in school yet feel blocked from success by the culture. J. R. Miller (1978) found that mothers very strongly interfered with the movement toward autonomy in success-fearing girls, but did so less with boys. This was attributed to the fact that independence and success are not congruent with the feminine role in our culture but were acceptable to the masculine one.

13. Freud's Support of Career-Oriented Women

The Paradox between Theory and Personal Relations

Although Freud was no admirer of feminism in his writings, in his personal and professional life he promoted the growth of a number of women who were career oriented and feminist. Characteristically, these women were either unmarried, separated, or if they were married their husbands were not important to them (Roazen 1984). Freud welcomed them into the psychoanalytic group; he found them less difficult and competitive than men. He enjoyed being closely surrounded by this group of talented, assertive, and ambitious women, and maintained not only professional contact but established sincere friendships with many of them that lasted through his lifetime.

These women analysts included Lou Andreas-Salomé, Marie Bonaparte, Dorothy Burlingham, Ruth Mack Brunswick, Helene Deutsch, Jeanne Lampl-de Groot, Hermine von Hug-Hellmuth, Anny Katan, Marianne Kris, Mira Oberholzer, Eva Rosenfeld, and Eugenia Sokolnicka. Some of them shielded him from visitors, arranged his vacations, and stood watch over his health. Just as he began life surrounded by his mother, his nanny, and later by five sisters, Freud ended his life surrounded by caring and protective women.

Traditionally in Victorian society, when men retired or died they passed on their occupational and family interests to their sons, usually the eldest. However, it was Freud's youngest daughter, Anna, who would carry his legacy of psychoanalysis, and not his sons. Anna happily accepted this mantle from Freud many years before he died. She proved to be a loyal daughter during his long and painful bout with cancer, which had required repeated surgery and the daily placement of an uncomfortable prosthesis into his mouth to enable him to eat and talk. Anna never married and devoted her life to him. Because Freud had difficulty talking, Anna gave his honorary speeches and read his scientific papers at psychoanalytic congresses. During Freud's lifetime, Anna cared for her father physically; after his death, she vigorously protected his work from attempts at revision by Melanie Klein and others within the British Psychoanalytic Society.

Freud also acknowledged the scientific contributions to psychoanalysis by women in his own writings. A number of these women were specially honored by being given the secret ring Freud bestowed upon his most talented and favorite analysts. Each ring contained a different intaglio stone, an engraved gem that ancient Romans had used as a seal. Freud's own ring had the head of Jupiter engraved into his ancient intaglio stone. Originally, in 1913, Freud had given a stone to each of the members of his secret committee, which consisted of Karl Abraham, Sandor Ferenczi, Ernest Jones, Otto Rank, and Hanns Sachs. At the suggestion of Jones, this group had been formed prior to the departure of Adler and Jung to protect the future of psychoanalysis. In a letter to Jones on August 1, 1912, about the secret committee, Freud wrote:

What took hold of my imagination immediately is your idea of a secret council composed of the best and most trustworthy among our men to take care of the further developments of psychoanalysis and defend the cause against personalities and accidents when I am no more. . . . I know there is a boyish and perhaps romantic element too in this conception, but perhaps it could be adapted to meet the necessities of reality.

Even though the committee dissolved and the rings lost their symbolic significance after World War I, Freud continued to give secret rings to those he considered closest to him. It was as if they were members of his personal family, with Freud assuming the role of a parental figure. These later recipients of the ring were no longer restricted to men. The women who received the ring, besides his daughter Anna, were Lou Andreas-Salomé, Marie Bonaparte, Ruth Mack Brunswick, Dorothy Burlingham, Gisela Ferenczi, Henny Freud, Edith Jackson, Katherine Jones, and Eva Rosenfeld. Freud expressed concern and admiration for their professional accomplishments. He carried on a lifelong correspondence with Lou

Andreas-Salomé, and sought her opinions and those of other women analysts concerning his new and evolving ideas in psychoanalysis. His unmarried sister- in-law, Minna Bernays, also appreciated and emotionally supported Freud's work.

Freud and his immediate family were rescued from the Nazis largely through the efforts of Marie Bonaparte, who remained one of Freud's closest friends and associates. It was she who also rescued Freud's letters to Fliess and had them published after his death. These letters provide an invaluable window into the daily life of Freud during the time he formulated psychoanalysis. Thus one can see a paradox between Freud's writings about women as second-class citizens and castrated males, and his valuing of women in his personal life. In turn, these women demonstrated esteem, intimacy, and loyalty to Freud.

Jensen's Gradiva and Freud's Preoedipal Mother

Freud considered his most significant discovery to be the Oedipus complex, which he felt formed the core of most neuroses. In his consultation room, he had placed on the wall at the foot of his analytic couch a reproduction of the picture by Ingres, "Oedipus Interrogating the Sphinx." Next to it there was a reproduction of the bas relief of a young woman called Gradiva. This location was the place of honor in his study. On this wall Freud's two great loves—archeology and psychoanalysis—met (Gay 1978). However, one can suspect there was further significance to these placements. On his trip to Rome in September 1907, Freud wrote his wife that he saw "a dear familiar face" at the Vatican museum. High up on a wall was the bas relief of Gradiva, which portrayed a young woman assertively stepping forward with confidence and grace. He bought a reproduction for his office and was overjoyed at this acquisition. Why was this sculpture a familiar face?

The previous year Freud had written a psychohistory based on the novel *Gradiva* by Wilhelm Jensen. Jensen's story was about a German archeologist, Norbert Hanold, who had given up his childhood girlfriend to pursue his career. On visiting Rome, Hanold saw this bas relief and named her Gradiva, "the girl who steps along." It portrayed the profile of a slender young Roman girl, with her head down, clothed in a flowing gown that is slightly raised at the ankle, briskly walking forward. After buying it, Hanold hung it on a wall of his study. Then he had a nightmare in which he saw Gradiva being buried under the ashes of Vesuvius in Pompeii.

However, instead of making this catastrophe occur in A.D. 79, he entertained the delusion that the eruption of Vesuvius occurred now. He immediately went to Pompeii, where he accidentally encountered his childhood girlfriend. She recognized his delusion and hoped to restore him to reality. Hanold asked her to walk in front of him; she complied and simulated the gait of Gradiva from the bas relief. By using his delusion, she was able to cure him.

Freud considered that in having the living girl copy the walk of Gradiva, Jensen had provided the key to the symbolism Hanold used to disguise the repressed memory of his love for his girlfriend. Freud felt that repression buries a memory and preserves it and, like archeology, is unearthed by psychoanalysis. However, even here one might comment that Hanold did not unearth his repressed memories and bring them into conscious awareness. Instead, his girlfriend acted them out for him.

I would further suggest that this bas relief of Gradiva and the story by Jensen had a special significance for Freud. Freud himself was like the hero Hanold of the novel in having lost a beloved girlfriend from his childhood. He had also devoted himself to his career and repressed his early longings. Like Hanold, Freud's work in psychoanalysis may have been a way of attempting to unearth these repressed feelings and memories. In the summer of 1872, Freud returned to his birthplace in Freiberg, Moravia. He was accompanied by two of his friends from the Sperlgymnasium, and they stayed with the Fluss family (Hardin 1988b). His parents had kept in touch with the family since leaving Freiberg thirteen years earlier. Freud, who was shy with girls, silently fell in love with their young daughter, Gisela. When she left, Freud felt bereft and mourned her loss by walking alone in the woods.

However, in a letter to his friend Silberstein (Clark 1980), Freud revealed that he had another passion as well—Gisela's mother. He commented that despite her bourgeois upbringing, Mrs. Fluss was a cultured woman with a wide breadth of knowledge, as well as a loving and nurturant mother. He wrote:

You should also see how she brought up her seven children and how she is still bringing them up; how they obey her, the older ones more than the younger ones, how no concern of any of the children ceases to be hers. . . . Other mothers—and why hide the fact that ours are among them; we shall not love them any the less for it— only look after the physical needs of their sons. Their spiritual development has been taken out of their hands . . . Frau Fluss knows no sphere that is beyond her influence. . . . She obviously recognizes that I always need encouragement to speak or to help myself, and she never fails to give it. This is where her dominion over me shows; as she guides me, so I speak, so present myself. . . . Enough of this. You see how words flow out of my heart and the letters out of my pen. (Clark 1980, 26)

Hardin (1988b) points out that Freud's infatuation for Gisela and Mrs. Fluss was overdetermined by the past losses, from early childhood, of his beloved mother and nanny. These memories had been repressed, and Freud was unconsciously driven as an adolescent to return to Freiberg to master the preoedipal traumas of his first three years of life. However, the loss of Gisela was again experienced as the loss of his young mother. Mrs. Fluss, an older loving mother figure who "cared for me as for her own child," was like his nanny, Resi.

Hardin also notes that it was not until the recent publication of *The Complete Letters of Sigmund Freud to Wilhelm Fliess* (Masson 1985), that time sequences were established. The first time Freud had a memory of the cupboard scene, where he thought his brother Philipp had put his mother into a chest, was also in 1872; therefore, the memory occurred at the age of sixteen, shortly after Freud returned from the Fluss home, and it recurred periodically thereafter. During his self-analysis, Freud reported it in a letter to Wilhelm Fliess on October 15, 1897. In this memory, which dates back to his being a child of two, Freud recalled that "I was crying my heart out, because my mother was nowhere to be found. My brother Philipp (who is twenty years older than I) opened a cupboard for me, and when I found that mother was not there either I cried still more, until she came through the door looking *slim* and *beautiful*" (Italics mine; Bonaparte et al. 1954, 222).

Freud was frightened that he would lose his mother just as he did his nanny. He knew Philipp was implicated in the loss of his nanny, and Freud feared that Philipp had been sexual with his mother and made her pregnant. Clearly, sexuality, pregnancy, and loss of his mother were equated into a triad. His mother would either give birth to another brother like Julius, and emotionally abandon him, or he might lose her permanently, as he did his nanny. His brother Philipp had indicated that his nanny had been put into a chest, a colloquial expression for being imprisoned. However, the chest probably meant a coffin and death to Sigmund, and he "cried his heart out." In all likelihood, Freud probably saw his dead brother Julius lying in a coffin at home. Thus, he dreaded that his mother might also die and be placed in a coffin, which he later dreamed in the dream about the bird-headed Egyptians carrying his dead mother on a bier.

When his mother stepped into the room as a slim woman, his fears were abated. His mother's slimness and no longer being pregnant was equated with her return. I suggest the *slim* and *beautiful* mother, who walked into the room in this memory, was the attractive young woman who assertively stepped forward in the bas relief of Gradiva.

On first seeing the name Gradiva, one is reminded of the word *gravida*, which means a pregnant woman, derived from the Latin word *gravidus*, a woman heavy with child. This is a word that Freud must have known, since it is widely used medically. Freud's mother had been pregnant with his sister Anna, and when he saw her again she had already given birth and was again slim and lithe. The word *diva* is also derived from the Latin, and means goddess. One could therefore speculate that to Freud the word Gradiva had a composite meaning: it might indicate a woman who was not pregnant, or one who had been but was now slim and able to move about freely again, like an idealized good mother or goddess.

As a small child, Freud had not wanted his mother to be pregnant, because he associated pregnancy with her loss. Her unpregnant state meant that she was available to him. Freud placed the bas relief of Gradiva, who represented his beloved unpregnant mother, next to a picture of the Oedipus complex. Even though he ignored the preoedipal period in his writings, in his actions he unconsciously acknowledged its importance.

Freud had been able to bring into conscious awareness his oedipal relationship with his father and to work it through analytically. Possibly, he was also trying to bring out of repression his early preoedipal relationship to his mother. However, like Hanold in Jenson's story, Freud was unable to lift the repression and needed to re-create and relive with women in the present his early relationship to his unpregnant mother. His unpregnant, slim mother was the goddess he had loved and lost in early childhood, the good preoedipal mother whom he needed to retrieve.

Hardin noted that during this same summer of 1872 in Freiberg, Freud first had the memory that he and his nephew John took Pauline's yellow dandelions away from her and ate delicious black bread, given to them by a peasant woman. Freud's associations to yellow were a yellow dress and the fantasy of marrying his niece Pauline. To bread, Freud associated earning his daily bread and living in the country. The memory incorporated two powerful forces—love and hunger. He had two repressed wishes: to deflower Pauline sexually, and to be fed and taken care of by the peasant woman, his nanny. Thus both oedipal and preoedipal wishes were being expressed. Another explanation might be that his snatching the flowers away from Pauline was an expression of his rage and an act of retaliation for feeling abandoned by his beloved mother and nanny.

Hardin also points out that when Freud returned from Freiberg at sixteen years of age, he recalled a Czech nursery rhyme. He did not know why he had remembered it, since its meaning was repressed. Like the other two memories he had at the time—of the chest and the dandelions— it also represented an expression of his lost and repressed love for his un-pregnant mother as well as his nanny during his first two years of life in Freiberg. What was especially traumatic for Freud was that he lost his comforting nanny shortly after he had lost his mother's attention because of her pregnancy. Pregnancy in his mind had turned his mother into the lost or unavailable bad mother, and her return, unpregnant, restored her as the good nurturant mother. This dynamic might have contributed to Freud's loss of sexual desire for his wife when she became pregnant in 1887.[1]

When Martha was not pregnant, Freud had idealized her and felt alive in her presence, just as he had with his unpregnant mother. When Martha became pregnant, she was no longer the good mother who was exclusively his, the preoedipal goddess who could nurture and restore his narcissism. Just as Freud had switched his attachment from his mother to his father, Freud switched his affection from Martha to Fliess. This appears to be a repetition of what had happened during his early childhood.

Since the traumatic loss of his mother had occurred during the rap-prochement stage of his development, before three years of age, boundaries between Freud and his mother probably had not been firmly established. This fused self-mother relationship enabled him to experience himself as his mother in other relationships. Most of the women surrounding Freud were not preoccupied with sex and motherhood, since many of them were unmarried or separated from their husbands. Their main concern was not to have babies but to advance their professional careers. They were strongly attached to Freud, most having intense transferences toward him. They experienced Freud as a parental figure for whom they actively competed. Freud could express himself as the good mother to them, making them feel included and protected, and feeding their narcissism. Because they showed ambition like men, Freud was able to identify them with himself more easily.

These women surrounding Freud represented Gradiva, his goddesslike

1. This dynamic might explain why Freud advised Ferenczi in 1916 not to marry Elma Palos, but to marry her mother Gizella, who was too old to bear children. Ferenczi was consciously aware of his need for mothering, since he was deprived as a child. However, did Freud give this advice because of his own fear that children were a threat to the relationship with the wife-mother? Grosskurth (1991) notes that Freud later felt "frightened" and "insecure" after giving this advice to Ferenczi.

unpregnant mother, to him. All were young and attractive women who were lithely and assertively stepping forward. His own daughter Anna remained unmarried and apparently chaste sexually throughout her life (Young-Bruehl 1989).

Anna was like the Greek goddess Athena, who was virginal and sprung forth from the head of her father Jupiter. Athena was not born as a result of her father's sexual intercourse with a woman. There was no pregnancy, birth, or attachment to a mother, and hence no danger of engulfment or abandonment. Eliminating sexuality meant there was no threat of her becoming a mother and losing her. It is interesting that Freud wore the image of the head of Jupiter on his intaglio secret ring. Perhaps Anna's unconscious pursual of this role of the asexual Athena fit with Freud's identification with Jupiter. Was she unconsciously pleasing her father by being what he required—asexual and faithful?

Anna apparently won an oedipal victory over her mother, since Freud seemed closer to Anna than to Martha. In addition, from 1918 to 1922 Anna was analyzed by her father, so that Freud participated in an oedipal acting out with his daughter. Anna then seemed unable to deal with her own fears of being overwhelmed by her sexual feelings, as revealed in her essay, "Beating Fantasies and Daydreams." Her sexual fantasies had been reinforced by reality, just as they had been for Freud in his childhood.

At this very time, 1919 to 1920, Freud wrote his work, *Beyond the Pleasure Principle*, describing the traumatic neurosis, mastery of separation, the repetition compulsion, and the death instinct, Thanatos. Freud's daughter Sophie died while he was writing this essay, and he observed her little son Ernst's play of throwing away and retrieving a toy reel in a repetitious and ritualistic manner. Freud became aware that the reel symbolized the lost mother, and that the little boy had experienced the death of his mother passively. By creating and undoing his loss in play, the boy took an active part in mastering his helplessness.

In *Beyond the Pleasure Principle*, Freud addressed himself to the topic of separation anxiety. He explored if the loss of the mother and not castration anxiety due to the father was responsible for certain neuroses. Freud experienced the loss of his daughter, and could see its traumatic effect on his grandson. This observation may have reawakened his own conflicts over abandonment by his preoedipal mother. As already noted earlier, Freud unconsciously seems to have associated sexuality and aggression with being punished and losing his own mother.

Like his grandson, Freud also may have had the need to undo and master his own helplessness over the feared traumatic loss of his mother.

Even though he was able to recognize the impact of separation anxiety in Ernst, he apparently was not able to contain it and analyze it, but needed to repeat it through action as well. To master his own helplessness, Freud appears to have reversed roles and acted his anxiety out with his daughter Anna instead. He unconsciously identified with the aggressor, and did to Anna what his mother had done to him.

Recall that Freud was overwhelmed at four years of age by the seductive experience of seeing his mother nude on the train trip from Leipzig to Vienna; serving as Anna's analyst now unconsciously repeated a seductive trauma with her. In this repetition compulsion, Freud became the active one and Anna the passive one in this "awesome" trauma with his mother. Since this seductive experience was possibly an act of aggression by his mother (or experienced as one by him), Freud's analysis of his daughter can be considered in a similar vein. Indeed, it was during his analysis with Anna in 1919 that Freud wrote his essay, "A Child Is Being Beaten." Mahoney (1990) suggests that the use of the grammatically present-progressive tense in the title reflected Freud's current ongoing clinical work with Anna, an unconscious seduction and abuse of his daughter.

In *Beyond the Pleasure Principle*, Freud developed his new life and death instincts, Eros and Thanatos, as well. In an earlier letter to Ferenczi in 1913, he admitted that Anna was the subject of his essay, "The Theme of the Three Caskets" (Mahoney 1990). Freud compared himself to King Lear and Anna to Cordelia. In the essay, Freud comments that Lear carries out the dead body of his faithful daughter, Cordelia: Cordelia is death. However, in the essay, Freud reversed the situation and thought of Cordelia as the death-goddess, like the Valkyrie of German mythology, carrying out the dead hero from the battlefield. Anna was like Thanatos, bidding him to renounce love and to make friends with the necessity of dying. Freud compared the three women symbolized by the three caskets to the mother. The mother gives birth to him, serves as the model in one's choice of a marital sexual partner, and, finally, is Mother Earth who takes him into her arms at death. Thanatos was defined by Freud as a regressive force and may have represented his unconscious need to repeat and relive with Anna the sexual seduction he experienced and the associated annihilation anxiety of his mother's death and loss. Anna became the good mother who would not abandon him throughout life, and would tenderly welcome him into her arms even in death.

Because Freud took Anna into analysis with him, she became like Gradiva (or Athena) throughout her life by repressing and sublimating her sexuality into her intellectual pursuits in psychoanalysis. But Anna was not the only one to fill the role of Gradiva for Freud. Just as he had several mothers during his preoedipal period, Freud had several women in his adult life who unconsciously filled this role. Who were the three main contenders for the role of Gradiva?

The Three Rivals for the Role of Gradiva

Most of the career women surrounding Freud were slim, youthful, vital, and attractive. Apparently Freud was also able to relive and partially master the preoedipal trauma experienced with his mother and nanny through these attentive women. He wanted them to fill the void in his adult life left from his childhood. However, he acted this out apparently without conscious awareness. The three main rivals for the position of Gradiva in Freud's life appeared to be Ruth Mack Brunswick, Princess Marie Bonaparte, and his daughter Anna.

Ruth Mack Brunswick. Ruth Mack was an American physician, fifteen years younger than Marie Bonaparte, who was forty-three when she started her analysis with Freud in 1925. Bertin (1982), Bonaparte's biographer, considered Ruth to be a threat to Marie. Ruth was "elegant and cultured," having both "charm and intelligence combined with a moral courage that Freud found very attractive." Ruth's father, Judge Julian Mack, was a famous jurist and philanthropist. She was graduated from Radcliffe College and completed medical school and a residency in psychiatry in the United States before going to Vienna to become an analyst. After arriving there she ended her marriage to Hermann Blumgart. She then met Mark Brunswick, a musical prodigy who was five years younger than she. Freud approved of Mark and took him into analysis before Ruth and Mark were married. He also analyzed Mark's brother David, as well as Ruth.

In the early years of Freud's relationships with women analysts, Ruth Mack Brunswick was his favorite. She came to dinner, visited him on vacations, and almost became a member of his family. Freud's daughter Anna was jealous, since he discussed his ideas with Ruth and even gave her, but not Anna, pages of his book on Woodrow Wilson to read. Roazen (1984) describes Ruth as charming and intelligent, outgoing and warm, as well as literate and verbal. She tended to be a domineering, unmotherly type. When Ruth had finished her analysis and established herself professionally with Freud's assistance, he presented her with a personal gift. Freud referred one of his most famous patients, the Wolf Man, to her

(Roazen 1984). Mack Brunswick also made contributions to the theory of psychoanalysis. Unlike the male analysts who emphasized the role of the mother in child development and were rejected by Freud, Mack Brunswick was able to do so tactfully. She also stressed the significance of the preoedipal period of child development but restricted the importance of the preoedipal period to the development of women, retaining the central position of the Oedipus complex. Freud accepted her contributions with no hint of rejection. He even acknowledged that she was the first analyst to treat a case of neurosis that was preoedipally fixated and had never attained the oedipal phase.

Marie Bonaparte. Princess Marie Bonaparte became the most important of Freud's female pupils by the end of his life (Roazen 1984). The great-grandniece of Napoleon, she entered an arranged marriage in 1907 to Prince George, the son of King George I of Greece. However, her husband was emotionally and physically distant from her. It was only later that Bonaparte discovered the reason: he had an ongoing and long-term homosexual relationship with his uncle, Prince Waldemar of Denmark. In 1913, she wrote: "The free blossoming of oneself is blighted within the walls of the conjugal home, and the soul and face take on that disheartened tinge one sees in so many wives. The oppression of marriage is a universal, if necessary malady, and I dare to believe there are more released widows than disconsolate ones" (Bertin 1982, 111).

After expressing these feminist sentiments, Bonaparte turned to other men for love, including Aristide Briand, the prime minister of France. In 1925 she began her personal analysis with Freud to resolve her sexual frigidity and other personal problems. In analysis, Freud astutely interpreted that she had witnessed the primal scene as a small child, which she had interpreted as an aggressive and murderous act. Bonaparte had unconsciously thought that sexual intercourse was responsible for the death of her mother, who had died a month after her birth. She decided to test out this interpretation and confronted her father's half-brother, Pascal. Pascal admitted to having repeatedly had sexual intercourse with Marie's nurse in front of Marie from the time she was six months old until she was three. In 1934 Bonaparte presented a paper on "Passivity, Masochism, and Femininity" at the International Congress of Psychoanalysis in Lucerne. She differed with Freud's notion that women who only had clitoral orgasms were immature. Based on his theory of bisexuality, Freud felt that vaginal orgasm was the hallmark of feminine maturity. According to Freud, women needed to shift from an active masculine clitoral orgasm to a passive

and masochistic vaginal one. He considered the clitoris the female equivalent of the male penis, and hence Freud considered clitoral orgasm to be
like male masturbation. Bonaparte stated that the clitoris and vagina
worked harmoniously together and were not separate. She also differed
with Freud and Helene Deutsch by not considering masochism as the
central feature of femininity. Her interest in female sexuality also included
transcultural studies to investigate the universality of the Oedipus complex.
She strongly objected to the widespread African custom of excision of the
clitoris, a custom that had existed from the time of the pharaohs in Egypt.
This painful practice deprived women of sexual pleasure and was used by
men as a means to control women; it represented an institutionalized
repression by society of female sexual pleasure. She published these topics
eventually in 1953 in *Female Sexuality*, which she felt exceeded Freud's
understanding of the topic.

In 1936 Bonaparte was able to buy the letters Freud had written to
Wilhelm Fliess between 1887 and 1902. During the Nazi occupation, she
smuggled them out of Vienna to Paris, where she deposited them at the
Danish legation. Anna Freud and Ernst Kris selected some of these letters
for publication, in 1950, in German and, in 1954, in English. With the
help of Ernest Jones and Ambassador William Bullitt, Bonaparte was able
to rescue Freud and his immediate family from the Nazis in June 1938.
Had she not succeeded, Freud and his entire family would have been
murdered by the Nazis in concentration camps, which is what happened
to four of his sisters. Freud died in London on September 23, 1939, and
was cremated three days later at Golders Green. The eulogies were given
by Stefan Zweig and Ernest Jones. Freud's ashes were placed into a Greek
vase that Marie Bonaparte had given him.

Anna Freud. Born in 1895, Anna Freud was the last of Freud's children.
She was not graduated from the *gymnasium*, but trained as a schoolteacher.
As a young adult, she audited her father's lectures and became interested
in analysis. In 1918, at the age of twenty-three, Anna began her psychoanalysis with her father. For an analyst to psychoanalyze a friend or relative
is considered a serious breach of the therapeutic frame. Gay (1988) considered this analysis by Freud of his own daughter to be a "technical error,"
and the "emotional costs" sustained by Anna "have yet to be calculated."
Freud's role as her analyst and his participation in this oedipal situation
made it impossible for Anna to resolve her erotic transference toward her
father. Just as Freud had experienced an oedipal triumph over his father
because of his mother's behavior, Anna also achieved an oedipal victory

over her mother. Freud preferred his daughter to his wife and shared his intimate thoughts and feelings with her rather than Martha.

Anna Freud's biographer, Young-Bruehl (1989), considers her first paper, "Beating Fantasies and Daydreams," presented in 1922 before the Vienna Society, to be autobiographical. Anna could not have obtained this material from a patient, since she had not yet seen one. The paper was derived from her analysis with her father, and it contained an incestuous love scene between a father and daughter, a beating scene, and the subject of masturbatory gratification. This was followed by the defense of sublimation, in which "nice stories" were made up. Young-Bruehl states that Anna's lifelong sexual asceticism was a sublimation of her Oedipus complex as described in this paper.

Freud may have been driven by an unconscious repetition compulsion to act out and master his own seductive experiences with his mother. As discussed earlier, Freud's mother may have used her nudity as an aggressive means to inspire terror in her young son on the train trip from Leipzig to Vienna. Even if this was not her intention, Freud experienced it as aggressively overwhelming and "awesome." Similarly, Freud was now seductive as well as intrusive and aggressive by analyzing his daughter. This would account for Anna's fantasy of incest and of being beaten.

Gay (1988) observes that Freud wished Anna not to be sexual, so that his little girl would remain attached to him. We can support this supposition based on the triad of sex, pregnancy, and loss. In view of Freud's association of sexuality with anger at his preoedipal mother's pregnancy and abandonment, Anna may have acted out her father's unconscious wish for her to be asexual and loyal to him alone. Freud would then not have to suffer another loss of his preoedipal mother, nor have to share her attention with other siblings.

Marie Bonaparte, who knew Anna Freud well, called her a "vestal" virgin, and, according to Young-Bruehl, Anna was chaste throughout her life. She never married, and after becoming an analyst in 1922, devoted her life to her career as a child analyst. Her patients became her sublimated children. She lived with Dorothy Burlingham and was involved with her children as well. One can speculate that Freud did not have to share Anna with any biological children of her own, as he had had to with his mother.

Anna Freud was a model of perfect loyalty to her father. Freud considered her as Athena to his Jupiter, Antigone to his Oedipus, or as Cordelia to his King Lear. More than any other woman analyst, Anna was the prototype of Gradiva. Her father was paramount in her affection, without any rival, and she attended to his needs and nursed him tenderly through his illness until his death. She was the good nurturant young mother that Freud did not have as a child, always sensitive to his emotional and physical needs. She never betrayed him by becoming pregnant and shifting her attention to a newborn child, as his mother had. After Freud's death, Anna continued her dedication by opening the Hampstead Clinic at 21 Maresfield Gardens, across from Freud's last residence.

14. Controversial Relationships with Women and Freud's Art Collection

Minna Bernays

One of the most intriguing riddles that has mystified many of Freud's biographers is the relationship between Freud and his wife's younger sister, Minna Bernays. Minna could be classified as another Gradiva. Peter Gay (1989) commented that "Freud's sharp-tongued, sharp-witted sister-in-law had been his confidante in psychoanalytic matters far more than his wife, even though he did not initiate Minna into all his intimate medical concerns." Almost from the moment when he fell in love with Martha, Freud was also drawn to her intellectual sister.

Gay (1989) traced the intimate relationship that Freud developed with Minna through a study of their extensive correspondence, which recently became available in the Library of Congress. In 1889 Freud wrote Minna of his boredom and loneliness while studying hypnosis with Hippolyte Bernheim in Nancy, France. In 1893 he wrote her about writing down his dream, which was the earliest record of Freud's interest in dreams. In a letter written by Minna to Freud in 1910, she mentions Freud's having discussed the case of the composer Mahler with her. Thus Freud shared many of his feelings and thoughts with Minna before and during his marriage to Martha.

Minna had been engaged for ten years to a Sanskrit scholar, Ignaz Schonberg, who died of tuberculosis in 1886. She was resigned, at age thirty, to remain unmarried. In 1895 she moved into the Freud home at

Berggasse 19 in Vienna, initially to help her sister with her last pregnancy. Freud and his family hoped that this situation would be temporary, and that Minna would either leave for university studies or marry. Neither prospect materialized, and Minna remained a part of the Freud household for the rest of her life. She was devoted to Freud and his work and conscientiously helped care for his six children.

The initial rumor that Freud had had a sexual affair with Minna came from Carl Jung. Jung revealed this information to John Billinsky, Carl Meier, and to his own mistress, Antonia Wolff. Jung stated that during his first visit to Freud in 1907, Minna wished to confide a secret to him. He claimed she told him that her relationship to Freud was "very intimate." This rumor has been picked up by other biographers, especially Peter Swales (1982). Using a detailed textual analysis of Freud's writings, Swales has speculated that Minna became pregnant by Freud and may even have had an abortion.

As evidence for this intimacy, Swales noted that Minna was alone with Freud at the time his father died in 1896, since Martha was visiting her mother in Hamburg, Germany. She was able to comfort Freud and become close to him. Beginning in 1898, Freud and Minna went on vacations alone without the family. Swales focuses his detective work to one vacation that Freud, Martha, and Minna took to Italy in August 1900. This was immediately after Freud had an argument with Wilhelm Fliess in Achensee in the northern Tyrol, marking the beginning of the end of their friendship. After several weeks, Martha returned home, leaving Freud and Minna alone. They traveled to Venice, Trent, Lake Garda, and Lake Maggiore. Then Freud took Minna to a spa in Merano to allow her to recover from tuberculosis. He then backtracked to Milan and Genoa before going home to Vienna.

Swales reasons that Minna was left at the spa to have an abortion, and not for the treatment of tuberculosis. Swales went to the spa to examine the records and noted that Minna indeed spent five months there. However, physicians would consider this very piece of evidence to militate against Swales's highly speculative idea. A spa is the appropriate place to recover from tuberculosis and not to obtain an abortion, which is performed in a hospital or medical clinic. Furthermore, physical recovery from an abortion takes days to weeks, while recovering from tuberculosis at that time could last months or years.

Swales also presents the following circumstantial evidence for his case. After returning to Vienna around September 14, Freud had a dream whose theme was his wish to experience "love that cost him nothing." The feelings in the dream were of guilt and self-reproach for being selfish. In the work Freud was involved in at the time, *The Psychopathology of Everyday Life*, he also mentioned his need to pay 300 Kronen to help cure a male relative. Swales speculates that this relative was really Minna, whose expenses at the spa Freud had paid. Swales then concluded that this was the cost Freud paid for his love for Minna. In this same work, Freud also says that he could not remember the meaning of the word "aliquis." Freud associated it to the blood of Saint Januarius, which legend contends miraculously liquefies each September (it did so as well when Garibaldi entered Naples). Swales interprets this to mean that Freud was worried about Minna's menstruation and possible pregnancy. He presents a highly speculative case, based on his own interpretations and circumstantial evidence.

An entirely different scenario can be concluded based on other circumstantial evidence. Freud's concern that he must pay for the love he got might consciously have something to do with the expectations of his mother, who demanded performance for her love and exploited his success. It could also represent his unconscious fear that the cost for sexuality was abandonment. But what about Saint Januarius? It is noteworthy that Freud's sister Anna was born on December 31, 1858, and he probably saw her for the first time the next day, January 1, and no doubt his mother was not available to him then. With the end of her pregnancy, his mother would menstruate again. But even more significant, his nanny Resi was arrested in January 1859. Her Catholicism might account for Freud's association of a saint. Thus January was a time involved in the loss of both mother figures for Freud. We also know that Freud associated Garibaldi with his father. Probably the liquefication of blood might signify menstruation. However, it also occurred when Garibaldi entered Naples. Entering Naples might possibly indicate sexual relations between his parents. One could speculate it was Freud's hope that his mother would miraculously not become pregnant after having sex with his father. She would continue to menstruate, and he would therefore not lose her. She would continue to remain his lithe and available preoedipal mother, his Gradiva.

Gay (1989) provides other evidence to refute speculations that Freud and Minna had an affair. Freud wrote to James J. Putnam, the famous American neurologist, that even though he stood for greater sexual freedom than bourgeois society considered proper, he had not himself taken advantage of it. Ernest Jones, Freud's Boswell, clearly stated Freud was "monogamic in a very unusual degree" and that Martha was the only woman in Freud's love life. Gay concludes that Jung was unreliable. It was Jung himself who had a number of affairs with other women besides his wife. Gay believes that writings of authors like Swales are "flights of conjecture, though ingenious, too inconclusive." It would seem highly unlikely that Minna would confide such a delicate and intimate secret to Jung, a perfect stranger whom she had just met.

Gay notes that Minna, like her sister Martha, referred to Freud as the "beloved old man," without any animosity. When Freud was forced to leave Vienna, he wrote his very last letter from there to Minna, and it was friendly. Minna had preceded him to London because of her deteriorating health. Freud had been delayed by the Nazi tax office, which had not given him the necessary papers to leave the country until Marie Bonaparte rescued him by paying the required ransom.

Gay concedes that he cannot be certain about his conclusions about Freud and Minna. A troubling factor is the gap in Freud's letters to Minna, which he numbered 95 to 160, that were dated from April 27, 1893, to July 25, 1910. If an affair had indeed occurred, these were the very years that would have been involved. Gay concludes that even though Freud did confide his emotions and share his thoughts and scientific findings with Minna, having a sexual affair was totally out of character for both of them. I would add that Freud's unconscious association of sex with abandonment and death, as discussed here, is another reason why this supposed affair with Minna is highly unlikely. He needed her to be an asexual Gradiva, not to become pregnant, and to remain a good asexual maternal figure. By having Minna live in the same household with his wife Martha, Freud could unconsciously create a childhood for himself and his children with two mothers, so as to relive and master the traumatic losses that occurred in his first few years of life.

Helene Deutsch

Helene Deutsch's two-volume edition of *The Psychology of Women* (1944, 1945) was the standard psychoanalytic texts on feminine psychology for many years. In the first volume, Deutsch stated that from the very beginning of her psychoanalytic work her goal was to present a systematic portrayal of female instinctual development and its relation to the reproductive function. The second volume was devoted to motherhood, including the issues of pregnancy, delivery, and child rearing; it ended with menopause. Her work essentially reflected most of Freud's basic ideas about feminine psychology. She remained within the conservative psychoanalytic camp, basically opposed to the revisions in female psychology suggested by Horney, Jones, and Klein.

Like Ruth Mack Brunswick, Helene Deutsch was a physician, but she had received her medical education in Vienna. In 1912 she was married to Felix Deutsch, an internist, and in 1918 she started her analysis with Freud. Roazen (1985) states that, according to Abram Kardiner, who knew her at the time, she was called "Helen of Troy, brilliant and beautiful, Freud's darling." She was one of the women analysts of whom Anna Freud was jealous as a rival for her father's attention. Helene Deutsch was not a motherly type, but one of the sophisticated career-oriented women surrounding Freud. She was clearly another attractive and youthful Gradiva figure for Freud.

Helene's husband, Felix, was Freud's personal physician. In 1923 Freud discovered that he had cancer of the mouth, a condition Felix had concealed from him. Freud felt betrayed and discontinued their professional relationship. Freud's anger at Felix also caused a rift between Freud and Helene, which in turn created tension in her marriage. She requested that Freud recommence her analysis, as a way of reestablishing their relationship. But Freud refused and instead referred her to his colleague, Sandor Ferenczi.

Rejecting Freud's suggestion, she chose Karl Abraham in Berlin as her analyst. This choice also gave Deutsch an opportunity to observe the procedures of the Berlin Psychoanalytic Institute, a model of well-run efficiency. Subsequently she organized the Vienna Institute, and later became its training director. During her analysis, Abraham showed her a letter from Freud that stated that her marriage was not to be disrupted by the analysis; Abraham and Deutsch complied to Freud's request. Despite a long, unhappy marriage, she remained married to Felix until his death in 1964.

In his book on Helene Deutsch, Roazen writes that her "clinical writings are also a disguised form of autobiography," into which she "poured the experience of her conflicted femininity" (Roazen 1985). Deutsch considered "the three essential traits of femininity" to be "narcissism, passivity, and masochism" (Deutsch 1944). She stated that narcissism arose from women's feelings of organ inferiority and the need constantly to compensate for this. In agreement with Freud, she saw the feminine woman as constitutionally passive, one who "does not love but lets herself be loved." She saw the innate masochism of women as a danger to their personality, but the personality was protected from loss by a woman's narcissism. These statements make sense in terms of Deutsch's masochistic compliance to Freud's intrusive demands that she stay married to a husband she did not love.

Concerning feminine psychology, Deutsch writes that "penis envy is not a primary factor, but a secondary one; it is essentially due not to external (seeing the male organ) but to internal developments; and if we did not realize this before, it is because we mistook the rationalization of the genital trauma for the trauma itself" (Deutsch 1944, 228).

Because the clitoris is small and the little girl is unaware of her vagina, Deutsch speculated that the little girl feels herself to be organless. The little girl's trauma is in perceiving herself as organless, and not simply in seeing a boy's penis. According to Deutsch, "The vagina—a completely passive, receptive organ— awaits an active agent (a man's penis) to become a functioning excitable organ." She reformulated Freud's idea about penis envy and stressed the effects on a girl when she considers herself to be without a sexual organ. She retained Freud's notion that the girl permanently felt biologically inferior to a boy because of physical differences. She acknowledged that penis envy existed and was significant, but saw it as arising from jealousy over the attention a newborn baby receives, especially if it is a boy.

Deutsch believed that "the tendency to identification, passive reception, masochistic renunciation in favor of others, the effects of intuition—all these are qualities that we have recognized as typical of the feminine woman." Although she acknowledged that culture influences women, Deutsch was unaware of how it totally pervaded and influenced her own thinking about femininity. Much of what she attributed to inborn constitutional factors are now clearly seen as the result of how patriarchal society shaped the personality of women. Women were supposed to be passive, masochistic, and selfless: this was the feminine ideal in the culture.

Helene Deutsch totally accepted Freud's erroneous ideas about inborn bisexuality, which served as a vehicle to rationalize the social stereotypes about women. Finally, she considered that a woman gained her identity as a person from the man she depended on and idealized. However, this simply mirrored the cultural stereotype about Victorian women. Women were blocked from achieving an identity of their own and needed to identify with and live vicariously through their husbands. Roazen (1984) points out that the man Deutsch identified with was not her husband, Felix, but Freud.

Freud's Art Collection

Freud not only surrounded himself with these career-oriented women to compensate for his lack of adequate mothering as a small child, but he also collected a large number of antique objects. Gay (1988) states that Freud's obsession with collecting antiquities was an aspect of his "addictive partiality for the prehistoric . . . second in intensity only to his nicotine addiction." It is suggested here that both of these addictions were probably due to the lack of adequate mothering during his early preoedipal period, his own prehistoric days.

Is there any evidence that Freud's nicotine addiction was related to the earliest years of his life? In the dream that Freud (1900) experienced at the time of his father's funeral, he recalled being in a railroad waiting room and seeing a sign, printed like a NO SMOKING notice, that instructed him to close an eye. I have speculated that the eye he closed was to the traumatic effect of his mother during his preoedipal and postoedipal periods of life (Slipp 1988b). His relationship with his mother remained a blind spot. The eye Freud kept open was to his feelings and thoughts concerning his father, especially the oedipal issues. Freud suffered a train phobia most of his life, trains being symbolic of the loss of his nanny and mother. In addition, it could be that Freud's nicotine addiction to cigar smoking was related to the early deprivation of his oral or dependency needs with his mother.

Freud's interest in ancient figures, such as those from Egypt, can be traced back to his fear of loss of his preoedipal mother. As mentioned earlier, when he was seven or eight years old, Freud dreamed that he saw his mother being carried on a bier, as if she were dead, by people who had falcon heads. This dream image reminded him of an illustration from the Philippson Bible, which his father would read to him, of Egyptian gods carrying a dead body on a bier. He also associated the birds with sex, and thus sexuality, death, and abandonment by his preoedipal mother were deeply etched into his unconscious.

One of the female figures from his collection was a terracotta image of the great mother goddess (Gamwell and Wells 1989). The figure was four and a half inches high; it originated from the Orontes valley of central Syria and dated from the early Middle Bronze Age (2000 to 1750 B.C.). These figures were commonly used in fertility rituals. However, this particular specimen of the great mother goddess was slimmer than most and did not have the exaggerated female sexual characteristics, such as large abdomen, hips, and breasts. Did Freud in fact select this figure of the great mother goddess precisely because she was slimmer and did not appear to be pregnant? Possibly so, making this particular great mother goddess a Gradiva figure, another example of his lithe and unpregnant mother.

Another figure that Freud valued highly was a bronze statue of Isis, the Egyptian great mother goddess. This particular example of the goddess is about eight and a half inches high, seated, and offering her breast to nurse her son Horus, who is lying across her lap; it is from the twenty-sixth Egyptian Dynasty (664–525 B.C.). Isis was the goddess of the fertile black soil of the Nile River valley and the goddess of love and maternity (Smith 1952). She was worshiped for her loving wifely and motherly qualities, as well as for being the mother and protector of each living pharaoh. According to the Egyptian myth, Isis remained faithful to her dead husband Osiris, who had been killed by his brother Set. Her only child, Horus, was conceived immaculately through the spirit of the dead Osiris. Isis nurtured and protected her child and hoped her son would avenge the murder of his father. When Horus was grown, he indeed fought and defeated Set, though the fight ended with one of Horus's eyes being torn out and Set's emasculation. Set then acknowledged Horus as the new monarch of the earth, and Thoth, the god of wisdom, replaced Horus's eye, restoring his sight. (Freud had a dream of closing one eye when his father died, and he had a marble statue of Thoth in his collection, in the image of a baboon.) Horus then reassembled the fragments of his father's buried body. Together with Isis, Thoth, and Anubis, the jackal god who invented embalming and sponsored the dead in the judgment hall, Osiris was restored to life and became the god of the underworld.

The cult of Isis later spread throughout the Roman empire, and many consider her to be the prototype of the kindly Christian Madonna and Child. For Freud, Isis probably had special meaning. She had only one child, not a plethora of children like his mother. She was the loving and faithful wife, who did not demean her husband, as his mother had done. In addition, Isis was a protective and nurturant mother figure, as he had wanted his own mother to be. Freud, like Horus, also sought to avenge the humiliation and soul murder of his father in an anti-Semitic Austrian society.

Freud also had a small terracotta head of the Greek great mother goddess Demeter, dating from the sixth century B.C. However, his favorite was his statue of the Greek goddess Athena, a bronze casting from Rome of the first or second century A.D. Athena, the virgin goddess of wisdom and war, measures four and a half inches high and is in a standing frontal pose. Her right hand holds a libation bowl and her left hand is raised to hold a spear, which is missing. Her head is covered by a Corinthian-style helmet, and over her draped dress she wears a breastplate containing a Medusa's head. Freud describes the meaning of the decapitated head of Medusa as follows:

This symbol of horror is worn upon her dress by the virgin goddess Athena. And rightly so, for thus she becomes a woman who is unapproachable and repels all sexual desires—since she displays the terrifying genitals of the Mother. Since the

Greeks were in the main strongly homosexual, it was inevitable that we should find among them a representation of woman as a being who frightens and repels (a male) because she is castrated. (Freud 1922, 274)

Bergmann quotes the poet Hilda Doolittle's experience as a patient of Freud's between 1933 and 1934. In referring to his statue of Athena, Doolittle quoted Freud as saying:

'This is my favorite.' He held the object towards me. I took it in my hand. It was a little bronze statue, helmeted, clothed to the foot in carved robe with the upper incised chiton or peplum. One hand was extended as if holding a staff or rod. 'She is perfect,' he said, 'only she has lost her spear.' I did not say anything. He knew I loved Greece. (Gamwell and Wells 1989, 178)

Bergmann comments that Pallas Athena was still perfect even though she did not have a penis. She symbolized an intellectual woman who denied her femininity and her sexuality. Athena represented the asexual, virginal woman who was not concerned about men and pregnancies, another example of Gradiva.[1] In addition, Athena was a goddess who had no relation to a mother, since she sprung full grown as an adult from the head of her father Jupiter. She was independent and self-fulfilling. This would make Athena especially appealing to Freud himself, since all his life he felt burdened by his obligation to achieve for his mother. Was Athena also symbolic of his virginal daughter Anna, who was his favorite?

In Vienna, Freud placed this figure of Athena in the center of his desk, since she was central in importance to him. As evidence of her emotionally charged value for him, Freud risked smuggling only this one statue of Athena out of Vienna in 1938, when his entire collection of antiquities was threatened to be confiscated by the Nazis. After he finally had his whole collection in London, he again placed Athena in the center of his desk.

These idols were probably transitional objects connecting him with his preoedipal mother and helping him to master his feelings of loss and abandonment by her in early childhood. However, it was the career-

---

1. At the traveling exhibit of Freud's artifacts in the United States (in New Orleans, May 1991), a statue of the goddess Artemis was shown, with the inscription that images of androgynous, childless women intrigued Freud. Artemis, like Athena, was a chaste, masculinized, and asexual goddess. Both were virginal and associated with aggression— Artemis had her arrows for the hunt and Athena her spear for war.

oriented women, especially his daughter Anna, he was surrounded by who actually helped fill the void by their devotion to his needs. Freud achieved the narcissistic supplies and the security from them that he had been deprived of in his first few years of life with his mother. Without any conscious awareness, he provided himself with these surrogate good mothers in order to relive and master his preoedipal trauma.

In turn, Freud offered an opportunity for professional growth in a new field to these women, and allowed them to surmount the limitations imposed by the patriarchal Victorian society. These women became leaders in the psychoanalytic movement and made seminal contributions in theory and treatment.

PART THREE

Current Issues

15. Freud and Jung

Jung's Views on Women and Jews

Many feminists have rejected Freud's work because of the patriarchal values reflected in his feminine psychology. Other women have turned away from psychoanalysis because of Freud's negative attitude toward spirituality. Thus, some women have turned to Jung in the belief that his analytic psychology favored females. According to Jung both sexes had masculine and feminine aspects to them, which he called the *animus* and the *anima*, respectively. In addition, Jung did not adhere to Freud's libido theory, which was a masculine sexual drive that was supposedly applicable to both sexes. For Jung, the libido was a more general life force, and he did not consider the Oedipus complex as the central issue in neurosis.

Freud chose Carl Jung as his disciple and heir to the psychoanalytic movement, despite Freud considering Jung to be anti-Semitic. Because Jung was Christian, psychoanalysis could not simply be condemned and dismissed as a Jewish-feminine-sexual science. Freud stated that Jung seemed "for my sake to give up certain racial prejudices which he had previously permitted himself" (Freud 1914). Jung did not consider himself to be anti-Semitic, although he thought and wrote in stereotypic racial and ethnic categories. However, he was a product of his culture and no more biased against women and Jews than most other Europeans. What indeed were Jung's attitudes toward women and Jews, as expressed by his actions and described in his writings?

In 1933 Ernst Kretschmer, the president of the General Medical Society for Psychotherapy in Germany, resigned over ideological differences with the Nazis. Jung had been vice-president since 1930, and he was asked to become president to prevent the Nazis from abolishing the organization altogether. With this intention, Jung became editor in chief and publisher of the organization's official journal, the *Zentralblatt*. According to Carden (1989), Jung differed with the leading German psychiatrist, M. H. Göring, a cousin of Hermann Göring, who attempted to exclude all non-Aryans from the Society. Although an "Aryan paragraph" existed for the German Society, Jung was able to set up an International Society so that Jewish doctors could remain in the organization and continue to publish in the journal. However, in keeping with the prevailing anti-Semitism and misogyny, in 1934 Jung wrote in his paper "The State of Psychotherapy Today" (1959b), that his own analytic psychology was Aryan and that Freud's psychoanalysis was a Jewish psychology. Jung compared Jews to women, who live off of men and look to manipulate and control them by becoming aware of men's weaknesses and vulnerabilities. Germanic people, Jung wrote, have greater creativity and intuitive depth of soul than Jewish people.

In "The Relations between the Ego and the Unconscious" (1953), Jung describes woman's world as limited to her family and husband, while the man's world is the nation, the state, business, and similar matters. The family is just a means to an end for a man, and the wife is not the only woman for the man. However, four years later, Jung resigned from the General Medical Society for Psychotherapy and compared the Nazi ideology to paranoid schizophrenia and Germany to a lunatic asylum. For this statement, Jung was placed on the Nazi blacklist in 1940.

What were Jung's other ideas concerning masculinity and femininity? Jung, probably using the ideas of Fliess and Weininger concerning bisexuality, considered that each person had masculine and feminine components. The anima, or female part, was related to emotionality, and the animus, the male portion, to reason. Jung wrote that people strove for integration and wholeness of these parts. Instead of attempting to explain this phenomenon in terms of learned gender identity development, Jung turned to philosophy. Employing the concept of *enantiodromia* from the Greek philosopher Heraclitus, Jung postulated that everything that exists turns into its opposite; for example, out of evil comes good, a concept also found in Chinese Taoist philosophy. Jung also saw the integration of opposites in the efforts of the medieval alchemists and in the symbolism of the tree.

However, Jung did recognize that men and women chose partners through whom they could vicariously live out split-off aspects of themselves. The result was that each gender did not itself have to own and take responsibility for these aspects, since they were expressed by the partner. In 1912 Jung wrote "Symbols of Transformation" (1956), describing how some men project their repressed doubts and insecurities into their wives in order to feel more adequate and decisive themselves. Jung recognized that some men sought personal completeness at the expense of scapegoating women. However, he felt that the animus and anima were biologically inborn in each sex and sought integration, and he did not see them as gender definitions that are learned from the culture. Emotionality is no more a feminine quality than rationality is a masculine one. He remained blind to the cultural stereotypes concerning women and men that were internalized from early childhood to form gender identity.

The Collective Unconscious

Jung (1959a) also speculated on the existence of a hereditary collective unconscious. He based this notion on his finding that the same ideas were repeated in the delusions of psychotics, in myths, folklore, religion, history, and anthropological findings. Jung assumed that the transcultural similarities he found were inherited; he considered them to be genetically preformed ideas and behaviors. This corresponded to the idea put forth by Plato in his concept of *eidos*. Jung then divided the collective unconscious into a racial part and a universal part. The racial part fit in with the Nazi ideology of a hereditary racial unconscious. Jung objected to Freud's attempt at finding a universal psychology of the mind. This also fit in with the Nazis' nationalist ideology that Jews, who did not have a homeland, wished to level and undermine national differences in order to impose homogeneity. (Although Jung was not a Nazi himself, his conflict with Freud represented the basic conflict between the Enlightenment's ideas about universalism versus the ideology of nationalism. Freud was an exponent of the Enlightenment, while Jung was influenced by the philosophy of nationalism.) In his "The State of Psychotherapy Today," Jung wrote: "In my opinion it has been a grave error in medical psychology up till now to apply Jewish categories—which are not even binding on all Jews—indiscriminately to Germanic and Slavic Christendom" (1959b, 157–73).

Within the hereditary collective unconscious, Jung felt there were what he termed "archetypes." An example of one of Jung's archetypes, from his "Symbols of Transformation" (1956), was the mother archetype, which was divided into positive and negative. The positive mother was protective, sympathetic, wise, nurturant, and growth enhancing; the negative mother was devouring, seductive, poisoning, terrifying, and associated with death. Jung connected these with the madonna/whore concepts of European culture as well as to the Indian goddess, Kali. However, these analogies across time and culture can be more simply understood by the fact that all infants experience their mothers and their world through the use of splitting, projection of fantasy, and magical thinking. This universal form of infantile thinking can explain how these fantasies could be found transculturally. Jung's error was in accepting the external, concrete manifestations of this infantile thinking as being genetically determined. What seems genetically inborn is the kind of thinking that infants use to perceive their worlds, and not any preformed ideas such as archetypes.

According to Melanie Klein (1948), during an early phase of development the infant relates to the mother as a part object, focusing on her breasts. When the breast is gratifying, it is perceived as good. When the breast is withdrawn or not gratifying, the child experiences rage toward the breast and wishes to destroy it. The mother's breast is *split* defensively and experienced as an all good or all bad object. To retain the pleasurable feelings toward the good breast/mother and to evacuate painful feelings, the infant uses projective identification. The nongratifying breast/mother is experienced as bad and persecutory. For Klein, the bad breast/mother became internalized as a destroyed and destroying object and formed the sadistic, persecutory part of the superego. The good, nurturant internalized breast/mother formed the ego ideal of the superego. Thus one can postulate that such transcultural concepts as the madonna/whore and the great mother goddesses, such as Kali, who are either nurturant or destructive are externalized projections of this early infantile splitting of the mother/breast into being all good or all bad. One can thus view Jung's idea of a collective unconscious, which was based on this transcultural finding, as not being hereditary and innately internal but a projection of this early primitive magical thinking persisting from infancy. The specific form of this externalized projection is shaped by each culture. What is genetic, is the universal form of thinking that infants use in their early adaptation. This developmental view is also suggested by some British Jungian analysts who have been influenced by Klein and Winnicott.

The Mystic Circle of the Mandala

Jung (1959a) was also interested in the symbolism of the *mandala*, which in Hindu mythology is a sacred circle. The mandala was a protective circle, subdivided internally into four sectors, symbolic of individuation. Jung felt it was related to the mother archetype in the collective unconscious, and was an antidote for chaotic states of mind.

One can speculate how other psychoanalysts might interpret this mandala symbolism differently. To a Kleinian, the mandala could be the good breast internalized by the infant during early development. The circle can represent the breast/mother and the superimposed cross, the infant fused with it. To an object-relations theorist, the mandala could be the fused good self of the infant with the good mother. Winnicott (1965) has stated that internalization of the good mother's functioning serves to organize and integrate the ego. Kohut (1977) stressed the importance, in self psychology, of the mother functioning as a self-object who provides self-enhancing reflections, or mirroring, during child development; this process facilitates cohesion of the self. Similarly, Kernberg (1975) believed that the fused good self-object image is formed internally in the infant by gratifying experiences with the mother; this good self-object image becomes the nucleus of the self and organizes the integrative functions of the ego. Jung was also intuitively aware of the integrative function of the internalized good self-mother image, but he accepted its external manifestations from mythology instead of tracing its origin to the early mother-child relationship.

The Influence of Philosophy

Another difference between Freud and Jung was Jung's stronger bent toward philosophy. It is undeniable that Freud's depth psychology was influenced by the philosophers of the Enlightenment as well as by Schopenhauer and Nietzsche; but Jung's ideas stressed the philosophies of the latter two Germans more strongly, especially their antirational, romantic, and mystical elements. Europeans felt that the ideals of the French Enlightenment had been betrayed by Napoleon's military adventures, and that rationalism and universalism could no longer be trusted; thus a crisis in ideology ensued (Kohn 1965). Durant ironically states that rationality "fell sick with Rousseau, took to its bed with Kant, and died with Schopenhauer" (1926).

The new philosophy of Schopenhauer and Nietzsche stressed a masculine world of will and power that elevated irrationality and subjectivism above reason. The crisis in ideology resulted in a revolt against paternal authority and asceticism of the Judeo-Christian culture. Reason in men had previously been elevated, while sexuality was projected onto women and considered sinful. This new philosophy reowned sexuality and irrational aspects of the personality from women. Sexuality and aggression were now validated as important for men's gender identity, endowing them with vitality, confidence, and creativity. However, even though these aspects were reowned by men, men remained superior; women continued to be inferior and needed to be controlled.

As a result of this new thinking, a crisis in meaning and in the way the world was perceived took place in nineteenth-century Europe that profoundly influenced psychology, literature, art, music, architecture, and politics. Schopenhauer felt that men were more influenced by the strivings of an inner will than by their intellect. The focus of this inner will was on sexual reproduction and endless life, which he felt explained why the Greeks worshiped the phallus and the Hindus the lingam. At the same time, he had contempt for women's beauty, intelligence, creativity, and ability to use language.

Nietzsche considered that man had an innate basic desire for power and a will to dominate, with the ideal being the superman. In the *AntiChrist*, he denounced the Jewish founders of Christianity, though he also rejected anti-Semitism (Kaufman 1974). While he liked the Old Testament, he disliked the New Testament. In *Beyond Good and Evil*, Nietzsche (1927) felt the Judeo-Christian culture fostered a slave mentality instead of a master morality. He believed that the Judeo-Christian religion advocated meekness, sympathy, obedience, and kindliness toward others, all of which he considered as weaknesses. He extolled the qualities of a healthy *male* animal such as courage, self-assertion, and freedom. In his book, *The Twilight of the Idols*, Nietzsche (1927) claimed that Christianity was "the anti-Aryan religion par excellence" (Kaufman 1974). Here he introduced the concept of the "blond beast," though it was not a racial idea or restricted to Germans; it included all peoples with strong animal impulses who had not been socialized.

The ideals that Nietzsche elevated were the will to power and autonomy, while pity, altruism, and caring for others were denigrated. The former traits were associated with masculinity and the latter with femininity. Women were considered to be inferior, incapable of "deep thought." Their place was in the kitchen, and their role was to bear male children who would be warriors. Women needed to be dominated, and to serve men. In *Thus Spake Zarathustra* (Nietzsche 1927), he wrote, "If thou goest to woman, do not forget thy whip!"

For Nietzsche, God was dead. To deal with this loss of faith in a paternal authority, he advocated that men give up the absolute moral values of the herd. His philosophy represented the apex of a "masculine" individualistic ideology that denigrated "feminine" values and communal relationships. He preached a form of individualism for superior men that was beyond good and evil and that negated social responsibility. To Nietzsche, these supermen were men of action and not thought or feeling who follow the will to power and make life worthwhile by seeking danger. Men could best test and prove their masculinity in the battlefield, which resulted in the creation of cults of manhood. Unfortunately, Nietzsche advocated a philosophy that fit in with German militarism, and parts of it were later adopted by Hitler and incorporated into Nazism.

Western culture, according to Nietzsche, needed to be revitalized by a reversion to pre-Judeo-Christian forms of religion, such as Roman, Greek, and pagan mythology. An example of the elevation of Greek phallic worship is in Nietzsche's (1927) *Birth of Tragedy*, where the Greek satyr was compared to the idyllic shepherd who longed for the primitive and natural, "the archetype of man, the embodiment of his highest and intensest emotions, the ecstatic reveler enraptured by the proximity of his god."

Jung (1959c) identified with this type of romantic phallic mysticism and the idealization of the irrational. He considered that "the blond beast," as described by Nietzsche, remained in the collective unconscious of Aryans: "As the Christian view of the world loses its authority, the more menacingly will the 'blond beast' be heard prowling about in its underground prison, ready at any moment to burst out with devastating consequences" (1959c, 3–28).

Freud's emphasis on the importance of unconscious sexuality and aggression as the motivating force for personality probably also stemmed from this type of thinking. However, even though Freud recognized that rationality was limited, he did not discard it. Indeed, Freud saw people's behavior as driven by irrational forces in the unconscious, but his aim in treatment was to recognize, integrate, and bring it under the control of the rational faculty, the ego. The ego mediated between the irrationality of the id and the social demands of outside reality. As Schopenhauer had analogized earlier, Freud compared the unconscious (the will) to a horse and the ego (the intellect) to its rider. For Freud, the ego is driven by the horse, but it can direct and control it. For Jung, the horse, which was guided by unconscious inarticulate reasoning, needed to be given free rein, since it was superior to the ego and surpassed conscious reasoning.

The Freud-Jung Conflict

Freud's great contribution was to champion courageously the importance of sex in a society that repressed sexuality. Sexual repression was particularly damaging to women, who suffered more than men psychologically. Sexual repression was used mainly to control women, but not men. Jews were also demeaned for being sexual, which contributed to anti-Semitism. Jung differed from Freud in believing that the libido was not sexual but a more general life force. Jung's position thus went along with the prevailing Victorian bias against sex, so that sexual repression could still be used against women and Jews. This conflict between Jung and Freud about the importance of sexuality resulted in a traumatic rupture of their relationship. Freud had suffered in Viennese society and in the medical establishment both because he was Jewish and because he had brought up the topic of sex. In a letter to Ferenczi on April 24, 1910, Freud wrote, "There one hears just the argument I tried to avoid by making Zurich the center. Viennese sensuality is not to be found anywhere else! Between the lines you can read further that we Viennese are not only swine but also Jews" (Adams and Sherry 1989, 3).

Because Freud was a Jew and his theories were sexual, they were considered invalid and not universally applicable by the medical establishment. Freud had welcomed Jung, who was Christian, into the psychoanalytic circle to minimize this bias against psychoanalysis as a Jewish-female-sexual science. In a letter to the Berlin psychoanalyst Karl Abraham on December 26, 1908, Freud specifically stated that "our Aryan comrades are really completely indispensable to us, otherwise psychoanalysis would succumb to anti-Semitism" (Adams and Sherry 1989, 2).

Although sexuality remains an important area in modern psychoanalysis, it no longer holds the central position. This is particularly true for personality disorders and the more severe forms of psychopathology. Jung had worked with schizophrenic patients, and had recognized that sexuality was not the prime factor here, but a defect in ego functioning. However, Jung also did not focus on early attachment to the mother or the way the child experiences its world. As in Freud's theory, preoedipal development and the mother-child relationship did not play a role in Jung's analytic psychology. However, Jung did recognize the importance of the mother and that the maternal imago overshadowed that of the father in both sexes. He was aware of the integrative function of the mother archetype in chaotic states of mind, which later analysts attributed to the internalized, fused, good self-mother image that occurred during early childhood. Jung was the first analyst to write about the self and the process of individuation, which is also paramount now. While Freud emphasized the oedipal period of child development, Jung recognized postoedipal and later stages of personality development throughout life.

Jung had intuitively grasped the primitive defenses of splitting and projective identification that were subsequently developed in modern object-relations theory. In addition, Jung struggled to integrate aspects of the self that were considered feminine and masculine, which we now know constitute gender identity. He was unaware of the importance of familial and cultural learning during early childhood, when gender identity is learned. Instead, Jung attributed masculine and feminine aspects of gender identity in each sex to inborn genetic factors. While Freud had emphasized male reason and the ego, Jung stressed feelings and the unconscious, with which he felt women were more in touch.

Although Jung recognized the role of the mother, his analytic psychology is no more pro-female than Freud's psychoanalysis. Essentially, Jung also appears to have expressed the prevailing phallocentric and anti-feminine positions then existing in European culture.

16. Modern Changes in Psychoanalysis

Masculine Reason and Feminine Emotion

Freud's quest for psychoanalysis was that he would discover the objective truths and general laws of nature for human behavior as existed in other sciences. Logos would replace myth, man's reason would overcome woman's irrationality and emotion. However, Freud presented a contradiction to these polarities. Paradoxically, the most outstanding contribution that psychoanalysis made was the discovery that unconscious irrational forces were more powerful than conscious rationality.

Women Patients' Influence on Psychoanalysis

Psychoanalysis during Freud's lifetime evolved considerably from what he originally formulated around the turn of the century in Vienna. Despite a marked intolerance for any deviation by others, Freud repeatedly changed his own psychoanalytic theory as well as its methods and goals of treatment. His revisions in theory and technique were a direct result of his listening carefully to his patients, who were mostly women, and considering issues brought up by them.

When Freud originally started working as a psychiatrist, most of his patients were women suffering from hysteria. At that time, his only goal was the elimination of neurotic symptoms. The first method he used was hypnosis, a technique learned in France from Charcot and Bernheim. Despite the cultural bias against women, Freud did not discount their talk as trivial or irrational. He listened to his women patients and acknowledged the importance of the memories they recounted. His sole aim was to bring into conscious awareness their traumatic repressed memories. In addition, Freud stressed that the release of the associated emotions was necessary in eliminating symptoms. He learned this cathartic technique from one of Breuer's female patients, Anna O, who termed it "chimney sweeping." Since emotions were seen as feminine in the culture, this was an acknowledgment of the importance of feminine aspects in treatment.

The next change in technique was to discontinue the use of hypnosis and to rely on free association. He learned this new technique again from his female patients suffering from hysteria, Frau Cäcilie M (Baroness Anna von Lieben) and Emmy von N (Baroness Fanny Moser). Here the patient expressed whatever came to mind, without censoring anything or trying to establish any logical order to the random thoughts that emerged. However, even though the patient now participated more than in hypnosis, all of Freud's patients remained in a passive position. The analyst was the only one to actively interpret the meaning of the patients' repressed memories. Freud thought that once these unconscious traumatic memories were made conscious by the analyst and the associated affect was released, the patients' neurotic symptoms would disappear. His motto was, "Where id was there shall be ego." Masculine logic would contain feminine emotion, with the analyst directing this process.

Freud had become aware of the importance of traumatic experiences in childhood that later produced neurotic symptoms in the adult. His patients, mostly women, recounted being sexually seduced during childhood. With girls the seducer was often the father or a male relative, and with boys it was frequently a maid or older sibling. However, Freud later concluded that these seductions had not occurred in reality but were products of the patient's fantasy. He abandoned his seduction theory and admitted that his own activity in the treatment might have influenced what his patients related to him. The driving force for neurosis was now considered to be unconscious fantasy, which was derived from the child's inborn infantile sexuality. Fantasy influenced how reality was perceived and remembered. Psychic reality, which could be considered as feminine by the standards of Victorian society, was more powerful than objective reality, which could be considered masculine. For example, during the oedipal period, a small boy might perceive his father as dangerous, because of the boy's sexual attraction to the mother. The boy would not see his father, who was actually benign and gentle, because the boy's perception was shaped by the irrational forces of inner fantasy and emotion, not reason.

The Case of Dora

In rejecting the seduction theory, Freud denied the importance of actual physical or emotional seduction and now attributed the neurosis of his patients to their inner sexual fantasies. He was now interested in tracing the sexual instincts and fantasies within the patient to validate his new theory of infantile sexuality. An example of this is in Freud's (1905a) report of the case of Dora (Ida Bauer). Dora's father was described as a narcissistic man, domineering, charming, intelligent, and promiscuous. Dora's father showed preference toward her and demeaned his wife. Dora had normal oedipal feelings toward her father, but he was emotionally seductive toward her. Thus, the oedipal fantasies Dora had were reinforced in reality by her father's behavior, resulting in an oedipal triumph over her mother. The boundaries between fantasy and reality became blurred instead of differentiated. Her father had secretly involved Dora as a confidante in his affair with his mistress, Frau K. Dora and her father shared this intimate secret, thus drawing Dora into a collusion with her father that betrayed the mother. Her father also fostered a relationship and identification of Dora with Frau K. Thus on an unconscious symbolic level, it was as if Dora and her father were having the affair.

What precipitated Dora into a hysterical neurosis was not only her feeling of being emotionally seduced but also by feeling betrayed and abandoned by her father (Slipp 1977). Frau K's husband attempted to proposition Dora while walking by a lake, saying that he got nothing from his wife. Dora reported the lake incident to her mother, who informed the father. The father then questioned the K's about this occurrence, which they both denied. Frau K claimed the story was only a fantasy and that Dora must have been sexually aroused by the stories they read together. Herr K also dismissed the reality of the lake incident. The father readily accepted this denial, since it maintained the cover for his affair with Frau K, despite invalidating, humiliating, and rejecting his daughter.

In describing her father to Freud, Dora said: "He was insincere, he had a strain of falsehood in his character, he only thought of his own enjoyment, and he had a gift for seeing things in the light which suited him best." Insightfully, she felt she had been traded off to Herr K, so that Herr K would tolerate her father's affair with Frau K. Dora then dreamed that her house caught fire and that she was rescued by her father while her mother was preoccupied with saving her jewel case. Freud interpreted this dream not as representing Dora's fear of losing her virginity, but as the opposite. She wished to give herself sexually to Herr K, who was a substitute for her father, since neither got anything from his wife. Freud interpreted that Dora entertained fantasies of fellatio, intercourse, and impregnation. He explained that her foot symptom was due to the consequence of this fantasy of wanting to make a "false step." However, another interpretation would seem to fit this dream as well (Slipp 1977). In reality, her father was not protective, but only stimulated her sexually. Thus the dream appeared to be a direct wishful fantasy that her father would protect her from the sensual hothouse in which she lived. She recognized that her own mother was unavailable, being concerned about preserving her own ego, genitals, and health. The reality was that her father had both syphilis and tuberculosis, and her mother eventually died of tuberculosis herself.

Freud denied the actual traumatic events that were happening. Just as the K's had invalidated Dora by claiming her story was due to her imagination, Freud also attributed Dora's neurosis to her sexual fantasies. Freud did not acknowledge that Dora's oedipal fantasies were being reinforced by events that corresponded to reality. Moi (1985) comments that Freud's interpretation of the above dream represented an effort to force Dora to admit to her sexual desire for Herr K, which Dora probably experienced as a repetition of Herr K's attempted seduction. Dora felt seduced, unprotected, invalidated, betrayed, and abandoned by Freud, just as she had been by her father and Herr K. Therapy repeated her trauma; she could not trust Freud either, and discontinued treatment. She later confronted the K's when one of their children died. Frau K did not deny the affair with her father, and Herr K admitted his attempted seduction of Dora by the lake. Dora then went back to see Freud with this evidence of the validity of her perceptions; she wanted to "finish her story." But Freud questioned her sincerity and discounted her story as being due to her vindictiveness. Dora did not return.

In 1922 Dora was seen by Felix Deutsch (1957). She presented herself as a helpless victim, suffering sexual frigidity—one who had remained distrustful of all men because they were "selfish, demanding, and ungiving." Treatment had been a failure or, perhaps even worse, reinforced her distrust and pathology. Freud attributed the failure in this case to Dora's vindictiveness and to his own lack of awareness of Dora's transference of Herr K and her father onto him.

Jacques Lacan (1982) considers that Freud himself unconsciously identified with Herr K. Lacan states that Freud's lack of awareness of his own countertransference shaped Dora's transference and eventually produced the negative outcome of treatment. Neil Hertz (1985), Steven Marcus (1985), Toril Moi (1985), and Madelon Sprengnether (1985) postulate that Freud forced his interpretations upon Dora, because they were based on Freud's defense against his own conflicts about bisexuality. Freud also unconsciously identified with Dora in his countertransference, and saw her as both being sexually attracted to women and to men.

This interpretation would fit the hypothesis presented earlier concerning Freud's psychic bisexuality, which resulted from maternal abandonment when he was two years old. As further evidence, Freud wrote the case of Dora during the time he was trying to resolve his own homosexual concerns in his self-analysis with Fliess.

One could also suggest that Freud's difficulty in treating Dora stemmed from his need to defend himself against his also having been the actual passive object who was seduced and abandoned by his nanny and mother. Was the case of Dora more a reflection of the unresolved preoedipal conflicts confronting Freud than Dora?

Greater Equality in Technique

As time went on, Freud became aware of the transference. He noted that patients were resistant to change during treatment, and lasting symptomatic cure often did not occur after treatment. The analyst simply taking an active stance and providing insight to a passive patient did not produce results. The patients resisted the analyst's attempt to bring painful unconscious instinctual material into consciousness. They protected their ego against loss of self-esteem or conflict by defense mechanisms such as denial, repression, projection, and so forth. The patients projected their past relationships onto the analyst, which in turn distorted their perception of the analyst. The patients relived these past relationships with family members in the present through their transference to the analyst. The analyst's interpreting the meaning of the material from the unconscious to consciousness was not enough. Past relationships experienced in the here and now in the transference to the analyst needed to be interpreted. In addition to this resistance, defenses also had to be worked through before a cure could be obtained.

As a result of these discoveries in technique, a shift in emphasis from symptom relief to helping the patient as a whole person followed. Freud (1926) reformulated his ideas about anxiety as he changed psychoanalysis from a mechanistic id psychology to a relational ego psychology. The mechanistic theory could be considered "masculine" and the relational one "feminine." Instead of simply tracking and releasing repressed unconscious instincts and fantasies from the id, he focused his attention on the ego. The ego was that part of the personality that facilitated adaptation. It mediated between the unconscious drives and demands of the conscience within the individual and outside reality. Previously, Freud had thought that anxiety had arisen directly from repressed instinctual material in the id. Now he saw anxiety as a danger signal emanating from the ego. This was a less mechanistic model of psychic functioning. A relational model of psychoanalytic treatment also gradually evolved, with more emphasis placed on the person's entire personality and his or her general adaptation to the environment.

In his further work on technique, Freud acknowledged the importance of the positive emotional relationship of the patient to the analyst, which facilitated a therapeutic alliance. Providing logical insight was not enough. The development of trust and a working alliance allowed the patient to lower resistances and defenses. The patient could then proceed along the difficult path of unearthing early childhood forms of thinking and reformulating them into adult reason. Freud further recommended that the therapist's logical interpretation needed to be given only when the patient was emotionally ready to accept it. He advocated that the analyst not listen to only what the patient said logically or contentwise, but to employ an "even-hovering attention" to gain a more holistic perception of what the patient was expressing. In this way the analyst's own unconscious could come into play and vibrate in harmony with the unconscious material produced by the patient. Freud was keenly aware of the interplay between these two processes of emotion and logic of conscious and unconscious material. Not only did this interplay enhance the therapeutic process, but this integration facilitated the creative reworking of the patient's personality during analysis.

Freud also attempted to understand the form of thinking that exists in early childhood as distinct from the rational logic used in adulthood. He did not discount the irrational part of the personality or attribute it to women or Jews. He noted that primary process thinking was evident in all children, primitive peoples, the unconscious, and in dreams. The primary-process thinking of the unconscious was fluid and emotional, with no sharp delineations or boundaries as to time, place, or person. Thoughts, feelings, and wishes were not differentiated from actions but were magically connected. Fantasy was not differentiated from external reality. The aim of primary process thinking was wish fulfillment, which was deter-

mined by the pleasure principle, that is, by seeking pleasure and avoiding pain. In secondary-process thinking, the ego made sharp distinctions between fantasies and actions and established firm boundaries as to time, place, and person. Secondary-process thinking took into account the rules of logic and the demands of the environment. It wa
by the reality principle and fostered adaptation to the external world. Freud considered that the secondary process needed to encompass and integrate the primary process to achieve normal adult functioning. In the production of psychological disturbances of personality and of symptom formation, Freud was able to see the continuing and powerful influence of the child's primary-process thinking that persisted in the unconscious of the adult. The goal of treatment was to bring to conscious awareness this primary-process thinking and to diminish its dominant influence through integration with secondary-process cognition.

For example, a small boy might have had sexual wishes for his mother and unconsciously continues to be fearful into adulthood that he would be punished for having these wishes. Since the small boy employed primary-process thinking, the wish was not differentiated from action and it created fear and conflict. By one's emerging awareness of these unconscious wishes in analysis, the boundary between one's wishing that something would happen in fantasy and it actually happening in the external real world is differentiated. In this way, the powerful emotions in the unconscious can be synthesized and integrated by the ego. Thus the ego would no longer be controlled by these irrational forces arising from early forms of thinking. The goal of analysis was to acknowledge childhood forms of thinking and to change them in the light of adult reason. This would enable the patient to function more adaptively to current reality.

Freud's work acknowledged that both the primary and secondary processes were important in all forms of creativity. The artist's subjective inner experience of the world becomes integrated and sublimated by the secondary process, which allows it to be expressed in a disciplined fashion in music, dance, sculpture, painting, poetry, and literature. Like the magic of primitives, the shapes, forms, and rhythms of music, dance, artistic line, and written words themselves are used for the expression of emotions and thoughts. However, in the magical thinking of primitives, the primary process of inner wish-fulfilling fantasy and emotion achieves primacy over the secondary process. Reality is overshadowed by myth, which is similar to neurosis, where reality is determined by unconscious fantasy.

Modern Psychoanalysis

Modern psychoanalysis recognizes the importance of the preoedipal period on the oedipal conflict and in later development. Freud had ignored the importance of the mother in child development and developed a one-person psychology for psychoanalysis. Modern developmental and object-relations psychoanalysis focus primarily on the early mother-child relationship, a two-person psychology.

The first complete development of a two-person psychology, taking into account the relation of mother and child, was by the British object-relations analyst, D. W. Winnicott (1965). His work accounted for both the intrapsychic and interpersonal dynamics between mother and child. Winnicott noted that prior to the birth of the child, the mother develops an increasing sensitivity to the needs of her baby, which he termed "primary maternal preoccupation." He found that when the mother is both need satisfying and comforting, the infant experiences "good enough mothering." The infant can then maintain the illusion of control over the mother and fuse with her. The concordance of object and self, of what is outside and inside, and between reality and fantasy enables the infant to develop basic trust and security. The mother's holding allows the baby to relate to its own body, and gradually to separate the "me" from the "not me."

Winnicott observed that around the end of the first year of life, the infant is able to transfer its attachment to a comforting, soft, cuddly object, such as a teddy bear or blanket. This object serves as a substitute mother, maintaining the fantasy of fusion with mother and defending against separation anxiety. Winnicott called this a transitional object, which is the first "not me" possession of the infant. It is both object, an extension of the mother, and subject, linked to the self. Play with the transitional object, which it can control, helps the infant deal with the dread of separation and helplessness. Winnicott called this play a *transitional space* in which the child can move back and forth between attachment and independence. Thus the child can participate in both fantasy and reality, while moving toward autonomy. If the mother is not too overprotective nor too physically or emotionally unavailable, the infant is able to cope with the distress of periods of mother's absence. Creative play in this transitional space enables the child to internalize the "good mother function," so as to be able to soothe and relieve tension by itself. This leads to gradual separation and individuation and eventually to autonomy.

The transitional object serves as a root for symbolic functioning, since it differentiates inner from outer reality, fact from fantasy, and facilitates reality testing. Winnicott (1971) extended this concept of the transitional space and play into later life as well. Acceptance of harsh reality is never complete throughout life. People can use real external objects to build a creative illusory world, thereby diminishing the strain between the subjective inner world of fantasy and the constant external world of reality. Winnicott noted that these transitional phenomena exist in adults in play, art, and religion.

Winnicott also noted that during child development, when the child is frustrated it perceives the mother as bad and she becomes the object of its aggression. When the mother provides a "holding environment" to contain the child's rage without retaliation or abandonment, further growth can occur. The child experiences that its anger did not destroy the mother, therefore reality becomes further differentiated from fantasy. The child learns that the mother has a separate existence in reality, is constant, and is not destroyed by fantasy. When the child learns "I am," it can move out of a narcissistic position to "I am responsible." The primary attachments between the parents and child, established during the preoedipal period, serve to contain later oedipal fantasies. This enables the child to experience these oedipal fantasies with trust in others and oneself that they will not be acted out.

If the mother is physically or emotionally unavailable or impinging, the child's survival is threatened by outside reality. It cannot use fantasy to cope with and differentiate fantasy from reality. The child may then experience "unthinkable anxieties" associated with abandonment or engulfment, such as the fear of falling apart or being annihilated. In later adult life, some of these individuals may fear being abandoned and not surviving when left alone. The organizing capacity of the ego is deficient with poor ego integration and development of a "false self" that is imitative and compliant. This developmental arrest during the preoedipal period also affects later developmental levels, including the Oedipus complex. If fantasy is not differentiated from reality, the oedipal child does not have the ability to creatively and safely play out incestuous and murderous fantasies toward its parents. Sexual and murderous fantasies toward the parents become extremely frightening, since they seem capable of becoming reality. If actual incest does occur, it not only destroys basic trust but also the transitional space to playfully test out possibilities. The boundary between fantasy and reality is lost, and fantasy is no longer fun or safe.

Probably Freud's invention of psychotherapy enabled him to create the transitional space he needed to partially cure himself of his own neurosis. Stone (1961) believes that analysis creates such a transitional space, which becomes a "serious make-believe." In this space the analyst serves as the mother who provides a safe holding environment that facilitates separation and individuation. The goal of analysis is to help the patient differentiate fantasy from reality. Freud started by enlisting his friend Fliess as a pseudo-analyst, onto whom his conflicts were transferred to work through and differentiate fantasies from reality.

Modern psychoanalytic practice has expanded its focus and is now concerned with the general functioning of the patient's total personality. This is exemplified in working with more severe forms of emotional disorders, such as borderline and narcissistic character disorders. One factor that has enabled this shift from working with symptoms to general problems of personality disorders is the change in focus from oedipal to preoedipal factors. In addition, there seems to be an apparent diminished incidence of hysterical and obsessional neuroses. This change in the prevalence of certain forms of disorders can be partly attributed to the influence of psychoanalysis on the culture. There is less hypocrisy and repression of sexuality and aggression, and there are better child-rearing practices. Instead of seeing children as little animals that need to be tamed and broken or as miniature adults, modern parents are becoming more and more attuned to the developmental needs of their children. Although the reduction in the number of cases of symptom neurosis is evident in clinical practice, it may be less than we think. With our increased skill in diagnosis, some of the cases that had been called hysterical or obsessional neurosis by Freud and others around the turn of the century would be diagnosed nowadays as a borderline or narcissistic character disorder.

Modern Changes in Technique

Recently, there have been further reformulations of some of Freud's basic ideas about technique as well. Freud eventually recognized the influence of countertransference. He defined it as the emotional reaction of the analyst to the patient, and saw it as a major resistance and impediment to psychoanalytic treatment. Freud considered all countertransferences to be unresolved neurotic reactions of the analyst to the patient. Analysts transferred their own unresolved problems onto the patient, and this interfered with the analysts' ability to be objective. Sandor Ferenczi (1919b) differed with Freud, noting that the analyst also reacted to the real personality of the patient, thereby influencing the countertransference. In turn, the patient responded to the analyst's countertransference, which if negative disrupted therapy, or if positive facilitated it.

A number of women analysts, sensitive to the nuances of relationships, brought about profound changes in technique. Helene Deutsch (1926) found that the analyst's identification with the patient's projected early objects in the transference, while maintaining objectivity, could facilitate empathic understanding and progress in treatment. Ella Freeman Sharpe (1930) also noted that the countertransference could either be interfering or helpful to treatment.

Donald Winnicott (1949), who had been influenced by Ferenczi and Klein, recognized Freud's formulation of the countertransference as *subjective*, but also acknowledged another form, which he termed *objective*. Objective countertransference was noted to occur in more disturbed, nonneurotic patients who needed to provoke hate in the analyst. Winnicott felt this represented a maturational need of the patient to re-create and repeat the early mother-child symbiotic relationship in treatment. He felt it was important for the analyst to recognize the hate provoked by the patient, to contain it, and to use it therapeutically. In this way the countertransference provided the therapist with an opportunity to help patients master their developmental arrest and to grow.

Further developments in the use of countertransference, were initiated by Kleinian analysts. Paula Heimann felt that the analysts' reactions to all their patients could serve as a therapeutic tool (Heimann 1950). These reactions were more important in empathically understanding the patient's unconscious than were purely intellectual judgments. Margaret Little (1951) agreed that countertransference feelings were unavoidable and always present, being provoked in the therapist through the patient's use of projective identification. Patients attempted to repeat early relationships with their parents in the treatment. Little felt that the therapist needed to openly reveal these induced responses and then work them through, so that the patient's perception of reality and trust could be bolstered. Heinrich Racker (1953, 1957) noted how the countertransference and transference interacted and influenced the patient's and therapist's perception of each other. If the therapist responds to the patient's ego and id, a "concordant" countertransference occurs, so that the therapist empathizes with the patient's feelings and thoughts. If the therapist identifies with the patient's unwanted aspects of the self or superego objects, the therapist may become judgmental or condemning and act out a "complementary" countertransference. In this latter instance, the patient's past trauma and pathology may be reinforced if the therapist acts like the patient perceived the parents. The patient may even induce such a persecutory response by projecting the superego or persecute the therapist by identifying with the superego and projecting unacceptable aspects of the self onto the therapist. Thus the countertransference could be useful in understanding and working with the transference.

This is the type of thinking that has entered the mainstream of psychoanalytic therapy today. The patient may attempt to split off unacceptable aspects of the internalized self or object representation and place it into the analyst. In this process, the patient unconsciously tries to manipulate the analyst into feeling, thinking, or behaving in accordance with this projective identification. For example, if the patient experiences the analyst as an angry father figure, the patient may project his or her object representation and subtly attempt to provoke the analyst into actually becoming angry. On the other hand, if the self-representation is projected, the patient may function as the angry father and do to the analyst what the patient had experienced as a child. Thus an intrapsychic problem becomes displaced into the interpersonal sphere and can be acted out there without any conscious awareness in the treatment. By the analyst's careful monitoring of the reactions to the patient, the objective countertransference may be used by the modern-day analyst as a way of empathically understanding and working with the unconscious issues within the patient.

Current Concepts about Bisexuality

Current scientific evidence does not support Freud's concept of bisexuality in feminine development. There are at least three issues he was trying to resolve. First, Freud was probably attempting to work through some of the issues around his own gender identity that may have been caused by the traumatic maternal losses when he was two years old. Second, he was aware of the discovery by Thiersch (1822–1895) that the fetus had a sexual bipotentiality, since forerunners of both female and male genitalia existed. The Wolffian ducts produced male genitalia but became vestigial in females, while the Mullerian ducts formed female organs but were vestigial in males. Third, Freud may have been attempting to bridge the polarity between the sexes that existed in the Victorian culture at the turn of the century.

When Freud originally returned from Paris after studying with Charcot, he challenged the prevailing notion that hysteria occurred only in women. The scientific community in Vienna vehemently opposed this finding.

Freud had not only opposed the established medical ideas, but was also shattering the cultural sexual stereotypes that demeaned women. Even though he himself accepted certain other aspects of these stereotypes, he was attacking the sharp boundary that distinguished gender identity between men and women.

In his theory of bisexuality, Freud also attributed masculine and feminine traits to be operative in both sexes, thereby blurring sharp gender boundaries. However, Freud's speculations concerning the innate biological bisexuality of both sexes is more complicated. He was aware of certain cultures where male homosexuality was sanctioned, such as in ancient Greece. However, there is a question of whether this was true homosexuality, which is characterized by homoerotic fantasies being experienced toward the same sex from early childhood onward. Homosexual activity can occur with heterosexual fantasies as a sexual release, or be used to express hostility or domination. There is ongoing psychoanalytic research by Richard Friedman (pers. com.) to test out the notion of innate bisexuality, whether heterosexuals have unconscious homosexual fantasies and vice versa. So far, this has not proven to be the case, although further research is needed.

Modern neuroendocrine research into the development of the human fetus does not show it to be bisexual before birth (Friedman 1988). Instead, the mammalian fetus has feminine structures during the earliest stages of its existence. Genetically, the male fetus has a YX set of chromosomes, while the female fetus has XX. Because of the Y chromosome, the male fetus is differentiated structurally from the female by the release and action of the androgen hormone, testosterone. In the human male fetus, this occurs from the sixth week to the third month of life. The female fetus develops biologically without this hormonal action in a straight line, and is found to be less complicated than the male.

In laboratory experiments with rats, when the mother is stressed during this crucial prenatal period, an inhibition of the release of testosterone occurs in the male fetus (Ehrhardt and Baker 1974). This inhibition is produced by the reduced activity of an enzyme essential for the synthesis of the androgen hormone testosterone. Because of the lack of androgen hormone at this time, some neurological pathways determining male sexual differentiation do not occur. The male infant rat that is born has no anatomical deficits, but later on functions with female-like sexual behavior. It will present itself sexually like a female when approached by another male rat. Although this sometimes occurs with normal rats, it is not as frequent as prenatally stressed males. The female fetus is not affected by the mother's prenatal stress syndrome. This research clearly indicates the psychobiological sequences that determine behavior, with each sex following a different pathway.

Although this animal research cannot be directly translated to humans, some have speculated that the development of a small subgroup of male homosexuality may be related to this maternal stress syndrome.[1] Possibly in humans as well, if the mother is stressed during this crucial period of hormonal neurological differentiation in the male fetus, androgens are not released, and the male may be born with feminine sexual responses.

Even if this is not the case, fetal research seems to indicate that neurological pathways are laid down differently for males and females during fetal life. Essentially, the female is the primordial or basic form of the fetus. Within the garden of Eden of the womb, it is Adam that arises out of Eve and not vice versa.

1. Simon LeVay (1991) recently reported that part of the anterior hypothalamus, which governs sexual behavior, in homosexually oriented men was anatomically more similar to women than to heterosexually oriented men. This could be taken as indicating the biological origin of male homosexuality as a natural variant of the brain, just as left-handedness is. It may also be due to the effect of prenatal low androgen level, as in the maternal stress syndrome. Left-handedness, which is also influenced by sex hormones, was found to be twice as likely in lesbian than in heterosexual women and more pronounced in gay men. Or it could be a result of a drop in androgen levels in the first two years of life while the brain is still being wired, which could explain why bisexuality may result from the stress of maternal abandonment. On the other hand, the anatomical brain difference may be the *result* of homosexuality and not its cause.

17. Toward a New Feminine Psychology

Changes in Psychoanalysis

A new psychology of women is gradually evolving in psychoanalysis as a result of research findings and the acceptance of analytic approaches that emphasize the mother-child relationship, the family, and the culture. These newer psychoanalytic theories do not view child development solely from an intrapsychic perspective. Bonding to the mother during the preoedipal phase of development is emphasized, and the quality and appropriate timing of mothering is considered crucial in child development. Freud's concept of bisexuality upon which he based his feminine psychology can no longer be considered valid. Sexual orientation is probably in most cases a biological given, and gender identity is *learned* around the second year of life. Even though the preoedipal mother is the first person to be internalized by both sexes to form the core of the ego, attachment and not sexuality is the basic concern of the infant during this early period.

During the second half of the preoedipal period, the child develops awareness of its sexual organs and begins self-stimulation. At this time Galenson and Roiphe (1974) have noted what appears to be penis envy in girls, but it is limited to the preoedipal period and is not significant in the development of femininity as Freud postulated. Femininity is inborn and determines the girl's turning to the father as a sexual object later in the oedipal period. Anthropological and transcultural studies also show that the Oedipus complex for boys is not a universal phenomenon, but occurs in those cultures where the father is empowered in the family and restricts sexual expression in the male child.

An advantage of these newer psychoanalytic theories is that they are testable, since the actual relationship between mother and child can be directly observed and evaluated. It was not possible to validate Freud's libido theory, since it was based solely on mental constructs without external referents. Being able to test the validity of a theory by research provides an avenue for developing a more scientific psychoanalytic theory of female development.

Research of the Mother-Infant Relationship

We will review some of the current observational research on humans and animals that will be helpful in developing a new feminine psychology. These studies have investigated how mothers' bond differently with boy and girl infants, and how infants of each gender attach to their mothers. We will explore the manner in which maternal attachment seems to determine later sexual, aggressive, and bonding behavior in males and females.

Charles Darwin (1872) was the first researcher to study maternal behavior in humans and animals. He was aware that animal behavior was genetically programmed, while human behavior was determined both by social and genetic factors. He attempted to differentiate these factors by comparing how emotions were expressed by animals and humans under a variety of circumstances. He investigated human infants and the insane; he submitted photographs and art to independent judges and did transcultural studies. Even though love, tenderness, and devotion were expressed differently in various cultures, Darwin concluded that female maternal behavior was instinctive in both humans and animals. Its goal was to enable survival of the species.

However, Darwin had no scientific way of differentiating genetic inheritance from learned behavior. Following his lead, many early psychoanalysts also considered much of human behavior as instinctive. The differentiation between nature versus nurture in animal and human mother-child interactions is now being studied by modern- day researchers. Although animal studies cannot be directly translated to more complex human behavior, they can offer us some valuable clues.

Helen Block Lewis (1976), in an extensive review of animal research, has discussed whether female mice, rats, and monkeys have personality characteristics that are congruent with maternal instinct. Since it is impossible to inquire about affectionate feelings in animals, scientists have noted that patterned sequences of maternal behavior, which they term "behavioral synchrony," occur in rats. They consist of a reciprocal interchange of stimulation between mother and infant, so that the mother sensitively adapts to the infant's changing needs.

Daniel Stern (1985), in his direct observations of human mother-infant relationships, noted interactive behavioral sequences that are similar to synchrony in animals. He found an "attunement" of mothers and infants, who interacted in a powerful and sensitive manner. This attunement manifested itself in mutual gazing behavior between mother and infant from the ages of three to six months. The mothers gave over control, and the infant seemed to regulate this engagement by initiating, maintaining, and terminating the interaction. Disengagement, which is an early way that infants assert their independence, could be accomplished by gaze aversion. Stern noted the mother could be reengaged, because of her sensitive and empathic connection, by the infant's gazing, smiling, or vocalizing.

This interactive finding bears some similarity to the concept of *mirroring* in self psychology. During later childhood, mothers and fathers respond in an admiring, empathic fashion to their children. The children then can internalize these self-enhancing reflections, which provide narcissistic supplies to form a cohesive self.

In animal research, Lewis further noted that before pregnancy, female rats preferred getting a food pellet to retrieving their growing pup. However, after delivery, they retrieved their newborn pup in preference to the food. Female rats quickly bonded to their own offspring, and they were able to discriminate and retrieve their own young from among others. The greatest level of bonding occurred shortly after birth and diminished as the pup grew and moved toward separation and independence. This maternal bonding response was found to be associated with changes in hormone levels, that is, an increase in estrogen and prolactin and a decrease in progesterone.

Maternal Preference for Female Infants

In another research study with mice, mothers showed preference in retrieving their female over their male pups. Among monkeys, mothers punished male infants more frequently and held, comforted, and paid attention to the females more often. It was not clear whether this happened because male infant monkeys were innately more aggressive. On the other hand, the mother's reinforcement of affectionate behavior in females and stimulation of aggression in males was considered to be adaptive for survival of the species. These behaviors were associated with the tasks these animals would assume as adults. Females needed to bond to their own young, and males needed to be aggressive to feed and protect the mother and child.

Doris Silverman's (1987a) extensive review of human research noted that a human mother's gender preference was also toward her female infants. The human mothers' bonding to female infants was more immediate and stronger than to male infants. It was difficult to tease out the genetic from the environmental factors, because from the very moment of birth parents respond differently to boy and girl infants. However, the average female infant was found to possess greater stability, showed less irritability or restlessness, and was easier to calm than the male. In addition, female infants were more alert, experienced earlier facial discrimination, and vocalized more than males. This finding was similar to the research of rhesus monkey infants, where females had earlier awareness and more intense attachment to the mother than males. This permitted females stronger bonding to the mother and earlier socialization than males.

Silverman's review showed there were sex-linked gazing patterns in both humans and animals. Infants tend to look at others of the same sex. Since mothers are more available than fathers, this pattern fosters greater connectedness for female infants. Females held their gaze at the mother longer, while male infants had shorter eye contact. Mothers also gazed more at female infants as well. Female infants had an earlier and more pronounced reflex smile, which facilitated a greater responsiveness from the mother. Mothers also responded to fussiness in males by physical handling, and in females by looking and vocalizing. With males, mothers vocalized more when the infant moved. Silverman notes that this overall pattern may reinforce a greater proclivity for motor responses in boys and for vocalization in girls:

In sum, the female neonates' developmentally more mature stable state system (e.g., greater calm, earlier and longer nighttime sleep, adaptability to environmental changes), her earlier sensory sensitivities, her initiation, maintenance, and interest in gazing, as well as her earlier vocalizations all are exquisite bonding facilitators. Female infants earlier become aware of their mothers and of the mother's impact; the process of socialization is thereby initiated sooner than in male infants.... The female infant who eventually becomes the mother is well programmed to be an effective bonder. (D. K. Silverman 1987a, 320–21)

Attachment, Not Instinctual Gratification, Is Primary

In Freudian psychoanalytic theory, attachment to the mother was not seen as significant during infancy. The infant's primary aim was gratification of its oral instinct, that is, being fed. To Freud, the newborn infant was protected by a stimulus barrier and lived in an autistic condition. It was unaware of the mother except as a need-satisfying object to gratify its oral needs. It was not until the rise of Kleinian and object-relations psychoanalytic theory that attachment to the mother became paramount.

The animal experiments conducted by Harry Harlow and his coworkers (1958) dramatically pointed out that the Kleinian and object-relations theories were more accurate than those of Freud. The need for attachment was much greater than for drive gratification of oral needs. Harlow found that baby rhesus monkeys preferred a cloth-covered imitation "mother," who provided contact-comfort but no feeding, to a wire-covered imitation "mother," who gave feeding but no contact-comfort. Harlow also found that if infant monkeys are deprived of an affectionate relationship to their mothers during childhood, they suffered disturbances in adult life. Maternally deprived male monkeys functioned poorly sexually when they matured, and female monkeys were not able to be effective mothers to their own young. Similar to Harlow's findings with monkeys, in humans the disruption of a boy's early attachment to the mother was found to be one of the causes for a gender identity disorder in adulthood (Coates and Friedman 1989). In all likelihood, disturbances in the early attachment to the mother determine later sexual functioning not only for men but for women as well.

The attachment of infants to their mothers has also been studied in some animals, notably birds, by naturalists in their experiments with imprinting. Chicks would bond to the object they gazed upon shortly after birth. Usually this object was the mother, and the infants would stay close and follow her about. However, if a human presented at this crucial period, the chicks made an attachment to him or her. Then they would exhibit childlike trust and follow behind the person, assuming that this was their mother (Lorenz 1966).

These findings on the importance of attachment over drive reduction also correspond to Bowlby's (1969–80) work with human infants. Here again, the human baby's bonding with the mother, not the feeding, was the most significant event. The baby's crying, clinging, grasping, and smiling all served the purpose of attachment. Neurologically, there is an inborn grasping reflex in infants during their first year of life. It is of interest that one of the diagnoses of autism in infants is the lack of a normal clinging response when it is twirled around.

In reviewing three hundred mother-child direct observational studies during the first two months of life, Emde and Robinson (1979) found that infants are programmed from birth to be stimulus seeking. Infants of both sexes were not passive, cut off from their environment, and only concerned about their own drive reduction, as Freud had theorized. They also found no stimulus barriers; newborn infants were not autistic. Infants needed to relate immediately, from birth onward. They were active and organized themselves around outside stimuli. Similar findings were replicated in the extensive reviews of infant research by Thomas and Chess (1980) and by Brazelton and Als (1979).

Stern (1985) and Sander (1980) noted that shortly after birth, infants preferred certain facial expressions and tonal ranges of speech. By two weeks, infants were able to discriminate their own mothers. Therefore, even fairly newborn infants were able critically to differentiate their environment. They found no linear progression in the direction of greater autonomy, as Mahler had noted. Infants could only entertain the symbiotic fantasy of oneness with mother after they developed a core sense of self and other. This corresponds to Lloyd Silverman's (1971) finding with adults in tachistoscopic studies: the subliminal maternal symbiotic merging message, "MOMMY AND I ARE ONE," is effective only when sufficient self-object differentiation exists.

Attachment and Female Development

A number of psychoanalytic writers have related the issue of attachment to women's sexual development. Ernest Jones (1927) was one of the first to consider that the girl's wish for a penis symbolized a composite father-penis fantasy. The little girl's desire for her father's penis was part of her attachment to him as a love object. It was only when she could not experience her father as a loving object that she experienced penis envy.

Such psychoanalytic writers as Balint (1954), Lampl-de Groot (1933), and Mack Brunswick (1940) considered that the girl's fantasy of having her father's penis enabled her to maintain her attachment to her mother, thereby being, like her father, a valued gratifier of mother. These analysts have commented that little girls may entertain the fantasy of having a penis so that they will be loved by the mother. This is especially the case if the mother rejects her daughter for her husband or a younger male sibling.

By entertaining this fantasy of possessing a penis, the little girl hopes to reestablish her attachment to mother. Thus, penis envy in all these instances seems to have only symbolic significance: to sustain the attachment to either the mother or father. Actual penis envy of little girls was noted in the direct observational research of Galenson and Roiphe (1974); however, it was limited to the preoedipal period of development and was not significant later.

Although castration refers to loss of the testes, men experience it more as a loss of the penis, which is a symbol of masculinity and bodily integrity. The use of the penis in sexual performance becomes important for men to maintain their gender identity and self-esteem. Therefore, the threat of loss of the penis strongly affects personality functioning in men. Ethel Person (1980) has pointed out that when a man is impotent, he feels that his masculinity is threatened, not just his sexuality. Men have to prove their masculinity by sexual performance. A woman can be inhibited or abstain from sex, but sexual performance is not as essential to her personality development as it is for a man. Therefore, Freud's psychology, centering on the penis and the threat of castration, seems applicable for men but not for women.

Women's Superego

What about Freud's ideas concerning the development of the superego in boys and girls? Melanie Klein differed from Freud in noting that the superego development begins during the first year of life for both sexes. In fact, Klein felt that superego development occurred first and then promoted the Oedipus complex. This progression was just the opposite of what Freud had theorized.

Modern infant observational research by Emde (1987) has validated Klein's ideas and not those of Freud. Emde found that young infants used "social referencing," that is, turning to the mother to regulate their behavior. For example, when the infant explored an object, it turned toward the mother to see her reaction. If the mother smiled, the infant would continue to explore; but if the mother showed fear, the infant would avoid the object. At the end of the first year of life, "positive affect sharing" occurred. The child looked to significant others to share an accomplishment. The child then learned "reciprocity," or how to take turns with others. By the end of the second year, the child was able to demonstrate "empathic" helping behavior. After it was two years old, the child could restrain its impulsivity in the *presence* of the parent. When it was three years old it could exhibit self- control even *without* the parent's presence. The child had internalized the mother's prohibitions sufficiently by three years of age to be able to control its impulsivity.

These findings indicated that superego development evolved from the first year of life by the child's gradual internalization of its relationship to its mother. The superego was considerably developed by the age of three, at which time the mother had become internalized. This is consistent with the psychoanalytic developmental idea of self and object constancy, which occurs at about three years of age. By then, the mother has become sufficiently internalized so that the infant can evoke her image in its memory when needed. The infant can then function toward itself as the actual mother had done earlier. Therefore, the infant can provide itself with comfort, nurturance, and guidance, and be more able to regulate its own self-esteem and ego functioning. Direct infant observational research does not validate Freud's notion that the superego comes into being at five years of age, after the resolution of the Oedipus complex and following internalization of the father. The superego is well in place by age three, because of internalization of the mother from birth onward.

Freud posited that because women were not threatened with castration, their Oedipus complex was not completely resolved, and thus the development of their superego was at a lower level than that of men. This statement is based on Freud's notion that the resolution of the Oedipus complex in males is accomplished by the threat of castration. However, the basic assumption—that the superego develops at five years of age after the resolution of the Oedipus complex—appears to be erroneous, as already noted. Thus Freud's notions about the inferiority of women's superego are invalid, since they proceed from the erroneous basic assumption that the superego originates at age five.

Feminists have also dismissed Freud's assertion that women have a deficient superego. Carol Gilligan (1977, 1982), basing her conclusions on three research studies, found that a woman's conscience was different but not inferior to a man's. A woman's superego spoke in another voice. Women's moral voice spoke about human connections and caring, while men were concerned about abstract principles. Methodologically, individuals were placed into a position of moral conflict that required a choice. Women were concerned about the effects of their choices, whether a person would be hurt or helped by them. Men were involved in abstraction, such as the justice of a decision. In previous studies of moral development, women were evaluated by arbitrary standards set up by men. The highest level achieved in those studies was the ability to reason abstractly. Therefore, women were judged often as being low-stage respondents in their moral development. The woman's "care voice" was not inferior to man's "justice voice": it was just different. Women cared about human relationships more than about abstract principles.

Critics of Gilligan, such as Linda Kerber, object to the apparent reinforcement of the stereotyped views that women are less aggressive and more nurturant than men (Prose 1990). Kerber felt that this research ignored social class and race, and that moral attitudes have less to do with gender than with power. Women are on the fringes of society and are less identified with the power structure. Gilligan's studies included a wide sample of economic, ethnic, and racial groups, but all were within the United States. Similar studies need to be conducted in non-Western cultures as well.

Are Men More Aggressive Than Women?

The issue of whether men are innately more aggressive than women has been hotly debated among scientists. Naturalists like Lorenz (1966) believe that male aggression is innate and adaptive to the struggle for survival. In animal studies, the competition for territoriality distributes the group and prevents the danger of exhausting food sources from one area of land. Male aggression also protects the family and the herd from outside predators. In rival fights for the female, the strongest most aggressive males will reproduce. In this way, nature fosters selective breeding and survival of the species.

What is the evidence for the notion that human males are genetically more aggressive than females? The physical expressions of aggression in the face and body and the physiological responses are similar and inborn for both sexes. The steroid hormone testosterone, found in a much higher concentration in the male, is known to increase muscle size and aggressiveness. Men are generally larger physically and more muscular than women. In addition, male children engage in rough and tumble play much more then female children.

In a review of research up to 1974, both Moyer (1974) and Maccoby and Jacklin (1974) concluded that in all cultures through recorded history, males are the more aggressive gender. Males commit more violent crimes and more acts of personal or organized social aggression than females. In a recent study of 4,462 Vietnam veterans, Dabbs and Morris (1990) found that men with high testosterone levels were more likely to have a history of delinquency, authority conflicts, substance abuse, and more sexual partners. Most of these men came from low-income economic groups; in men of higher status, the particular profession or social conditions may influence whether or not their aggression is sublimated and expressed in *social* dominance instead.

However, genetics is not the sole factor in aggression. Environmental influences play a significant role as well. The body responds biologically to emotions arising from current experiences. In a study by Booth et al. (1989), the level of testosterone in men was found to fluctuate 20 to 30 percent following competitive activities. Testosterone levels went up after a triumph and down after a defeat. They noted that the testosterone level is closely linked to the establishment of dominance hierarchies, as found in all primates, including man.[1]

Culture also plays a significant role in the expression of aggression. Ashley Montagu (1968) has pointed out that among the Bushmen of South Africa, the Pygmies of the Ituri Forest, the Eskimos of the Arctic Circle, and elsewhere there is no evidence of a heritage of aggressive territoriality. In most groups, territorialism is more related to tribalism and social forces. Besides, in a great number of cultures, such as the Pueblo Indians, Eskimos, Bushmen, Australian aborigines, Pygmies, and so forth, men are not aggressive and warlike. Not all cultures foster or teach fighting and aggression. Both nature and nurture are important and interactive on the question of aggression. However, given all of the evidence, one can conclude that men have a greater potential for aggression than women.

There is also evidence from child development about the greater innate aggressiveness of men. Doris Silverman (1987a) has pointed out that from earliest infancy, the less stable state system of the male creates greater

1. Davis and Fernald (1990) found that social hierarchy directly influenced the brain structure and sexual functioning in African cichlid fish. Dominant male fish had larger preoptic neuronal cells in the hypothalamus, causing the pituitary gland to release the gonadotropin hormone, which increased male gonad functioning. They were brilliantly colored, claimed territory, and mated with females. Submissive fish had much smaller cells in the hypothalamus; they had immature gonads, did not mate or claim territory, and had sand-colored scales like females. Since the colored males were more visible and prone to be eaten, some males who were formerly submissive became dominant and underwent the above changes in their hypothalamus, pituitary, gonads, coloring, and territorial-mating behavior. Although this research cannot be directly applied to human males, the cycle of brain-pituitary-gonad-hormone-sexual behavior is similar.

irritability, which leads to more soothing and calming by the mother instead of socialization. Some observational research has also shown that the face of the mother tends to overstimulate the male infant, who is more unstable and vulnerable. This results not only in greater irritability, but also in the need for autonomy and distance from the mother by gaze aversion.

Chodorow (1978) states that during the preoedipal period, boys have to differentiate from their all-powerful mother to achieve a masculine gender identity. Girls can maintain their identification with the mother of early childhood, and their personality structure is not threatened by dependency on her. The boy's need to strive for autonomy and independence apart from the mother results in an increased necessity for aggression and control in adult males.

The Future

Most psychoanalytic writers depict a developmental continuum from infancy to adulthood of increasing individuation and independence. Autonomy, not dependence, is viewed as the ideal in Western culture generally, a view that has influenced psychoanalytic theory. Freud's thinking mirrored these Western attitudes, resulting in a denigration of attachment and an elevation of masculine strivings for autonomy. As we recognize the limitations of either an individualistic or a collectivist society, further changes in theory will occur. People need to belong, to be attached to others, as much as they need to be independent.

According to Silverman and others, given the strong attachment proclivities of women, psychoanalytic theory makes it appear that this essential part of feminine psychology is a kind of developmental failure. Mental health becomes equated with autonomy, and sickness with dependency. Instead, women's natural bonding abilities need to be recognized and acknowledged in a modern feminine psychology. Both autonomy and the ability to relate to others are important and essential to the mental health for both sexes.

Carol Gilligan's new research confirms some of the cultural blocks toward achievement that exist for girls and that foster a submissive role for them (Prose 1990). She found that girls were strong and confident in their convictions during their preadolescence, but they became transformed into apologetic and hesitant teenagers. Gilligan attributes this change in adolescent girls to their coming up against "the wall of Western culture." Adolescent girls experience their assertiveness and clearsighted-ness as dangerous and learn "to think in ways that differ from what they really think." Gilligan found that girls lose their sense of authority as they become part of the current culture that states, "Keep quiet and notice the absence of women and say nothing." Gilligan's conclusions were similar to those found in the girls of our tachistoscopic study of high-school underachievers. Girls felt blocked from social achievement and self-expression, but were able to succeed once they were given a subliminal message permitting them to achieve.

Society is changing, however, and the bars to gender equality are grad-ually being eliminated. A poll conducted by the *New York Times* in 1989 indicated that the gap of inequality between men and women has become narrower over the last twenty-five years, both at work and at home. There is greater opportunity for women to advance at work, and men are tending to share more of the housework at home. Women have begun to enter fields that were traditionally restricted to men, such as police work, fire-fighting, and construction; the clergy and the military; and they have found jobs as business executives, astronauts, supreme court justices, and poli-ticians. Twenty years ago, only 7 percent of doctors and 3 percent of lawyers were women. Now one out of every five in these professions are women. Although fewer than 2 percent of women are currently in the top management of the largest corporations, a study by Korn Ferry In-ternational expects this level to rise to 16 percent by the year 2000. Al-though the gains are slow, the goals of the women's movement for gender equality are being met. The *New York Times* poll indicated that the women's movement has made the relationship between the sexes in the middle classes more open and honest, with greater friendship and intimacy. Par-adoxically, there are a larger number of women also living in poverty who are single parents with children.

As men value and become more involved in sharing the nurturing of infants, a number of assumptions in feminine psychology will need to be changed. If the father is also intimately involved in child rearing, the male child may not need to distance himself from an all-powerful mother in order to differentiate and achieve a male gender identity. The male infant will have bonded to the father as well as to the mother at the earliest stages of development. The male child can identify with the father as a nurturant person, just as the female child does with the mother. The male child may not have to distance himself from the mother and other relationships in order to achieve a masculine identity. Therefore, those aspects of the personality that had been labeled as feminine need not be denied, split off, and projected by men onto women. In adulthood, this may manifest itself by men no longer needing to control and distance themselves from women. Chodorow's statement about current feminine psychology, that women need to seek out other women for emotional intimacy, should become a relic of the past. Men need not be trapped in current cultural stereotypes. Men can become more capable of emotionality and genuine friendship with women, since it will become part of the accepted male identity. Just as women achieve their feminine gender identity through their relationship with the mother, men can develop their masculine identity in their relationship to a nurturant father. Intimacy should no longer be a threat to a man's individuality and masculinity. If women also identify earlier with their fathers, they should no longer feel blocked from achievement and enjoy the freedom to use their intellectual and creative abilities. Being feminine does not mean that girls need to suffer an identity crisis during adolescence, to give up their independence and become submissive in order to establish relationships with boys.

These prognostications about the unfolding of male and female gender identity seem to be validated when the father is involved in child care. In a longitudinal study by Kyle Pruett at the Yale Child Study Center (Salk 1990), boys and girls were followed in sixteen families where the fathers were primarily responsible for child care and the mothers worked full-time. These children were found to be different from their classmates in ways that one would expect from Chodorow's and Gilligan's work. At age four, girls did not desert the building-blocks corner and boys did not leave the doll corner. Each gender continued to spend time in both areas, unlike their classmates. When they were eight to ten years old, boys also enjoyed nurturing babies and girls also remained interested in the workplace. The core gender identity of these children was expanded yet firmly established in each sex. The study indicated that valuing both relationships and independence can be equally important for girls and boys.

Not only are child-rearing practices changing, but society itself is gradually becoming more egalitarian. More and more opportunities are opening up for women to achieve on an equal footing with men. The Freudian mystique of feminine psychology, so much influenced by the Victorian culture, is disappearing in modern psychoanalysis. As the culture changes, so will many of the assumptions held by current theories of feminine psychology. A new feminine psychology is evolving to keep up with the progress of modern society and scientific research. Women as well as men can be more whole and complete personalities, both enjoying autonomy and the capacity for a more sharing and intimate relationship.

18. Epilogue: The Evolution of Feminism and Integration with Psychoanalysis

Early Feminists

In the eighteenth century, the early feminists had focused on the constriction and injustices that women suffered. This was part of the more general movement of the time for political emancipation and equality that spread throughout Europe and America. It was a reflection of Enlightenment thinking, which considered that social reform could occur by an appeal to reason and education. The first feminists were characterized by profound idealism and by the trust that writing about the social injustice suffered by women would bring about change.

Gaining the Vote in America

Unlike the first feminists, nineteenth- and twentieth-century feminists did not restrict themselves to an appeal to reason. Firestone (1971) has pointed out that in the United States, feminists joined together into a movement that was always socially active, since this country was founded after the Enlightenment and Industrial Revolution. Feminists were further spurred on to political involvement by the abolitionist movement. In the early nineteenth century the Women's Rights Movement was organized, with Elizabeth Cady Stanton and Susan B. Anthony among its most militant advocates. The first convention was held in Seneca Falls, New York, in

1848. The organization objected to the overall lack of civil rights for married women, and to the legal treatment of unmarried women as if they were minors. Women did not have the right to vote, sign a will, or have custody of their children in the case of divorce. After American women were granted the vote in 1920, the feminist movement became inactive, since its goal had been achieved. They had assumed that gaining the vote would automatically secure other legal gains; they had not yet sought social equality in the workplace or at home.

Women in the Work Force

During the Civil War and World War I, women left the home to do volunteer and charity work. However, it was not until World War II that women joined the labor force in large numbers out of necessity, since the men were away fighting. After World War II, women were induced to give up their jobs on their own volition. The returning servicemen needed the work, and society proclaimed that the best place for women was in the home. This social value—that women were supposed to seek happiness and fulfillment in domesticity— was termed the "feminine mystique" by Betty Friedan (1963). The feminine mystique reached its peak during the 1950s, when togetherness, "homemaking," and motherhood were emphasized as the primary goals for women. However, the improvements in birth control, health care, household appliances, and governmental social services gradually enabled American women to have greater control over their own lives.

Charles Darwin and Herbert Spencer

Because of Charles Darwin's (1809–1862) theory of evolution, an emphasis on inborn biological factors occurred in the scientific thinking of the nineteenth and early twentieth centuries. Darwin emphasized that natural selection occurred as a result of the biological transmission of certain hereditary traits. Herbert Spencer extended this thinking into Social Darwinism, the belief that only the innately fittest humans won the struggle for survival in society. A number of groups used Social Darwinism to justify their ideological biases— that is, that men were superior to women and that certain races were "better" than others. Some eugenicists wanted to improve humanity by selective breeding, thereby eliminating the disabled and insane. Friedrich Nietzsche evolved an even more elitist philosophy: not only were men better than women, but certain men were supermen, above other men. Unfortunately, these ideas served to form the core of Nazi ideology concerning race and gender.

Freud, like most scientists of his era, was also strongly influenced by Darwinian ideas, and he emphasized hereditary sexual and aggressive instincts as causes for human behavior. This biological orientation was especially true in Freud's theory about feminine psychology, that is, inborn bisexuality, the Oedipus complex, penis envy, masochism, and primary narcissism: "Anatomy is destiny." Despite this biological bias concerning inborn instinctual elements, Freud did listen to his patients talk about the life experiences that had been traumatic to them. Freud also attempted to integrate this nature versus nurture controversy by emphasizing that symptoms were not simply the effect of a traumatic environment, but how the individual perceived and reacted to their experiences. However, Freud's emphasis was not on the external event but on its perception, which remained influenced by inborn hereditary instinctual forces.

Ruth Benedict and Margaret Mead

Two anthropologists, Ruth Benedict and Margaret Mead, challenged the notion that people, especially women, were molded primarily by hereditary instinct. Each undertook transcultural studies to compare our own society to primitive ones. Benedict (1946) studied the Zuni Pueblo American Indians, a traditional, strongly socialized group (termed "Apollonian" by Benedict); the American Plains Indians, who sought individualized sensations and escape through drugs and rituals (termed "Dionysian" by Benedict); the Dobu near New Guinea, a competitive and suspicious society; and the Kwakiutl Indians on the northwest coast of America, a group characterized by exhibitionism and shame. Benedict felt the recognition of this cultural relativity could help change the existing biases and stereotyping about gender and race.

In *Sex and Temperament in Three Primitive Societies* (1935), Margaret Mead concentrated on how gender roles differed markedly in various societies. The book was based on her anthropological study of primitive cultures in the South Pacific that began in 1925. Specific gender rules in each society impacted upon and shaped the roles and identity of both males and females. Mead's findings, like Benedict's, questioned the Western notions, including those held by Freud, that male and female characteristics were biologically inborn and that they determined sexual roles. It challenged associating temperamental traits such as activeness or passivity and dominance or submissiveness as being "naturally" feminine or masculine. For example, among the Arapesh, both men and women are unaggressive and gentle; among the Mundugumor, both are aggressive and angry and the women dislike children; in the Tchambuli, men adorn themselves, gossip, and are interested in art, while women are unadorned and efficient. Sexually stereotyped behavioral traits were forced upon boys and girls by society, whether they fit the individual's temperament and endowment or not. Mead acknowledged that there were innate biological and physiological differences between the sexes, but that they interacted with and were strongly shaped by cultural forces. She recommended that the gifts of all individuals, whether male or female, be recognized and not stereotyped as male or female.

Simone de Beauvoir

Simone de Beauvoir's book, *The Second Sex* (1961), was first published in France in 1949. It sensitized women to the constricted social conditions under which they lived and contained a critique of the anthropological, economic, psychological, and social factors that affect women. In psychology, her main thesis was that boys were socialized to be active and to "do" things. Boys looked forward to becoming something "important" in the future, enabling them to live a life of transcendence. On the other hand, girls were trained to be passive and simply to "be," even though innately they were able to "do." This restricted a woman to a life of immanence that was limited to the present, without ambition or a future shaped by her own efforts.

Boys' identities were formed in terms of this ability to live a life of transcendence. Girls' identities evolved around a life of immanence. By being able to be active and plan for the future, the boy experienced himself as the subject. By being passive and living in the present, the girl saw herself as the object. Men could further define themselves as the subject, since women become the object. As an object, women achieved their sense of self by identifying with the man. Women were not able to reverse this process to achieve reciprocity because of their upbringing and their continued psychic oppression. Because of this lack of equality, women became "the second sex," a term coined by de Beauvoir.

On a deeper psychological level, de Beauvoir commented that women became the container for aspects from which men feel alienated in themselves. Woman became man's "Other," the "intermediary" between him and nature. Even though de Beauvoir was not familiar with the concepts of object-relations psychoanalysis, she framed her thinking in a way remarkably consistent with it. What she was describing is the process of projective identification. Men projected unacceptable and dissociated aspects of themselves, such as their dependency, emotionality, and human vulnerability into women, who became their container. Men then induced women into identifying with and expressing these aspects for them. In this way, women became the Other and were denied a unique and separate identity of their own.

De Beauvoir further traced feminine development in the family and society, noting that the small girl willingly accepts her feminine role at first, since she wishes to rule like her mother. Mothers appear to be the privileged and empowered group during early childhood. However, later, when she emerges from the maternal circle through her schoolwork, reading, and experiences, she becomes aware that men are the truly powerful ones who control the world. It is this revelation, much more than discovering the penis, that alters the girl's conception of herself.

De Beauvoir rejected Freud's concept of penis envy in favor of women's envying the greater power that men have in society. The penis was only a symbol of this domination by men, being the same view that was proposed by Horney, Jones, and others mentioned earlier in this book. Similar to these psychoanalysts, de Beauvoir considered Freud's theory as androcentric, viewed solely from a man's perspective. She objected to the emphasis on the centrality of sexual conflict, which had been the cornerstone of Freud's theory. This is also in keeping with modern psychoanalysis that focuses less on sexuality and more on the preoedipal issues of attachment and separation from the mother. De Beauvoir felt the real conflict for women was either to assert their own liberty or to accept the role of object. De Beauvoir considered that existentially women have the ability and power to choose to be active. Women did not have to accept alienation from themselves as a full person. Women did not have to see themselves only as an object for men. De Beauvoir showed the pathway and validated the new possibilities that were open for women. Women needed to seize the moment, to be the *subject*, and proceed in their emancipation.

Betty Friedan

This evolution continued with the publication of *The Feminine Mystique* by Betty Friedan in 1963. This book was extremely successful and made a tremendous impact throughout the world. Friedan did not rely only on the written word, but was politically active and galvanized women into the second feminist movement. In 1965, she helped found the National Organization for Women (NOW). It became a national organization and the nucleus of the women's movement in the United States. NOW fought against all forms of sexism in advertisements, discrimination in employment, as well as legal inequalities. This second feminist movement also expanded into a supportive social network to raise feminine consciousness to seek gender equality.

In *The Feminine Mystique*, Friedan described the currently existing "happy housewife heroine" as an updated version of the German prescription for women: Kinder, Küche, Kirche. This was a feminine mystique grafted onto old patriarchal prejudices and stereotypes. Women who tried to have a career were seen as being envious of men and were condemned for not finding fulfillment in their "feminine" nature. Women were supposed to be passive, dominated by men, and to assume a reproductive-maternal role. By encouraging girls to avoid a commitment to school and career through the promise of fulfillment in marriage, the feminine mystique arrested the development of women and deprived them of a personal identity.

Friedan saw Freud's theory of women as arising in a historical context and contributing to the continuation of Victorian patriarchal prejudices. Friedan noted that much of what Freud saw as universal and biological or instinctual is now shown to be culture-bound. Friedan favored the replacement of Freud's emphasis on sexuality as the primary human need with the impulse for human growth. She noted that as the child's mind and body grew, the ability to master and understand one's environment increased. Thus Friedan's thinking was more consistent with Karen Horney's, Melanie Klein's, and object-relations psychoanalytic psychology. In modern psychoanalytic thinking, less emphasis is placed on sexual conflict and more on developmental arrest during early childhood, which is now seen as more crucial in causing psychopathology.

In *The Second Stage* (1981), Friedan recognized the emerging issues that have come about as a result of the feminist movement. She advocated that feminists go beyond "sexual politics," which saw men as the enemy of women. The women's movement had focused on achievement in a men's world by men's values and terms. The issues facing women now concern the integration of their new role in the workplace with that of wife and mother. Friedan maintains that changes in the workplace and in the home must occur to relieve the stress on women today. She notes that men must be enlisted as cooperating participants in this change. Men and male-oriented institutions need to become sensitized to and acknowledge feminine values. Husbands need to take an equal part in sharing the responsibilities of the home with their working wives. Women need to be given time off from work after birth or adoption, and provided with more flexible hours and better child-care facilities. Child rearing, as well as caring for elderly parents, is important. The modern feminist movement is now dealing with these new issues, which have arisen from the shift toward greater gender equality at work and in the home.

Current Feminist Theories

This first wave of twentieth-century feminists could be called egalitarian, since they sought equal rights with men. A second wave emerged after 1968 that emphasized women's radical difference from men and demanded the right to remain outside of male-defined, phallocentric structures and institutions (Kristeva 1977). Even in *The Second Sex*, de Beauvoir had stressed the oppressiveness of motherhood as an institution and rejected maternity as a way for women to achieve transcendence. In opposing these views, Helene Cixous (1986) considered this rejection of maternity by feminists as a patriarchal trap that perpetuates the denial of women to experience their bodies.

Second-wave notions of universal gender differences between men and women have been critiqued by other feminists. According to Teresa de Lauretis (1985), focusing on these gender differences keeps feminist thinking bound to the terms of patriarchy itself. It constrains feminist thought within an oppositional conceptual frame, polarizing men and women. It also makes it difficult to look at the differences between individual women and the universal woman, and between women of different races, classes, and ethnicity. It perpetuates theories that privilege one sex at the expense of the other, thereby continuing the war between the sexes and not motivating men to join with women to effect social change.

Feminist Psychoanalytic Theory

Freud's theory about women has been criticized by the feminist movement as being patriarchal, phallocentric, ignoring the mother, and too biologically oriented. The first dissent within psychoanalysis that emphasized the importance of the mother in child development came from Carl Jung, Otto Rank, and especially Sandor Ferenczi. Opposition to Freud's ideas about the castration complex and penis envy in feminine psychology resulted in the long debate between Freud and Ernest Jones that lasted from the 1920s into the 1930s. While Helene Deutsch defended Freud's biological theories concerning women, Melanie Klein developed her own concepts concerning child development that emphasized the mother, and Karen Horney pursued a culturalist approach.

Melanie Klein investigated the preoedipal period of childhood that emphasized attachment to the mother, and considered drives not as mechanistic forces but as fantasies that accompany relationships. Klein (1937) theorized that infants fantasize the preoedipal mother as the bountiful breast/mother containing oral supplies. Frustrating experiences with the mother lead the infant to wish to steal her oral supplies, thereby having a fantasy of damaging the mother. However, Klein felt that during the later depressive position, the infant's concern for the mother also produced reparative fantasies to undo this damage. She also speculated that due to an inborn primordial feminine sexuality, the girl has an unconscious knowledge of her vagina.

Klein did not formulate a comprehensive theory concerning gender development; however, D. K. Silverman (1987b) points out that Klein did differentiate genders in terms of their ambivalent greedy-destructive versus loving-reparative fantasies toward the mother. Klein felt that because boys had a penis they experienced less envy, destructiveness, and guilt, thereby loosening their bond to the mother. Since girls' destructive fantasies were more intense, their reparative needs and ties to the mother become greater. Klein also speculated that this was one reason why girls tend to bond more strongly than males.

The other analytic group that questioned Freud's ideas of feminine development were the neo-Freudians, especially Karen Horney and Clara Thompson. They were influenced by the cultural findings about gender uncovered by the new research in anthropology and sociology. Although the sexes were biologically determined, they noted that ideas concerning femininity and masculinity were a product of culture. In addition, the neo-Freudians were the first psychoanalytic group to become engaged with the feminist movement, and attempted to integrate feminist theory with psychoanalysis. The neo-Freudians rejected Freud's notion of a single, inborn, male developmental route for both sexes and believed there was a different path for each sex. They rejected Freud's constructs about women concerning the castration complex and penis envy leading to the oedipal period. They also emphasized postoedipal development, where culture has its most obvious input. Although the neo-Freudians were correct about gender identity being learned from cultural sexual stereotypes, one crucial area remained unexplored. It is now known (Stoller 1968) that gender identity begins during the preoedipal period, a time that neither the neo-Freudians nor the Kleinians had investigated sufficiently.

To answer questions about gender development during the preoedipal period, two trends have emerged in recent feminist psychoanalytic writings. The first draws on object-relations theory and is developed in the work of Dorothy Dinnerstein's *The Mermaid and the Minotaur* (1976), Nancy Chodorow's *The Reproduction of Mothering* (1978) and *Feminism and Psychoanalytic Theory* (1989), and Jane Flax's "The Conflict between Nurturance and Autonomy in Mother-Daughter Relationships and within Feminism" (1978). The second trend is derived from the thinking of the French psychoanalyst, Jacques Lacan, and is reflected in Helene Cixous's "The Laugh of the Medusa" (1976) and *The Newly Born Woman* (1986), Luce Irigaray's *This Sex Which Is Not One* (1985a) and *Speculum of the Other Woman* (1985b), and Julia Kristeva's *Polylogue* (1977; see also 1987).

Despite considerable theoretical differences, both of these psychoanalytic groups emphasize the preoedipal period of child development. The preoedipal period is seen as a gynocentric space that celebrates maternal bonding and may be recaptured by women as a rebirth away from patriarchal cultural images to rework women's position in society.

Dorothy Dinnerstein (1976) extended Kleinian theory into child development to explain why women are seen as "the other," as part of nature, dehumanized, and exploited. During earliest infancy the mother, who is the primary caretaker, is seen as a part-object, an "it," as if part of nature. However, by the time the father becomes a significant object, the infant has already developed a separate self, an "I." The infant then experiences the father as a whole and separate object, another "I." Since girls identify with the mother, the mother then also becomes more humanized and becomes an "I" to the girl. On the other hand, since the mother originally had been experienced as an "it" to the girl, she may also experience herself as less of an "I," that is, more of an object and less of a subject.

Nancy Chodorow (1971) noted that in almost all societies women were physically, politically, and economically dominated by men. She considered that neither sex could attain a stable gender identity because of sex-role ideology and socialization. Men needed to prove their masculinity by "doing," because of their insecurity about their male gender identity. Women's "being" represented a resignation to their devalued and inferior role, instead of a genuine acceptance of the self. In *The Reproduction of*

Mothering (1978), Chodorow noted that during the preoedipal stage, the mother was experienced as dominant. However, on entering the oedipal stage, a reversal in power structure occurred, with the child becoming aware of male social dominance. The suppression of women in later life by men may partly be a result of the residual fear and resentment of the powerful preoedipal mother. What evolves, Chodorow suggests, is a defensive masculine identity and a compensatory ideology of male superiority.

In *Feminism and Psychoanalytic Theory* (1989), Chodorow strives to further integrate feminist theory with object-relations psychoanalysis, even though object-relations theory has not developed an adequate explanation for gender differentiation. Using Margaret Mahler's developmental timetable, Chodorow notes that during the separation-individuation phase of early child development, both intrapsychic and interpersonal space are established. The struggle between isolation and fusion with mother that occurs during this early developmental phase also continues throughout the rest of life. There is both a distancing from—as well as a longing for—fusion with the lost "all good" symbiotic mother of the preoedipal period. She theorizes that girls feel at ease in their connection to the preoedipal mother, since they belong to the same sex. However, boys experience a sense of danger to their identity by engulfment and need to disconnect from the preoedipal mother as a person of the opposite sex. To do this, boys tend to repress "affect," "relational needs," as well as a "sense of connection." Men's selves are more involved in distancing in order to defensively establish firm ego boundaries and deny interpersonal connections. Women's selves are concerned more with relationships and more open-boundary negotiations.

Other feminist object-relations theorists also emphasize the need of boys to *differentiate* from the mother to achieve a male identity, while girls can *identify* with the mother. These differences are reinforced further by mothers' differential treatment of the sexes. According to Chodorow, Dinnerstein, and Flax, mothers identify more strongly with female children, and they encourage boys to separate and become autonomous. To resolve this imbalance, Chodorow, Dinnerstein, and Flax suggest that both parents share in parenting equally, enabling men and women to become more fully human.

There has been some criticism of object-relations feminist theory. It questions whether men would be willing to share in the mothering role, in view of their need to differentiate from the mother to achieve a male identity. According to object-relations feminist theory, men need to distance themselves and oppose the engulfing preoedipal mother, and not identify with her.

In response, one can state that the core identity of the self for both sexes is considered to be a result of internalization of the mother during the earlier symbiotic stage of development. Furthermore, the need to separate from the mother may not be limited to early child development, but can continue to exist throughout childhood and into adulthood.

If a patriarchal society prevents the mother from achieving her own identity, she may interfere with the autonomous strivings of her children, especially her sons. Because a patriarchal phallocentric Victorian society limited a woman's ability to find her own self-fulfillment, she was forced to identify with her husband's social success to sustain her self-esteem. If her husband was not successful, she could pressure and control her son to achieve socially and live vicariously through his success. Thus, in a patriarchal society the son may need to oppose a close-binding mother to establish a separate identity, which may persist as a continuing struggle into adulthood. As previously mentioned, this appeared to be the case for Freud, who did not analyze his early preoedipal and postoedipal relationship to his mother, but limited his theory to the oedipal relationship with the father.

Object relations theory views the intrapsychic structure as evolving out of the interpersonal dynamics that become internalized. Thus as culture becomes less patriarchal, relationships change and in turn intrapsychic dynamics of the individuals change. With the present greater social equality between the sexes due to more economic opportunities for women, gender roles also appear to have become less rigid and stereotyped.

In the American middle class, fathers have become increasingly involved in mothering their infants because their wives also work, and caretaking is not considered a reflection on their masculinity. Women are also attaining their own identities, being more assertive and able to achieve outside the home as well, without success being condemned as unfeminine or as a phallic-masculine protest. With mothers finding self-fulfillment and their own identity, there is little need for a mother to bind the son to her and live vicariously through him. Because of these role changes at least, boys should experience less difficulty differentiating from a mother who is experienced as all-powerful, engulfing, and controlling. The need of men to distance themselves and control women later in life should also be reduced or eliminated as patriarchal society changes. As fathers also become involved in child care, the boy can bond with a nurturant father so that separating from the mother and achieving a male gender identity is facilitated. The lack of bonding with a father figure has become a core issue in an emerging male movement.

The other feminist psychoanalytic group—Cixous, Irigaray, and Kristeva—relies on the work of Jacques Lacan. Lacan (1987) reformulated Freud's psychoanalysis by abandoning its biological metaphors and substituting linguistics and logic. Of the various revisions of Freud, the Lacanian is paradoxically the most radical and at the same time the most conservative. While Horney and object-relations theorists recognize the role of culture, they consider that there is also an inborn femininity. Lacan, however, discounts the role of biology and considers femininity as simply a reflection of language and culture.

On the conservative side, he does not emphasize the importance of the preoedipal period (which corresponds to his term, the Imaginary) but gives priority to the oedipal period (which he calls the Symbolic). Thus the role of the mother is minimized and the father's importance is emphasized. What is most important is that he retains the phallocentric structure of Freud, even though he considers it a patriarchal cultural fraud. Lacan believes that it is the linguistic, cultural concept of the phallus (not the biological penis itself) and the castration complex that differentiate the sexes.

Lacan (Mitchell and Rose 1982) considers that there is a preoedipal "mirror stage" in which the infant gazes at the mother for its reflection and identity. While Winnicott sees the mother mirroring the child to itself, Lacan sees the mother as giving an image, which is a misrepresentation, to the child. The child's ego is split, and an "Imaginary" image is developed. This mirror image serves as a model of ego functioning, permitting the subject to function as an "I."

It is the father who disrupts the exclusive relationship between the mother and child and who represents the conventional systems of meaning, the "Symbolic." According to Lacan, linguistic consciousness occurs when the infant recognizes itself as being separate from its mother. It is the loss of the mother that furthers the development of an identity. The Imaginary is replaced by the Symbolic identity. This separation is experienced by the infant as a loss of a sense of wholeness, of not being one with the mother, and of a loss of *jouissance* (unspeakable enjoyment, as in the pleasure of sexual orgasm) that this bond engendered.

The pain of this separation and loss results in a repression of this preoedipal relationship into the unconscious. The infant then attempts to reestablish a relationship with an "Other" through discourse and communication. The Other (representing the idealized lost mother) is experienced as having the power to make good this loss and to complete the subject. However, this desire can never be satisfied, since symbolic language cannot recoup the primary identification with the mother.

The child experiences the loss of the mother as due to the mother's desire for a phallus, because she does not have one. The loss of the unmediated *jouissance* that characterized the preoedipal bond to the mother is symbolized by the father's phallus in Lacan's schema. The phallus symbolizes the father's privilege of possessing the mother and accompanies masculine gender identity. Despite Lacan's claim that the signification of the phallus in Western patriarchy is a fraud, it is a prevalent fraud in the culture. Lacan says that girls experience that they lack the value this potent sign designates, that is, the belief that the mother desires a phallus, which is what the girl lacks. Women then become relegated to the status of a castrated Other and are devalued, since they lack the affirmative qualities associated with the phallus. Women are then unable to represent themselves as subjects, since they also define themselves as "not men." They see themselves as an object and men as a subject, and seek to affirm themselves through men as their Other. In addition, Lacan notes that women are presented as the mysterious Other, who (like God) secures for man his own self-knowledge and truth. He states that both these perceptions of women as castrated or mysterious Others are the products of male fantasy, and are not based on reality.

Clinicians, especially those in the United States, have found Lacan's writing almost unintelligible and his rejection of biology unacceptable. However, many feminists have embraced Lacan's theories that discount biology and consider language and culture as primary, since change in gender structure and identity seems more possible. In particular, women need not take the postures of the masochistic object or idealized mysterious Other. It is precisely for these reasons, that Cixous, Irigaray, and Kristeva deploy metaphor as a tool to represent that which is not (in Lacan's terms) currently in discourse. Reliance on Lacan's work also allows these feminist theoreticians to analyze the problem of male motivation. The phallus is viewed as only a cultural symbol, a signifier and not the actual organ, that is used to divide the genders. They consider that men delude themselves into believing that they possess the omnipotence that the phallus represents. It is also in men's interest to deal with their helplessness concerning the loss of the preoedipal mother and to go beyond their culturally reinforced fantasies.

Cixous (1986) points out that historically witches and hysterics have challenged the Symbolic order. They disrupt the phallocentrism that suppresses the realm of the Imaginary, women, and their bodies. She considers that Freud's case of Dora is a prime example of the rebellion against the exchange of women that, as Lévi-Strauss noted, has historically sustained patriarchy. She disagrees with Lacan's disregard of the mother in his formulations, and she emphasizes the female body and its sexual and maternal functions.

Irigaray (1985a) comments that Freud could not comprehend female homosexuality, since he considered a single male sexual model for both genders. She traces the effacing of the womb in Plato's philosophy as a way of denying birth and death in order to establish the law of the father. To undermine phallocentrism and to express Imaginary-feminine discourse, she writes in a poetic style that disrupts the linear order of sentences.

Kristeva (1986) also emphasizes the Imaginary, which she feels contains the creative energy of the preoedipal drives. She disagrees with Irigaray's efforts to speak within the Imaginary. The Imaginary continues to exist within and becomes expressed in Symbolic language by poetry and music. Kristeva reviews the practice of worshiping the great mother goddess and the suppression of women and their bodies.

A criticism that can be directed at these Lacanian feminist theoreticians is that they reintroduce the familiar Freudian presentation of woman as the castrated victim or Other. Even if the images the feminist Lacanians offer are different in some respects from those of Freud and others, it is not clear how their scripts of preoedipal determinism, the Imaginary, can bring about the changes they intend. Even though symbolic language is dualistic, with a subject and an object, it is questionable how elevating the Imaginary, with its magical primary-process thinking, can facilitate social change. Indeed, as presented in Part One of this book, it is precisely the preoedipal form of thinking, the Imaginary, with its use of magic and primitive defense mechanisms that has been shown to be responsible for the historical evolution of both patriarchy and phallocentrism. The suppression of women is not based on rational symbolic logic, but on irrationality. People have institutionalized in their culture the same magical methods of coping with helplessness as are used by the preoedipal child. To elevate women from the position of object into being a subject will not occur by a return to prelogical, primitive, magical ways of thinking and communicating. Indeed, women already seem to have more access to nondiscursive symbolism, which is more fluid, metaphorical, and imagistic as well as more personal, emotional, and intimate, as described by Langer (1942) in chapter 3 of this book. Even though one can disagree with the solution offered by the feminist Lacanians, one can agree with the goal of ultimately viewing both men and women as subjects and men becoming more capable of intimacy.

Irrespective of how we view the differences between Lacanian (or Western patriarchal) presentations of women and those presented in feminist Lacanian revisions, the overall effectiveness of their theories is still at issue. Finally, Spivak (1981) has noted that Lacanian writings do not include the experiences of non-Western women, women of color, poor women, and many gay women. As both political agenda and therapeutic cure, their writings seem to fall short of their well-intended goal.

Sprengnether (1990) considers that both Lacanian and object-relations psychoanalysis present other limitations for feminist theory. Neither one alters the cultural notion that women are identified primarily with their reproductive functions and consequently constitute a threat to masculinity and phallic civilization. Even though object-relations theory focuses on the preoedipal mother, it is still from the child's perspective of the mother as only a nurturer—one who is gratifying or nongratifying of the child's needs. Lacan seems altogether indifferent to the mother, except that she represents the Imaginary. Sprengnether notes that while Lacan negates biology and emphasizes linguistics, which seems to undermine phallocentrism in the culture, there are two disadvantages in Lacanian theory for women. First, if women deny the importance of sexual differences, it is difficult for them to create a presence in discourse, since historical, material, and physiological issues are denied. Second, Lacan's placement of the Symbolic (oedipal) over the Imaginary (preoedipal) in language makes the feminist writings only subversive and inhibits cultural change. This is especially the case for the above three Lacanian feminist writers who have attempted to diminish the power of the Symbolic, which represents the father. They emphasize the Imaginary, the figure of the mother, and the female body. Sprengnether then concludes that while Chodorow attempts to move object-relations theory toward cultural interpretation, the female Lacanians shift from a nonbiological and cultural approach to one of innate biological femininity: "What this situation suggests is that psychoanalytic feminism needs a way to account for femininity in both biological and cultural terms."

In this book, particularly in chapters 8 and 12, I have offered a bridge that connects individual dynamics, interpersonal relations, the family, and society. Instead of viewing the mother only from the child's perspective, we need to see her in terms of her own dynamics as well as her interactions with the family and society. The object-relations family typology presented, especially the depressive form, serves as a way to relate these various levels of interaction.

In chapter 17, an effort was made to develop a feminine psychology that is multidetermined, and not reductionistic and limited to a single perspective. It does not follow Freud's dictum that anatomy is destiny, nor Lacan's belief that language is destiny. Modern understanding of gender identity rests on a number of factors. The infant is born with certain genetic and prenatal givens that include temperament, intelligence, creative gifts, the potential for certain physical and emotional ills, and some gender-specific behavior. However, these are influenced and molded by important interpersonal relationships with the mother, the father, and siblings, by the family as a system, by society, and by the culture. Even within a given society there are various determinants, such as race, ethnicity, religion, and socioeconomic factors.

The challenge for the future is to confront the more difficult task of emphasizing the multiplicity of female expressions without effacing the equally important cultural as well as biological differences between and within the sexes. Feminist psychoanalytic theory has been developing with enormous speed into a sophisticated and respected discipline in its own right. It should continue to grow and develop to meet the challenges of a rapidly changing society.

References

Abraham, K. 1911. "Manic depressive states and the pregenital levels of the libido." In *Selected Papers on Psychoanalysis*. London: Hogarth Press, 1965.

Adams, M. V., and Sherry, J. 1989. *Significant Words and Events: Jungians, Freudians, and Anti-Semitism*. New York: C. G. Jung Foundation.

Arieti, S. 1962. "The psychotherapeutic approach to depression." *American Journal of Psychotherapy* 16:397–406.

Balint, A. 1954. *The Early Years of Life: A Psychoanalytic Study*. New York: Basic Books.

Benedict, R. 1946. *Patterns of Culture*. New York: Mentor Books, New American Library.

Bergmann, M. S. 1989. "Science and art in Freud's life and work." In *Sigmund Freud and Art*, edited by L. Gamwell and R. Wells. New York: Harry N. Abrams.

Bernays, A. 1988. "Shrinking Freud." *Lears Magazine*, November–December, 92–94.

Bertin, C. 1982. *Marie Bonaparte: A Life*. New York: Harcourt Brace Jovanovich.

Bieber, I.; Dain, H. J.; Dince, P. R.; Drellich, M. G.; Grand, H. G.; Gundlach, R. H.; Kremer, M. W.; Rifkin, A. H.; Wilbur, C. B.; and Bieber, T. B. 1962. *Homosexuality: A Psychoanalytic Study*. New York: Basic Books.

Binford, S. R. 1982. "Are goddesses and matriarchies merely figments of feminist imagination?" In *The Politics of Women's Spirituality: Essays on the Rise of Spiritual Power within the Feminist Movement*, edited by C. Spretnak. New York: Anchor Books, Doubleday.

Bion, W. R. 1961. *Experience in Groups*. New York: Basic Books.

Blum, H. P. 1983. "The prototype of preoedipal reconstruction." In *Freud and*

His Self-Analysis, edited by M. Kanzer and Jules Glenn, chap. 9. New York: Jason Aronson.

———. 1990. "Freud, Fliess and the parenthood of psychoanalysis." *Psychoanalytic Quarterly* 59:21–39.

Bonaparte, M.; Freud A.; and Kris, E. 1954. *The Origins of Psychoanalysis: Letters to Wilhelm Fliess, Drafts and Notes: 1887–1902*. New York: Basic Books.

Bonime, W. 1959. "The psychodynamics of neurotic depression." In *American Handbook of Psychiatry*, edited by S. Arieti. Vol. 3. New York: Basic Books.

Booth, A.; Shelley, G.; Mazur, A.; Tharp, G.; et al. 1989. "Testosterone and winning and losing in human competition." *Hormones and Behavior* 23:556–71.

Bowlby, J. 1969–80. *Attachment and Loss*. 3 vols. New York: Basic Books.

Brazelton, T. B., and Als, H. 1979. "The early stages in the development of mother-infant interaction." In *The Psychoanalytic Study of the Child*, edited by A. J. Solnit, R. S. Eissler, A. Freud, M. Kris, and P. B. Neubauer. Vol. 34. New Haven: Yale University Press.

Briffault, R. 1929. "Sex in religion." In *Sex in Civilization*, edited by V. F. Calverton and S. D. Schmalhausen. Garden City, N.Y.: Garden City Publishing Co.

Brownmiller, S. 1975. *Against Our Will: Men, Women and Rape*. New York: Simon and Schuster.

Bulfinch, T. 1964. *Bulfinch's Mythology*. London: Spring Books.

Campbell, J. 1988. *The Power of Myth*. With Bill Moyers. New York: Doubleday.

Canovan-Gumpert, D.; Garner, K.; and Gumpert, P. 1978. *The Success-Fearing Personality: Theory and Research with Implications for the Social Psychology of Achievement*. Lexington, Mass.: D. C. Heath.

Carden, N. L. 1989. "Critics' anti-Semitism accusation of Carl Jung is unwarranted." *The Psychiatric Times*, April, 22–24.

Chodorow, N. J. 1971. "Being and doing." In *Women in Sexist Society*, edited by V. Gornick and B. K. Moran. New York: Basic Books.

———. 1978. *The Reproduction of Mothering: Psychoanalysis and the Sociology of Gender*. Berkeley: University of California Press.

———. 1989. *Feminism and Psychoanalytic Theory*. New Haven: Yale University Press.

Cixous, H. 1976. "The laugh of the Medusa." *Signs: Journal of Women in Culture and Society* 1(4):875–93.

———. 1986. *The Newly Born Woman*. Minneapolis: University of Minnesota Press.

Clark, R. W. 1980. *Freud: The Man and the Cause*. New York: Random House.

Coates S. 1985. "Extreme boyhood femininity: Overview and new research findings." In *Conflict in Gender Identity of Boys*, edited by Z. De Fries, R. C. Friedman, and R. Corn. Westport, Conn.: Greenwood Press.

Coates, S., and Friedman, R. C. 1989. "Conflict in gender identity of boys." Presented at the American Academy of Psychoanalysis Meeting, New York, January 21. In press as "Ontogenesis of boyhood gender identity disorders" in *Journal of the American Academy of Psychoanalysis*.

Cohen, N. 1974. "Explorations in the fear of success." Ph.D. diss., Columbia University.

Dabbs, J. M., and Morris, R. 1990. "Testosterone, social class, and antisocial behavior in a sample of 4,462 men." *Psychological Science* 1:209–11.

Darwin, C. 1872. *The Expression of the Emotions in Man and Animals.* London: John Murray.

Davis, M. R., and Fernald, R. D. 1990. "Social control of neuronal soma size." *Journal of Neurobiology* 21:1180–88.

De Beauvoir, S. 1961. *The Second Sex.* New York: Bantam Books.

De Lauretis, T. 1985. *Technologies of Gender.* Bloomington: Indiana University Press.

Deutsch, F. 1957. "A footnote to Freud's 'Fragment of an analysis of a case of hysteria.' " *Psychoanalytic Quarterly* 26:159–67.

Deutsch, H. 1926. "Occult processes occurring during psychoanalysis." In *Psychoanalysis and the Occult*, edited by G. Devereux. New York: International Universities Press (reprint 1953).

———. 1944. *The Psychology of Women: A Psychoanalytic Interpretation.* Vol. 1. New York: Grune & Stratton.

———. 1945. *The Psychology of Women: A Psychoanalytic Interpretation.* Vol. 2, *Motherhood.* New York: Grune & Stratton.

Dinnerstein, D. 1976. *The Mermaid and the Minotaur.* New York: Harper and Row.

Dundes, A. 1988. *The Flood Myth.* Berkeley: University of California Press.

Durant, W. 1926. *The Story of Philosophy.* New York: Simon and Schuster.

Eckardt, M. H. 1978. "Organizational schisms in American psychoanalysis." In *American Psychoanalysis: Origins and Development*, edited by J. Quen and E. Carlson. New York: Brunner-Mazel.

Ehrhardt, A. A., and Baker, S. W. 1974. "Fetal androgens, human central nervous system differentiation and behavior sex differences." In *Sex Differences in Behavior*, edited by R. C. Friedman, R. M. Richart, and R. L. VandeWiele. New York: Wiley.

Emde, R. N. 1987. "The role of positive emotions on development." Presented at Pleasure Beyond the Pleasure Principle Conference, Columbia University Center for Psychoanalytic Training and Research, New York.

Emde, R. N., and Robinson, J. 1979. "The first two months: Recent research in developmental psychobiology." In *Basic Handbook of Child Psychiatry*. Vol. 1, edited by J. D. Noshpitz. New York: Basic Books.

Ferenczi, S. 1919a. "Nakedness as a means of inspiring terror." In *The Selected Papers of Sandor Ferenczi, M.D.: Further Contributions to the Theory and Technique of Psycho-Analysis*, edited by J. Rickman. New York: Basic Books (reprint 1953).

———. 1919b. "On the technique of psycho-analysis." In *The Selected Papers of Sandor Ferenczi, M.D.: Further Contributions to the Theory and Technique of Psycho-Analysis*, edited by J. Rickman. New York: Basic Books (reprint 1953).

————. 1932. "Confusion of tongues between adults and the child." In *The Assault on Truth* by J. M. Masson. New York: Farrar, Straus, and Giroux (reprint 1984).

Firestone, S. 1971. "On American feminism." In *Woman in Sexist Society*, edited by V. Gornick and B. K. Moran. New York: Mentor.

Flax, J. 1978. "The conflict between nurturance and autonomy in mother/daughter relationships and within feminism." *Feminist Studies* 4(1):171–89.

Frazer, J. G. 1922. *The Golden Bough.* New York: Macmillan.

Freud, M. 1983. *Sigmund Freud: Man and Father.* New York: Jason Aronson.

Freud, S. 1899. "Screen memories." Standard Edition, vol. 3.

————. 1900. *The Interpretation of Dreams.* Standard Edition, vol. 4.

————. 1901. *The Psychopathology of Everyday Life.* Standard Edition, vol. 6.

————. 1905a. "Fragment of an analysis of a case of hysteria." Standard Edition, vol. 7.

————. 1905b. *Three Essays on the Theory of Sexuality.* Standard Edition, vol. 7.

————. 1909. "Analysis of a phobia in a five-year-old boy." Standard Edition, vol. 10.

————. 1910. *Leonardo da Vinci and a Memory of His Childhood.* Standard Edition, vol. 11.

————. 1912. *Totem and Taboo.* Standard Edition, vol. 13.

————. 1913. "The theme of the three caskets." Standard Edition, vol. 12.

————. 1914. "On the history of the psycho-analytic movement." Standard Edition, vol. 14.

————. 1920. *Beyond the Pleasure Principle.* Standard Edition, vol. 18.

————. 1921. *Group Psychology and the Analysis of the Ego.* Standard Edition, vol. 18.

————. 1922. "Some neurotic mechanisms in jealousy, paranoia and homosexuality." Standard Edition, vol. 18.

————. 1925. "Some psychical consequences of the anatomical distinction between the sexes." Standard Edition, vol. 19.

————. 1926. *Inhibitions, Symptoms, and Anxiety.* Standard Edition, vol. 20.

————. 1927. *The Future of an Illusion.* Standard Edition, vol. 21.

————. 1930. *Civilization and Its Discontents.* Standard Edition, vol. 21.

————. 1931. "Female sexuality." Standard Edition, vol. 21.

————. 1933. *New Introductory Lectures on Psychoanalysis.* Standard Edition, vol. 22.

————. 1937a. "Analysis terminable and interminable." Standard Edition, vol. 23.

————. 1937b. "Constructions in analysis." Standard Edition, vol. 23.

————. 1939. *Moses and Monotheism.* Standard Edition, vol. 23.

Freud, S., and Breuer, J. 1895. *Studies on Hysteria.* Standard Edition, vol. 2.

Friedan, B. 1963. *The Feminine Mystique.* New York: Norton.

————. 1981. *The Second Stage.* New York: Summit Books.

Friedman, R. C. 1988. *Male Homosexuality.* New Haven: Yale University Press.

Friend, M. R.; Schiddel, L.; Klein, B.; and Dunaeff, D. 1954. "Observations on the development of transvestism in boys." *American Journal of Orthopsychiatry* 24:563–74.

Galenson, E. 1980. "Sexual development during the second year of life." *Psychiatric Clinics of North America* 3:1, 37–44.

Galenson, E., and Roiphe, H. 1974. "The emergence of genital awareness during the second year of life." In *Sex Differences in Behavior*, edited by R. C. Friedman, R. M. Richart, and R. L. VandeWiele. New York: Wiley.

Gamwell, L., and Wells, R. 1989. *Sigmund Freud and Art: His Personal Collection of Antiquities*. New York: Harry N. Abrams.

Gay, P. 1978. *Freud, Jews and Other Germans: Masters and Victims in Modernist Culture*. Oxford: Oxford University Press.

———. 1988. *Freud: A Life for Our Time*. New York: Norton.

———. 1989. "Sigmund and Minna? The biographer as voyeur." *New York Times*, Book Review Section, 29 January, 1, 43–45.

Gilligan, C. 1977. "In a different voice: Women's conception of self and morality." *Harvard Educational Review* 47:481–517.

———. 1982. *In a Different Voice: Psychological Theory and Women's Development*. Cambridge: Harvard University Press.

Gilman, S. 1986. *Jewish Self-Hatred: Anti-Semitism and the Hidden Language of the Jews*. Baltimore: Johns Hopkins University Press.

Gimbutas, M. 1974. *The Goddesses and Gods of Old Europe: 7000 to 3500 B.C. Myths, Legends and Cult Images*. Berkeley: University of California Press.

———. 1989. *The Language of the Goddess*. New York: Harper and Row.

Goldberg, B. Z. 1930. *The Sacred Fire: The Story of Sex in Religion*. New York: Grove Press.

Greenberg, S. 1980. "An experimental study of underachievement: The effects of subliminal merging and success-related stimuli on the academic performance of bright, underachieving high school students." Ph.D. diss., New York University.

Grinstein, A. 1968. *On Sigmund Freud's Dreams*. Detroit: Wayne State University Press.

Grosskurth, P. 1991. *The Secret Ring: Freud's Inner Circle and the Politics of Psychoanalysis*. Reading, Mass.: Addison-Wesley.

Hardin, H. T. 1988a. "On the vicissitudes of Freud's early mothering: II, Alienation from his biological mother." *Psychoanalytic Quarterly* 57:72–86.

———. (1988b). "On the vicissitudes of Freud's early mothering: III, Freiberg, screen memories, and loss." *Psychoanalytic Quarterly* 57:209–23.

Harlow, H. F. 1958. "The nature of love." *American Psychologist* 13:673–85.

Heimann, P. 1950. "On countertransference." *International Journal of Psycho- analysis* 31:81–84.

Heller, J. B. 1956. "Freud's mother and father: A memoir." *Commentary* 21:418–21.

Hertz, N. 1985. "Dora's secrets, Freud's techniques." In *In Dora's Case: Freud,*

Hysteria, Feminism, edited by C. Bernheimer and C. Kahane. New York: Columbia University Press.

Horney, K. 1922. "On the genesis of the castration complex in women." In *Feminine Psychology,* edited by H. Kelman. New York: W. W. Norton (reprint 1967).

———. 1926. "The flight from womanhood: The masculinity complex in women as viewed by men and by women." *International Journal of Psycho-analysis* 7:324–39.

———. 1932. "The dread of women." In *Feminine Psychology,* edited by H. Kelman. New York: W. W. Norton (reprint 1967).

———. 1937. *The Neurotic Personality of Our Time.* New York: W. W. Norton.

———. 1939. *New Ways in Psychoanalysis.* New York: W. W. Norton.

Irigaray, L. 1985a. *This Sex Which Is Not One.* Ithaca, N.Y.: Cornell University Press.

———. 1985b. *Speculum of the Other Woman.* Ithaca, N.Y.: Cornell University Press.

Jacobson, E. 1971. *Depression.* New York: International Universities Press.

Janik, A., and Toulmin, S. 1973. *Wittgenstein's Vienna.* New York: Touchstone, Simon and Schuster.

Jones, E. 1927. "The early development of female sexuality." *International Journal of Pycho-analysis* 8:459–72.

———. 1953. *The Life and Work of Sigmund Freud.* Vol. 1, *The Formative Years and the Great Discoveries, 1856–1900.* New York: Basic Books.

———. 1955. *The Life and Work of Sigmund Freud.* Vol. 2, *Years of Maturity, 1901–1919.* New York: Basic Books.

———. 1957. *The Life and Work of Sigmund Freud.* Vol. 3, *The Last Phase, 1919–1939.* New York: Basic Books.

Jung, C. G. 1953. "The relations between the ego and the unconscious." *Collected Works,* vol. 7. New York: Bollingen.

———. 1956. "Symbols of transformation." *Collected Works,* vol. 5. New York: Bollingen.

———. 1959a. "Archetypes of the collective unconscious." *Collected Works,* vol. 9. New York: Bollingen.

———. 1959b. "The state of psychotherapy today." *Collected Works,* vol. 10. New York: Bollingen.

———. 1959c. "The role of the unconscious." *Collected Works,* vol. 10. New York: Bollingen.

Kaufman, W. 1974. *Nietzsche, Philosopher, Psychologist, AntiChrist.* Princeton, N.J.: Princeton University Press.

Kernberg, O. F. 1975. *Borderline Conditions and Pathological Narcissism.* New York: Jason Aronson.

Kety, S. S.; Rosenthal, D.; Wender, P. H.; and Schulsinger, F. 1968. "The types and prevalence of mental illness in the biological and adoptive families of adopted schizophrenics." In *The Transmission of Schizophrenia*, edited by D. Rosenthal and S. S. Kety. Oxford: Pergamon Press.

Klaf, F. S. 1964. *Kama Sutra of Vatsyayana*. New York: Lancer.

Kleeman, J. 1976. "Freud's views on early sexuality in light of direct child observation." *Journal of the American Psychoanalytic Association* 24 (suppl.):3–28.

Klein, D. B. 1981. *Jewish Origins of the Psychoanalytic Movement*. New York: Praeger.

Klein, M. 1928. "Early stages of the oedipal conflict." In *Love, Guilt, and Reparation & Other Works, 1921–1945*. New York: Dell (reprint 1975).

———. 1937. "Love, guilt and reparation." In *Love, Guilt, and Reparation & Other Works, 1921–1945*. New York: Dell (reprint 1975).

———. 1948. *Contributions to Psychoanalysis*. London: Hogarth Press and the Institute of Psychoanalysis.

Kohn, H. 1965. *Nationalism: Its Meaning and History*, rev. ed. New York: D. Van Nostrand.

Kohut, H. 1977. *The Restoration of the Self*. New York: International Universities Press.

Kristeva, J. 1977. *Polylogue*. Paris: Editions de Seuil.

———. 1986. *The Kristeva Reader*. Edited by T. Moi. New York: Columbia University Press.

———. 1987. "Talking about polylogue." In *French Feminist Thought*. Edited by T. Moi, 110–17. Oxford: Oxford University Press.

Krull, M. 1986. *Freud and His Father*. New York: W. W. Norton.

Lacan, J. 1982. "Intervention on transference." In *Feminine Sexuality*, edited by J. Mitchell and J. Rose. New York: W. W. Norton.

———. 1987. *Ecrits: A Selection*. New York: W. W. Norton.

Lampl-de Groot, J. 1933. "Contribution to the problem of femininity." *Psychoanalytic Quarterly* 2:489–518.

Langer, S. K. 1942. *Philosophy in a New Key: A Study in the Symbolism of Reason, Rite, and Art*. Cambridge, Mass.: Harvard University Press.

Leavy, S. A. 1964. *The Freud Journal of Lou Andreas-Salomé*. New York: Basic Books.

LeVay, S. 1991. "A difference in hypothalamic structure between heterosexual and homosexual men." *Science*, August 30, 1034–37, and "Is Homosexuality Biological?" *Science*, August 30, 956–57.

Lévi-Strauss, C. 1968. *Structural Anthropology*. London: Penguin Press.

Lewin, K. 1935. "Psycho- sociological problems of a minority group." *Character and Personality* 3:175–87.

Lewis, H. B. 1976. *Psychic War in Men and Women*. New York: New York University Press.

Lidz, T., and Lidz, R. 1988. *Oedipus in the Stone Age*. New York: International Universities Press.

Little, M. 1951. "Countertransference and the patient's response to it." *International Journal of Psycho-analysis* 32:32–40.

Lorenz, K. 1966. *On Aggression*. New York: Harcourt, Brace, and World.

Maccoby, E. E., and Jacklin, C. N. 1974. *The Psychology of Sex Differences*. Palo Alto: Stanford University Press.

McGrath, W. J. 1986. *Freud's Discovery of Psychoanalysis*. Ithaca, N.Y.: Cornell University Press.

Mack Brunswick, R. 1940. "The pre-oedipal phase of the libido development." *Psychoanalytic Quarterly* 9:293–319.

Mahler, M. S., and Furer, M. 1968. *On Human Symbiosis and the Vicissitudes of Individuation*. Vol. 1. New York: International Universities Press.

Mahler, M. S.; Pine, F.; and Bergman, A. 1975. *The Psychological Birth of the Human Infant: Symbiosis and Individuation*. New York: Basic Books.

Mahoney, P. J. 1990. "Freud, family therapist." Paper delivered at Third Hannah Conference, Freud and the History of Psychoanalysis, October 12–14, Toronto, Canada.

Malinowski, B. 1929. *The Sexual Life of Savages*. New York: Harcourt, Brace, and World.

Marcus, S. 1985. "Freud and Dora: Story, history, case history." In *In Dora's Case: Freud, Hysteria, Feminism*, edited by C. Bernheimer and C. Kahane. New York: Columbia University Press.

Masson, J. M., ed. 1985. *The Complete Letters of Sigmund Freud to Wilhelm Fliess, 1887–1904*. Cambridge, Mass.: Harvard University Press.

Matlin, M. W. 1987. *The Psychology of Women*. New York: Holt, Rinehart and Winston.

Mead, M. 1935. *Sex and Temperament in Three Primitive Societies*. New York: Morrow.

Miller, J. B. 1976. *Toward a New Psychology of Women*. Boston: Beacon Press.

Miller, J. R. 1978. "The relationship of fear of success to perceived parental attitudes toward success and autonomy." Ph.D. diss., Columbia University.

Mitchell, J. 1974. *Psychoanalysis and Feminism: Freud, Reich, Laing, and Women*. New York: Vintage.

Mitchell, J., and Rose, J. 1982. *Feminine Sexuality: Jacques Lacan and the Ecole Freudienne*. New York: W. W. Norton.

Moi, T. 1985. "Representation of patriarchy, sexuality, and epistemology in Freud's Dora." In *In Dora's Case: Freud, Hysteria, Feminism*, edited by C. Bernheimer and C. Kahane. New York: Columbia University Press.

Money, J., and Ehrhardt, A. A. 1972. *Man and Woman, Boy and Girl: The Differentiation and Dimorphism of Gender from Conception to Maturity*. Baltimore: Johns Hopkins University Press.

Montagu, A. 1968. "Animals and man: Divergent behavior." *Science*, September 6.

Moyer, K. E. 1974. "Sex differences in aggression." In *Sex Differences in Behavior*, edited by R. C. Friedman, R. M. Richart, and R. L. VandeWiele. New York: Wiley.

Niederland, W. G. 1958. "Linguistic observations on beating fantasies." *Journal of the Hillside Hospital* 8:202–7.

———. 1965. "An analytic inquiry into the life and work of Heinrich Schliemann." In *Drives, Affects, Behavior*. Vol. 2, edited by M. Schur. New York: International Universities Press.

Nietzsche, F. 1927. *The Philosophy of Nietzsche*. New York: The Modern Library, Random House.

Person, E. S. 1980. "Sexuality as the mainstay of identity: Psychoanalytic perspectives." In *Women: Sex and Sexuality*, edited by C. R. Stimpson and E. S. Person. Chicago: University of Chicago Press.

Piaget, J. 1954. *The Construction of Reality in the Child*. New York: Basic Books.

———. 1963. "Realism and the origin of the idea of participation." In *The Child's Conception of the World*, edited by C. K. Ogden. Patterson, N.J.: Littlefield Adams.

Prose, F. 1990. "Carol Gilligan studies girls growing up: Confident at 11, confused at 16." *New York Times Magazine*, 7 January, 22–46.

Rabuzzi, K. A. 1989. Review of *Lady of the Beasts: Ancient Images of the Goddess and Her Sacred Animals* by B. Johnson. San Francisco: Harper and Row. In *New York Times* Book Review Section, 11 February, 22.

Racker, H. 1953. "A contribution to the problem of countertransference." *International Journal of Psycho-analysis* 34:313–24.

———. 1957. "The meanings and uses of countertransference." *Psychoanalytic Quarterly* 26:303–57.

Remmling, G. W. 1967. *The Road to Suspicion: A Study of Modern Mentality and the Sociology of Knowledge*. New York: Appleton Century Crofts.

Roazen, P. 1984. *Freud and His Followers*. New York: New York University Press.

———. 1985. *Helene Deutsch, a Psychoanalyst's Life*. New York: Doubleday.

Rossi, A. S. 1973. *The Feminist Papers: From Adams to de Beauvoir*. New York: Bantam.

Salk, L. 1990. "Raising boys, raising girls." *McCall's*, December, 84–86.

Sander, L. W. 1980. "New knowledge about the infant from current research: Implications for psychoanalysis. *Journal of the American Psychoanalytic Association* 28: 181–98.

Schorske, C. E. 1981. *Fin-de-Siècle Vienna: Politics and Culture*. New York: Vintage.

Schur, M. 1972. *Freud: Living and Dying*. New York: International Universities Press.

Seligman, M. E. P., and Maier, S. F. 1967. "Failure to escape traumatic shock." *Journal of Experimental Psychology* 74:1–9.

Sharpe, E. F. 1930. "The technique of psycho-analysis." In *Collected Papers on Psycho-Analysis*, edited by M. Brierley. London: Hogarth Press, 1950.

Silverman, D. K. 1987a. "What are little girls made of?" *Psychoanalytic Psychology* 4:315–34.

———. 1987b. "Female bonding: Some supportive findings for Melanie Klein's views." *Psychoanalytic Review* 74(2):201–15.

Silverman, L. H. 1971. "An experimental technique for the study of unconscious conflict." *British Journal of Medical Psychology* 44:17–25.

Silverman, L. H., and Wolitzky, D. L. 1982. "Toward the resolution of controversial issues in psychoanalytic treatment." In *Curative Factors in Dynamic Psychotherapy*, edited by S. Slipp. New York: McGraw- Hill.

Slipp, S. 1969. "The psychotic adolescent in the context of his family." Paper
presented at the annual meeting of the American Medical Association, and in
The Emotionally Troubled Adolescent and the Family Physician, edited by M. G.
Kalogerakis. Springfield, Ill.: Charles C. Thomas, 1973.

———. 1973. "The symbiotic survival pattern: A relational theory of schizophrenia." *Family Process* 12:377–98.

———. 1976. "An intrapsychic-interpersonal theory of depression." *Journal of the
American Academy of Psychoanalysis* 4:389–409.

———. 1977. "Interpersonal factors in hysteria: Freud's seduction theory and the
case of Dora." *Journal of the American Academy of Psychoanalysis* 5:359–76.

———. 1984. *Object Relations: A Dynamic Bridge between Individual and Family
Treatment*. New York: Jason Aronson.

———. 1986. "Psychoanalytic treatment of depression." In *Verständnis und Ther-
apie der Depression*, edited by S.K.D. Sulz. Munich, Germany: Ernst Reinhardt.

———. 1988a. *The Technique and Practice of Object Relations Family Therapy*.
Northvale, N.J.: Jason Aronson.

———. 1988b. "Freud's mother, Ferenczi, and the seduction theory." *Journal of
the American Academy of Psychoanalysis* 16:155–65.

Slipp, S., and Nissenfeld, S. 1981. "An experimental study of psychoanalytic
theories of depression." *Journal of the American Academy of Psychoanalysis* 9:583–
600.

Smith, H. W. 1952. *Man and His Gods*. Boston: Little, Brown.

Spence, D. 1987. *The Freudian Metaphor: Toward a Paradigm Change in Psychoanalysis*. New York: W. W. Norton.

Spivak, G. C. 1981. "French feminism in an international frame." *Yale French
Studies* 62:154–84.

Sprengnether, M. 1985. "Enforcing Oedipus: Freud and Dora." In *In Dora's Case:
Freud, Hysteria, Feminism*, edited by C. Bernheimer and C. Kahane. New York:
Columbia University Press.

———. 1990. *The Spectral Mother: Freud, Feminism, and Psychoanalysis*. Ithaca,
N.Y.: Cornell University Press.

Spretnak, C. 1982. *The Politics of Women's Spirituality: Essays on the Rise of Spiritual
Power within the Feminist Movement*. New York: Anchor Books, Doubleday.

Steinfels, P. 1990. "Idyllic theory of goddesses creates storm." Science Times, *New
York Times*, 13 February.

Stern, D. N. 1977. *The First Relationship: Infant and Mother*. Cambridge, Mass.:
Harvard University Press.

———. 1985. *The Interpersonal World of the Infant: A View from Psychoanalysis and
Developmental Psychology*. New York: Basic Books.

Stoller, R. J. 1968. *Sex and Gender*. New York: Science House.

Stone, L. 1961. *The Psychoanalytic Situation*. New York: International Universities
Press.

Summers, M. 1951. *Malleus Maleficarum*. London: Pushkin Press.

Swales, P. J. 1982. "Freud, Minna Bernays, and the conquest of Rome: New light on the origins of psychoanalysis." *The New American Review*, Spring/Summer, 1–23.

Thomas, A., and Chess, S. 1980. *The Dynamics of Psychological Development*. New York: Brunner/Mazel.

Thompson, C. 1950. *Psychoanalysis: Evolution and Development*. New York: Grove Press.

Tienari, P.; Sorri, A.; Lahti, I.; et al. 1984. "The Finnish adoptive family study of schizophrenia." Paper presented at the International Symposium on the Psychotherapy of Schizophrenia, New Haven, Conn.

Unger, R. 1990. "Oh, goddess! Feminists and witches create a new religion from ancient myths and magic." *New York Times*, 4 June, 40–46.

Vida, J. 1989. "Presentation on Sandor Ferenczi in the panel on the psychoanalytic understanding of female sexuality from Freud to the present." American Academy of Psychoanalysis, 5 May.

Voth, H. M. 1972. "Some effects of Freud's personality on psychoanalytic theory and technique." *International Journal of Psychiatry* 10:48–69.

Winnicott, D. W. 1949. "Hate in the countertransference." *International Journal of Psycho-analysis* 30:36–74.

———. 1965. *The Maturational Process and the Facilitating Environment*. New York: International Universities Press.

———. 1971. *Playing and Reality*. London: Tavistock.

Young-Bruehl, E. 1989. *Anna Freud: A Biography*. New York: Summit Books.

Name Index

Abraham, 41
Abraham, Karl, 16, 121, 125, 142, 158
Adam, 41
Adams, Abigail, 49
Adams, John, 49
Adams, M. V., 158
Adler, Alfred, 125
Alcott, Louisa May, 50
Alexander, Franz, 19
Alexander the Great, 55
Als, H., 179
Andreas-Salomé, Lou, 101, 102, 124, 125–26
Anthony, David, 23
Anthony, Susan B., 188
Aquinas, Thomas, 44
Arieti, Silvano, 83
Aristotle, 45, 51
Augustine, Saint, 44
Austen, Jane, 50

Bachofen, J. J., 24 n.2
Baker, S. W., 106, 172
Balint, A., 179
Balint, Michael, 16
Bauer, Ida (Dora case), 162–64
Beethoven, Ludwig van, 51
Benedict, Ruth, 190–91
Bergman, A., 103
Bergmann, M. S., 42 n.1, 146

Bernays, Anne (granddaughter of Anna Freud Bernays), 92
Bernays, Eli (brother-in-law of SF), 92
Bernays, Minna (sister-in-law of SF), 78, 126, 138–41
Bernheim, Hippolyte, 138, 160
Bertin, C., 17, 133, 134
Bieber, I., 85
Billinsky, John, 139
Binford, Sally, 23
Bion, Wilfred, 114–15, 119
Blum, H. P., 75, 101, 108–10, 111
Blumgart, Hermann, 133
Bonaparte, Marie, 17, 55, 66, 84, 94, 124, 125, 126, 133, 134–35, 136
Bonaparte, Pascal, 134
Bonime, W., 83
Booth, A., 183
Botticelli, Sandro, 75
Bowlby, John, 63 n.1, 178
Brazelton, T. B., 179
Breuer, Josef, 54, 83–84, 110, 161
Briand, Aristide, 134
Briffault, R., 38, 40, 43
Broca, Paul, 47
Brontë sisters, 50
Brownmiller, S., 25
Brucke, Ernst, 110
Brunswick, David, 133
Brunswick, Mark, 133

Subject Index

Abandonment, 65, 84, 130; sex and, 71–79, 140, 141, 144; fear of, 82, 92, 93, 168; fear of, in Freud, 64, 68, 75, 83, 95
Abolitionist movement, 188
Achievement, 193; in girls, 184–85, 186
Activeness, 191
Activity, and masculinity, 12, 87
Adaptation, 33, 37, 166; cultural, 3–4; ego and, 165; magical form of, 3; to nature, 20, 21; preoedipal form of, 115; symbiotic, 115–16
Addictions (Freud), 143–44
Adjective Rating Scale, 120
Adonis, 39
Aggression, 13, 95, 169, 177; in infancy, 92; in men, 7, 182–84; toward mother (Freud), 5, 101; as motivating force for personality, 157; sexuality and, 73 n.1, 74; validated, 156
Agricultural societies, 23, 24, 37–38
Altruistic love, 43, 156
Ambivalence: failure to integrate, 118; integration of, 35, 65, 104
Ambivalence toward mother, 35, 36, 65, 99; of Freud, 6, 62, 66, 80, 86, 90, 91, 95, 100; Freud's denial of, 83–85
American Academy of Psychoanalysis, 19
American Plains Indians, 190
Anaitis (goddess), 22

Anal phase, 92
"Analysis Terminable and Interminable" (Freud), 98
Analytic psychology (Jung), 7, 151, 152, 158–59
Ancient cultures, 3
Androgens, 172, 173
Anger: in depressives, 119; in family, 119; of Freud, 65, 66; projection of, 118; repressed, in Freud, 83–85, 90, 91–92. See also Rage toward mother
Anima, 151, 152–53
Animals, associated with goddesses, 22, 24
Animus, 151, 152–53
Annihilation anxiety, 5, 34, 114, 115, 168; in Freud, 6, 64, 82, 86, 132
Anthology from a Pragmatic Point of View (Kant), 51
Anthropology, 2, 195
AntiChrist (Nietzsche), 156
Anti-Semitism, 1, 4, 7, 63, 76, 152, 158; influence on Freud's theories, 54–57; of Jung, 151; misogyny and, 51–54; rejected by Nietzsche, 156
Anxiety, 18, 164–65; in preoedipal period, 63; "unthinkable," 168
Aphrodite (goddess), 39, 40
Apollonian society, 190
Arapesh (people), 191
Archeology, 3, 126, 127